THE PENGUIN POETRY LIBRARY

W. B. YEATS

William Butler Yeats was born in Dublin in 1865 into an artistic family and spent his childhood in Sligo, Dublin, and London. In Dublin he enrolled at the Metropolitan School of Art in 1884. The next year he became a founder-member of the Dublin Hermetic Society; in time this led him to the Esoteric Section of the Theosophical Society and the Hermetic Order of the Golden Dawn (1890). He developed a life-long interest in magic, the occult and the supernatural, which influenced much of his thinking and writing, and which achieved its most complete expression in the expository speculations of *A Vision* (1925; revised version 1937). His early poetry was influenced by Victorian models, which he largely came to reject in the search for a personal utterance and for a voice which was distinctively Irish.

Yeats's permanent home was in London, though he visited Ireland frequently. For a while he was close to the politics of Irish nationalism, not least because of his long infatuation with the revolutionary Maud Gonne, to whom he unsuccessfully proposed on many occasions throughout his life. From an early stage, he devoted his energies much less to direct political action than to the cause of an imaginative nationalism which involved him in the collection of folklore (notably in *The Celtic Twilight*, 1893), in the creation and management of a national theatre for which he wrote a body of plays (five of which presented the epic hero Cuchulain), and in the critical reinterpretation and advancement of the Irish literary tradition. Like his plays, Yeats's poetry constantly redefined itself; it is particularly remarkable for its expansive development after *Responsibilities* (1914) and for the imaginative rigour of its frequent revisions.

In 1915 Yeats refused a knighthood from the British government; in 1922 he became a Senator of the newly-founded Irish Free State, and finally settled in Dublin with Georgie Hyde-Lees, whom he had married in 1917 and whose automatic writing became the basis of *A Vision*. In 1917 he also purchased a Norman stone tower in Ballylee Co. and this provided the symbolic focus for *The Tower* (1928) which is, arguably, his richest collection of poetry. Yeats left a vivid record of his life

and of his friends and acquaintances in the volumes which were collec-
ted as *Autobiographies*, also published by Penguin, and in the franker
Memoirs (not published until 1972). He died at Roquebrune, France, in
January 1939.

W. B. YEATS

Selected Poetry

**EDITED WITH AN INTRODUCTION
AND NOTES BY
TIMOTHY WEBB**

PENGUIN BOOKS

PENGUIN BOOKS

Published by the Penguin Group
Penguin Books Ltd, 27 Wrights Lane, London W8 5TZ, England
Penguin Books USA Inc., 375 Hudson Street, New York, New York 10014, USA
Penguin Books Australia Ltd, Ringwood, Victoria, Australia
Penguin Books Canada Ltd, 10 Alcorn Avenue, Toronto, Ontario, Canada M4V 3B2
Penguin Books (NZ) Ltd, 182–190 Wairau Road, Auckland 10, New Zealand

Penguin Books Ltd, Registered Offices: Harmondsworth, Middlesex, England

This selection first published in Penguin Books 1991
7 9 10 8

The acknowledgements on p. xliii constitute
an extension of this copyright page

Printed in England by Clays Ltd, St Ives plc
Filmset in 10 on 11 pt Monophoto Ehrhardt

CONTENTS

✦✦✦✦✦✦

v

CONTENTS

THE WIND AMONG THE REEDS

IN THE SEVEN WOODS

CONTENTS

CONTENTS

THE WILD SWANS AT COOLE

CONTENTS

CONTENTS

THE WINDING STAIR AND OTHER POEMS

From A FULL MOON IN MARCH

NEW POEMS

CONTENTS

ACKNOWLEDGEMENTS

I should like to express my particular indebtedness and gratitude to earlier editors of Yeats, especially to Peter Allt and Russell K. Alspach, whose *Variorum* editions of the poems and the plays are an invaluable resource to all readers of Yeats. The bibliography provides some indication of my other major debts, but, among editors, I should like to name the following with warmth: Denis Donoghue, Richard Finneran, John Frayne, George Mills Harper, John Kelly and Eric Domville, Philip Marcus, Warwick Gould, Michael Sidnell, George Brandon Saul and Allan Wade. Daniel Albright's edition of the poems has appeared just in time for me to see that my own edition would have profited greatly had his example been available at an earlier stage. I have also been much influenced and informed by the work of Curtis Bradford, Richard Ellmann, Thomas Parkinson and Jon Stallworthy. To Derry Jeffares I owe a double debt: first, for his pioneering *Commentary*, which puts all later editors under obligation to his researches; secondly, for his personal encouragement and for initiating me into Anglo-Irish literary studies when I was in the School of English at the University of Leeds. I should also like to thank my former colleagues at the University of York for providing a congenial and stimulating environment in which I was able to teach a special paper on Yeats; nor should I forget the many students who took part in those seminars and whose responses to Yeats, both oral and written, have greatly helped to enrich my thinking. I also owe particular debts to the following: to David Pierce for Yeatsian counsel; to Catherine Ellen for her work on the typescript; to Debbie Johnson for generous help with proofs; to Donna Poppy for her patience, skill and tact in copy-editing and for her extensive knowledge of Yeats; to Paul Keegan for accepting this project; and to my wife Ruth for helping to make it possible.

INTRODUCTION

❖❖❖❖❖❖

According to his biographers and the registrar of births, deaths and marriages, William Butler Yeats was born in Dublin on 13 June 1865 and died at Cap-Martin on 28 January 1939. The seventy-three years which separated these two dates saw the appearance under his name of critical essays, stories, autobiographical works, plays in verse and prose and, recurrently and centrally, a body of poems, narrative, dramatic and, predominantly, lyrical, which is the basis of his reputation as one of the greatest writers of his time. Yeats was playwright, literary journalist, critic, editor, public speaker, student and recorder of oral tradition, genuine and independent investigator of the occult, mythologist and mythmaker, theatre director, and promoter of national literature. The range and diversity of these activities and of their creative elements may be surprising to those who know Yeats only vaguely and peripherally as the creator of a handful of lyrics or of 'Easter 1916', which has achieved a particular national significance. The simplifications of popular literary history usually tend to minimise or to ignore the prose works of a poet, so the achievements of *Autobiographies*, or *A Vision*, or 'The Tables of the Law' (which James Joyce knew by heart), have not received their due, and the prose is more often treated as a key to the mysterious gates of the poetry. The poetry is Yeats's greatest achievement, arising from a capaciousness of imaginative endeavour and a consistency of application, and embracing a variety of literary forms and a variety of interests which can be seen as diverse yet, ultimately, interconnected.

Some contemporary interpreters of literature might prefer to approach Yeats in terms of textual phenomena, of the word and the phoneme, of poems, prose and plays on the page, rather than in the conventional terms of biography. The historical record shows a compelling and influential presence who left a personal impress on Irish public life and on the course of modern literature; his life has seemed to shape and articulate a persuasive version of the figure and function of the poet.

Yeats the man was a vivid and forceful personality who was proud of his family origins and who thought about ancestry, though he might also have agreed that his identity was not so much a given or a solid and stable entity as an artificial construct. He was acutely sensitive to the ways in which we fabricate our own identity and to the artificiality and even the theatricality of our self-presentation. Even the history of a nation might be interpreted as a sacred drama and its dominant figures as 'Artificers of the Great Moment' who could be equated with poets and with actors. This led him to evolve his doctrine of the 'mask' ('the image of what we wish to become'), which had major consequences both for his own life and for his work as a poet. In his poetry (and in some of his prose) he evolved a series of personae which helped him to project certain possibilities or aspects of character and to articulate and dramatise the divisions and the conflicts within himself.

At a fairly simple level this strategy can be observed in his two autobiographical novels: *John Sherman*, which was published in 1891, and *The Speckled Bird*, which went through a number of drafts but which never resolved itself sufficiently to appear in Yeats's lifetime. Yeats's efforts in these novels to fictionalise his emotional life offer a suggestive parallel to his practice as a poet. Sometimes, as in the love poetry, the use of a persona must have helped both to distance his emotions and to objectify them. For instance, a number of poems in *The Green Helmet and Other Poems* (1910) were first published under the general heading of 'Raymond Lully and his wife Pernella'. As Yeats later pointed out in an embarrassed note, this was a slip of the pen: he had intended to write the name not of the Catalan philosopher but of the Parisian scribe and alchemist, Nicolas Flamel, whose devotion to his wife and fellow worker had become legendary. Through another error, one version of the story 'Rosa Alchemica' had also transformed Lully's wife Pernelle into 'Parnella', thus satisfying by a slight alteration the claims of alchemy and of patriotism; this happy coinage has found its way into at least one recent study of the alchemical tradition. Whatever the names, Yeats's prevailing terms of reference were alchemy and fidelity in love. In his own life he had seen the close conjunction between Flamel and his wife as a model for his relationship with Maud Gonne. Later he removed the alchemical associations from the title, so that poems such as 'A Woman Homer Sung' and 'No Second Troy' were no longer filtered through this medium. Indeed, any reader of Yeats might now be surprised to discover such *pentimenti*, such evidence of earlier thoughts no longer visible to the unaided eye. This might seem to show that the invocation of Flamel was largely external to the life of the poetry and provided nothing more than a convenient frame for a sequence of love poems whose directness required some complication and refrigeration. Yet the alchemist was central to Yeats's conception of the poet at this stage of his career. As he explained in a Preface to *Poems* (1906): 'All art is in the last analysis an endeavour to condense as out of the flying vapour of the world an image of human perfection, and for its own and not for the art's sake, and that is why the labour of the alchemists, who were called artists in their day, is a befitting comparison for all deliberate change of style.' Yeats's elaborate strategy for the dramatising of the personal also reveals a concern which is highly suggestive and a practice which is consistent with many other poems, especially in his earlier years.

A more complicated example of Yeats's use of the persona is provided by the first edition of *The Wind Among the Reeds* (1899). In this case many of the poems were distanced from Yeats by their attribution to a range of speakers, imagined, legendary and historical: 'Hanrahan reproves the Curlew', 'Michael Robartes remembers Forgotten Beauty' (the version itself remembered and rejected by Joyce's Stephen Dedalus), 'Aedh wishes for the Cloths of Heaven', 'Mongan thinks of his Past Greatness'. In earlier versions it was O'Sullivan Rua who reproved the curlew, remembered forgotten beauty ('O'Sullivan Rua to Mary Lavell') and addressed the secret rose, while a number of the poems ascribed to Aedh (or Aodh) were originally addressed specifically to 'Dectora' (a name which later appeared in *The Shadowy Waters*, a play with strong autobiographical associations). Contemporary readers who are familiar with this volume in its final form may be surprised by the apparent precision of these attributions, since in later versions Yeats removed all specificity, and poems are characteristically headed 'The Lover mourns for the Loss of Love', 'The Poet pleads with the Elemental Powers' and 'He wishes for the Cloths of Heaven'. Aedh, Hanrahan and Robartes had all appeared in the stories which were collected as *The Secret Rose* (1897), where they were characterised in some detail (see notes to *The Wind Among the Reeds*); in this collection of poems Yeats used them 'more as principles of the mind than as actual personages'. Mongan was a legendary wizard and king. O'Sullivan Rua (or the Red) was Eoghan Ruadh Ó Súilleabháin or, in Anglicised form, Owen Roe O'Sullivan (1748–84), a peasant poet who still figured powerfully in the oral tradition. His name was originally attached to a number of the early stories; later he was entirely eliminated to be replaced in most cases by the fictional Hanrahan.

The figure of Red Hanrahan allowed Yeats an opportunity to explore the traditions of Gaelic poetry and of a Gaelic way of life from which he had been partially separated, though not alienated, by his Protestant upbringing and by his ignorance of the Irish language. 'Red Hanrahan's Song about Ireland', which was published in three different versions, is an expression of 'the tragic patriotism of Catholic Ireland' and provides some kind of counterbalance to Yeats's involvement with the values of the Anglo-Irish and the landed gentry which centred around Coole Park and the Gregory family. Hanrahan's relation to his audience may also offer one version of a more unified Irish culture, 'Before the merchant and the clerk/Breathed on the world with timid breath'. In 'The Tower' Yeats included his own fictional Hanrahan in the same imaginative context as Homer and Anthony Raftery, the blind Gaelic poet of the early nineteenth century who, like Hanrahan, was associated with the oral traditions of the west of Ireland. The second section of this powerfully reflexive and self-scrutinising poem concludes with Yeats's invocation of the character he had created. Yeats turns to Hanrahan with a sense of shared experience and of complicity in the painful mysteries of love in a way which suggests both that there is a central identity between the poet and the fictional character who is one of his personae and that the character has an external reality and an authority of his own:

> Old lecher with a love on every wind,
> Bring up out of that deep considering mind
> All that you have discovered in the grave,
> For it is certain that you have
> Reckoned up every unforeknown, unseeing
> Plunge, lured by a softening eye,
> Or by a touch or a sigh,
> Into the labyrinth of another's being;
>
> Does the imagination dwell the most
> Upon a woman won or woman lost?

The most enduring of Yeats's personae was Michael Robartes. He never attained the centrality which Stephen Dedalus assumed for Joyce, but he was more closely identified with the operations of the Yeatsian imagination than Aedh or Hanrahan or (in later years) Aherne, who provided the title of 'Owen Aherne and his Dancers', and whom Yeats afterwards referred to as John Aherne. In the early story 'Rosa Alchemica' he is characterised in terms of contrasting and conflicting qualities: his 'wild red hair, fierce eyes, sensitive, tremulous lips and rough clothes, made him look . . . something between a debauchee, a saint, and a peasant'. In this portrait his red hair aligns him in Celtic brotherhood with Owen Roe O'Sullivan and Red Hanrahan. After *The Wind Among the Reeds* Robartes seems to be dormant until Yeats has passed into his fifties. He features in 'The Double Vision of Michael Robartes' and 'The Phases of the Moon', which is essentially a dialogue between himself and Aherne, and later in 'Michael Robartes and the Dancer', which is the title-poem of the 1921 collection. In 'A People's Theatre' (1919) Yeats complicated his relationship with Robartes by attributing two poems from *The Wild Swans at Coole* to his authorship: 'Are we approaching a supreme moment of self-consciousness, the two halves of the soul separate and face to face? A certain friend of mine has written upon this subject a couple of intricate poems . . . which are my continual study'. Again in 'Ego Dominus Tuus', which itself is a dialogue between two speakers, Hic describes Ille as walking under his tower 'where still/A lamp burns on beside the open book/That Michael Robartes left': here a Yeatsian interlocutor reminds a version of Yeats of the influence of one of his own personae which, as in the case of Hanrahan, seems to have a reality beyond that of his own creating.

Robartes appears to have had a particular association with Yeats's occult activities and with the more esoteric significances of his work. In *Michael Robartes and the Dancer* Yeats's lengthy explanatory notes for 'An Image from a Past Life' and 'The Second Coming' are both attributed to Robartes, and the Preface expresses a hope that 'my selection from the great mass of his letters and table talk' may soon be published. Yeats once intended that *A Vision* should be formed by a series of Robartes papers; the second version included 'Stories of Michael Robartes and his Friends' (which had first been published separately in 1931) as well as 'The Phases of the Moon', though it omitted 'Appendix of Michael Robartes' and 'Michael Robartes Foretells' (both of which have been published only recently). There is some danger in assuming complete identity between the character in the early fiction and the subtle author and explicator of the later 'texts for exposition' or even in assuming continuity or exchangeability between poetry and prose. Yet, when all due reservations have been made, we must observe that Yeats himself has taken trouble to suggest the possibility of some such continuity. There may be something playful in his deliberate confusing of the distinction between himself and Robartes, yet in his later manifestation Robartes is closely linked to some of Yeats's deepest concerns. In 1933, for example, Yeats was excited by a rereading of Balzac's *Louis Lambert* and responded by considering the alternative possibilities 'of making "Michael Robartes" write an annotation or even of doing it myself'. In the event, the essay appeared in the *London Mercury* in July 1934 and was attributed to W. B. Yeats. The reappearance of Robartes coincided with the renaissance of Yeats's interest in the occult and the supernatural after his marriage in 1917 and his wife's discovery of automatic writing. And his crossing of the boundary between poetry and prose suggests a unity of thought beyond the superficial distinctions of genre.

Few poets have been more explicitly attentive to the deliberate creation of a poetic self. In 'A General Introduction for my Work', which was written towards the end of his life, Yeats set down the following principle for the benefit of his readers:

A poet writes always of his personal life; in his finest work out of its tragedy, whatever it be, remorse, lost love, or mere loneliness; he never speaks directly as to someone at the breakfast table, there is always a phantasmagoria ... Even when the poet seems most himself, when he is Raleigh and gives potentates the lie, or Shelley 'a nerve o'er which do creep the else unfelt oppressions of this earth,' or Byron 'and the soul wears out the breast' as 'the sword outwears its sheath,' he is never the bundle of accident and incoherence that sits down to breakfast; he has been reborn as an idea, something intended, complete.

Here Yeats seems to be claiming that the poet is never isolated by the individuality of his existence since he is part of an imaginative and psychological history ('a phantasmagoria') which informs his own life and which can be drawn on as a poetic resource. In Yeats's own poetry this dimension can be tangibly experienced in the legendary, the mythological, the occult, the supernatural and in that mysterious energy which gathers round images and symbols such as the rose or the rough beast of 'The Second Coming', which are both highly personal and part of an ancient tradition.

This investment in phantasmagoria is both an enrichment and a protection against the insidious forces of individuality or the misguided modern desire for originality. As Yeats expressed it later in his essay: 'all that is personal soon rots; it must be packed in ice or salt ... Talk to me of originality and I will turn on you with rage. I am a crowd, I am a lonely man, I am nothing. Ancient salt is best packing.' Protected by ancient salt against the corrupting possibilities of direct self-expression or of verse which is merely confessional, the poet is enabled to translate the biographical particulars of his personal life into the durability of art. The breakfast table seems to stand for the crude material of everyday life, not yet mediated through the transforming agency of art; so in 'Ego Dominus Tuus' Yeats equated the works of painters and writers who love the world and serve its purposes with the 'struggle of the fly in marmalade'. Failure to understand this may produce poetry which is merely personal. Or, as in the case of Wordsworth, it is possible to fail if the poet is not sufficiently 'theatrical': this diagnosis may owe something to an Irishman's feeling that there was something cumbrously moralistic in nineteenth-century English literature, though it also derives from a firmly held belief in the importance of calculated self-projection and of gesture. Without these protecting and enriching properties or strategies, the poet remains merely a man, a 'bundle of accident and incoherence'; with their help he is 'reborn as an idea, something intended, complete'. The random, the arbitrary and the formless are replaced by the shaping of 'the conscious mind's intelligible structure'. The emphasis here on the willed and the chosen should not be ignored; the poet is not the man who falls into casual conversation with his neighbour or who appears to be sitting at the breakfast table in the seemingly unquestionable completeness of everyday identity but an artificial construction or concept, which is the result of a deliberate act of the poetic imagination. For some of Yeats's readers this emphasis on artifice, this flouting of the imperative of sincerity or of self-expression, is difficult to understand or to accept. Yet Yeats correctly implied that he is in the great tradition of European poetry, citing Dante, Milton and Shakespeare, and he insisted that even Romantic poets such as Byron and Shelley, who are so close to the quick of their own lives and who appear to make poetry out of their own biographical circumstances, are in fact distanced from life by the self-consciously formalised articulations of their poetry. 'Art is art because it is not nature', as he liked to remind himself, providing his own version of Goethe's statement.

This insistence on the artfulness of art is a major concern of a number of Yeats's finest poems such as 'Sailing to Byzantium', 'Byzantium', 'Meditations in Time of Civil War' and 'The Circus Animals' Desertion'; like many of his deepest convictions, it is subject to question and sometimes it seems less than adequate when matched against the 'fury and the mire of human veins', the 'foul rag-and-bone shop of the heart' or 'That dolphin-torn, that gong-tormented sea'. Increasingly in his later poems Yeats acknowledged the body and the material world, the forces which pull us away from pure mind and the closed gardens of art; increasingly he matched the value of poetry against the value of a life of action or of life itself. It is characteristic of Yeats to admit the struggle, to allow his readers to feel 'the stirring of the beast underneath'. Yet there is a recurrent and antithetical insistence on the virtues of art, of technique, of the refrigerating strategies of the poet. In *Autobiographies* Yeats admitted: 'as I look backward upon my own writing, I take pleasure alone in those verses where it seems to me I have found something hard and cold, some articulation of the Image which is the opposite of all that I am in my daily life, and all that my country is'. So in 'The Fisherman' he declared his ambition to write for his ideal audience 'one poem maybe as cold/And passionate as the dawn': here the balancing of *passionate* and of *cold* gives expression to Yeats's belief that 'imagination ... must be carried beyond feeling into the original ice'. There is a tension in Yeats between images of the poet as craftsman and as hero. Ruefully he admitted to the tension in 'All Things can Tempt Me' (probably written in 1908 and first published in 1909), where he remembered: 'When I was young,/I had not given a penny for a song/Did not the poet sing it with such airs/That one believed he had a sword upstairs'. This poem acknowledges that in earlier years love and politics had distracted him from the 'craft of verse'; now, it expresses a deeper disillusionment and a desire to be 'Colder and dumber and deafer than a fish'. This seems to combine a sense of the ultimate futility of the poetic vocation with a resentment of the 'accustomed toil' of versemaking. Yeats continued to write like a poet who had a sword upstairs; indeed, a section of 'Meditations in Time of

Civil War' is specifically devoted to exploring the significance of the Japanese sword which lay on his table in the tower at Ballylee, his symbolically resonant home at various times during the 1920s. And there is more than a touch of the swordsman in the magniloquence of much of Yeats's rhetoric, in the dramatic force of its gestures and in the authority of its declarations: for example, 'I write it out in a verse', 'I spit into the face of Time/That has transfigured me', 'Irish poets learn your trade,/Sing whatever is well made'.

Yet, recurrently, the high talk could seem inflated, even to Yeats himself. Frequently, and quite as characteristically, he thought of the poet not as a flamboyant figure but as a worker in metal, or miniature, or mosaic, or even as a stitcher: 'we achieve, if we do achieve, in little sedentary stitches as though we were making lace'. The contrast is vividly expressed in *The Trembling of the Veil*, where Yeats insists on the danger of 'that violent energy, which is like a fire of straw' and which 'consumes in a few minutes the nervous vitality':

Our fire must burn slowly, and we must constantly turn away to think, constantly analyse what we have done, be content even to have little life outside our work, to show, perhaps, to other men, as little as the watch-mender shows, his magnifying-glass caught in his screwed-up eye. Only then do we learn to conserve our vitality, to keep our mind enough under control and to make our technique sufficiently flexible for expression of the emotions of life as they arise.

Here the emphasis falls on studied and vocational impersonality and on dedication to the absorbing and demanding requirements of technique. Here, as in Yeats's other figures of the poet as miniaturist or craftsman, the emphasis also falls on the uncongeniality of the medium and on its distance from the threatening pluralities and fecundities of everyday life. This is skill, craft, painstaking and meticulous application: the punitive discipline of the artisan rather than the lofty utterance of the inspired artist. It is characteristic of Yeats that he should not remain content even with this formulation; perhaps the image of the absorbed watch-mender suggests an extreme polarity which could not remain totally satisfying. So in 1936 he reacted against the difficulty of modern verse by aligning himself with the circus and with the grand simplicities of popular art: 'These new men are goldsmiths working with a glass screwed into one eye, whereas we stride ahead of the crowd, its swordsmen, its jugglers, looking to right and left.' The poem 'High Talk' seems to develop the exuberantly positive implications of striding 'ahead of the crowd' in its central image of the stilt-walker; yet here the figure of Malachi Stilt-Jack seems like a translation of poetic flamboyance into something self-mocking, grotesque and precarious in the shaky dignity of its temporary elevation.

Elevation is regularly countered by ironical insistence on the unromantic. To write poetry is not necessarily to take part in a dignified vocation: it is to be excluded from the world of action and condemned to 'sedentary toil' (the word *sedentary* acquires a peculiar bitterness in Yeats). In 'Adam's Curse' Yeats put this view of the pains of poetry into a wider context. He recalled a conversation in which he had said,

> . . .'A line will take us hours maybe;
> Yet if it does not seem a moment's thought,
> Our stitching and unstitching has been naught.
> Better go down upon your marrow-bones
> And scrub a kitchen pavement, or break stones
> Like an old pauper, in all kinds of weather;
> For to articulate sweet sounds together
> Is to work harder than all these, and yet
> Be thought an idler by the noisy set
> Of bankers, schoolmasters, and clergymen
> The martyrs call the world.'

The physical intensity of the language and the directness of words such as *scrub* and *break stones* carry a high charge of resentment, and the punishment of the poet gives rise to a kind of inverted romanticising which invests him with negative glamour. Breaking stones may suggest the making of what Yeats elsewhere called *road metal*; in the nineteenth century particularly, public works such as road-building involved the convict as well as the pauper, and poverty was a condition scarcely distinguishable from penal servitude. The image is put to savage use in a late epigram on Parnell, where stone-breaking seems to be associated with the unchanging condition of the ordinary Irishman or perhaps of fundamental man largely unaffected by the grand march of 'politics': 'Parnell came down the road, he said to a cheering man:/"Ireland shall get her freedom and you still break stone."' 'Adam's Curse' goes on to suggest that the curse imposed on Adam as a result of the Fall includes both the painful articulations of the poet and, in the case of woman, the labour to be beautiful. According to Yeats's philosophy, feminine beauty was the product of a 'discipline':

> How many centuries spent
> The sedentary soul
> In toil of measurement
> Beyond eagle or mole,
> Beyond hearing or seeing,
> Or Archimedes' guess,
> To raise into being
> That loveliness?

So the beautiful woman, be she Maud Gonne or Helen of Troy, is in a sense an artist, the artificer of her own beauty. In this she resembles the poet who does not exist within his own poetry as a simple translation of the man at the breakfast table but who is 'reborn as an idea, something intended, complete'. The recurring principle is artifice by which life is transformed into art, whether through the heroic discipline of the looking-glass or through an engagement with the resistant medium of poetic form.

In 'A General Introduction for my Work' Yeats explained the importance of form. He recalled his discovery of 'a powerful and passionate syntax, and a complete coincidence between period and stanza', and he defended his use of traditional verse form:

If I wrote of personal love or sorrow in free verse, or in any rhythm that left it unchanged, amid all its accidence, I would be full of self-contempt because of my egotism and indiscretion, and foresee the boredom of my reader. I must choose a traditional stanza, even what I alter must seem traditional . . . Ancient salt is best packing.

This passage might usefully be compared with T. S. Eliot's essay 'Reflections on *Vers Libre*', as indeed the whole essay might be compared with 'Tradition and the Individual Talent'. Yeats required the ancient potencies of symbols which have emerged out of the fibrous darkness of tradition and the formal control provided by a strictly regulated and received verse form, which is frequently stanzaic. While 'Meditations in Time of Civil War', for instance, employs a variety of forms, it also exhibits a recurrent attraction towards the sonorities and formalities of *ottava rima*, or of the eight-line rhyming stanza. This may extend the range of traditional rhyme (binding, for example, *man* with *stone* and *terraces* with *deities*); it also counters the centrifugal force of the subject matter with the recognisable regularity of the traditional metrics and rhyme scheme. The terrible annunciation of 'Leda and the Swan', with its intimations of the violations of history, is miraculously compressed in the form of a sonnet. 'The Second Coming' is not stanzaic (though it began as a poem in rhyme), yet it packs its images of a disintegrating world in the ancient salt of blank verse and a syntax which manifests a strong controlling intelligence. Both Yeats's politics and his understanding of poetic discipline required that the vehicle for his vision of a world in which 'the centre cannot hold' should be a verse form which embodied and enacted the gravitational pull of the centre. Against the 'accidence and incoherence' of a collapsing world he sets an alternative accidence: the random and the accidental is held at bay by the grammar of civilised discourse. The contrast with *The Waste Land* is instructive. Eliot, the self-declared classicist, employs a technique which is expressionist and mimetic, which to some extent participates in the fragmentation which it laments. On the other hand, Yeats, the self-declared Romantic, approaches the subject of impending anarchy with a formal control which might be described as classical.

This classical discipline is exercised not only to exclude or control the mire and blood of an unregenerate world, as in 'Byzantium', where the marbles of the dancing floor 'Break bitter furies of complexity'; it is also at the same time an exercise in self-control, self-presentation and, ultimately, in the creation of the self. For Yeats, the poet as man was inseparable from the utterance which he achieved in his poetry; therefore the development and perfection of poetic technique was not merely the specialised drudgery of the craftsman but an activity which was inseparable from the expression of self. This necessary conjunction was set out in a suggestively declarative verse which Yeats included as an epigraph in the second volume of his *Collected Works* in 1908:

> The friends that have it I do wrong
> When ever I remake a song,
> Should know what issue is at stake:
> It is myself that I remake.

Remake is a significant and favourite word: recalling in 1910 his poetical friends of the 1890s, he explained how he had been 'worn out with a nervous excitement' and how he had renounced the lyrical mode of this 'Tragic Generation' in order that 'I might remake myself'. Seen in this light, the line of Yeats's stylistic progression is both a history of aesthetic development and a sequence of chapters in the writing of a self. For the poet himself, the search is not for self-expression in the ordinary sense of the term but for a poetic identity which is achieved with increasing precision, rendered absolute only by his death. So the style of Yeats's poetry changes over the years and so his poems, most particularly those of the early period, are revised and rewritten under pressure from the changing circumstances of his life and in keeping with the evolving demands of his aesthetics. The final versions of his poems are, effectively, those which appeared in the *Collected Poems* of 1949, after his death; in spite of some textual inadequacies and limitations, this volume represents the final stage of Yeats's poetic evolution, the ultimate point in his process of making and remaking and the poetic version of himself which he wished to bequeath to posterity. To acknowledge this, however, should not prevent us from recognising that this final version of Yeats was possible only because of the existence of its many predecessors.

The present edition is designed to draw attention to this process of development and to widen the reader's sense of what constitutes Yeats and the Yeatsian. In historical terms, this has an obvious advantage over the procedure of *Collected Poems* and most later editions of Yeats. Two striking and famous examples are provided by 'The Sorrow of Love' and the poem which in its later versions was known as 'The Lamentation of the Old Pensioner'. Both were rewritten so extensively as to become in effect new poems. In 1890 the old pensioner concluded his lament in a style which was essentially sentimental:

> The road-side trees keep murmuring –
> Ah, wherefore murmur ye
> As in the old days long gone by,
> Green oak and poplar tree!
> The well-known faces all are gone,
> And the fret is on me.

In the final version the sound and the syntax are harsher and the last two lines have a savagely physical vigour which completely transforms the mood:

> There's not a woman turns her face
> Upon a broken tree,
> And yet the beauties that I loved
> Are in my memory;
> I spit into the face of Time
> That has transfigured me.

Yeats's diction holds together *spit* and *transfigured* in a creative tension which was not available to him in the 1890s, nor indeed till much later. The final version of this poem did not appear till 1925, although it is actually printed in at least one recent edition with the date 1890.

The final stanza of 'The Sorrow of Love' was published in 1892 in the following version:

> And now the sparrows warring in the eaves,
>   The crumbling moon, the white stars in the sky,
> And the loud chanting of the unquiet leaves,
>   Are shaken with earth's old and weary cry.

Three years later *crumbling* was changed to *curd-pale* and *chanting* to *chaunting*. This remained the canonical version until 1925, when it was replaced by a stanza which was more in keeping with that phase of Yeats's career which had recently produced 'The Second Coming' and which would produce within a few years the resonant complexities of *The Tower*:

> Arose, and on the instant clamorous eaves,
> A climbing moon upon an empty sky,
> And all that lamentation of the leaves,
> Could but compose man's image and his cry.

Not everyone has preferred the revision. Louis MacNeice, for one, claimed that although the new poem is 'no longer languid ... it no longer rings true'. In his view, 'Yeats, with a different poem in his mind's eye, has distorted it.' Whatever the relative merits of the two versions, they do exhibit a striking dissimilarity, and they both bear the impress of the period in which they were written. Yet, if one turns to *Collected Poems*, one finds 'The Sorrow of Love' (like 'The Lamentation of the Old Pensioner') under the heading of *The Rose*, which is dated 1893. This heading is a retrospective invention and editorial device, since Yeats never published a volume called *The Rose*; indisputably, too, 1893 is a misleading date for a poem which was written thirty years later. One doesn't have to prefer the first version to feel that such an arrangement is historically deceptive. By eliminating the first version, Yeats also does less than justice to the distinctive achievement of an earlier phase of his career. These two poems provide, perhaps, the most perfect and complete examples of a process which was crucial to Yeats's poetic development.

This process of creation and revision can be observed from several perspectives. Yeats's manuscripts have not yet yielded all their secrets, though fascinating materials have already been published by a number of pioneering scholars. In due course the Cornell Edition will provide a comprehensive guide; for the present, most readers will turn to the books of Jon Stallworthy and David Clark, and to the examination of manuscript material in the works of Ellmann, Jeffares, Parkinson and others. For printed versions only, the evidence is much easier to accumulate. At its most fundamental level, the complete process of change and revision in printed texts can be traced through the pages of *The Variorum Edition of the Poems of W. B. Yeats*, edited by Peter Allt and Russell K. Alspach. However, this book is very large and difficult to use. Limitation of space has made it impossible to represent poems in more than one version, and the table of textual variants at the bottom of the page is a challenge to the patience and the reconstructive abilities of the reader. From such materials it is hard to recapture the identity of earlier versions of the poems or to experience anything of their original inscape or impact.

It is one of the aims of the present edition to simplify such matters for the reader and to ensure, as far as possible, that an encounter with the variations of Yeats's text should be removed from the forbidding associations of scholarship and integrated with the actual experience of reading. The best and clearest examples of this procedure are those poems which are represented in two or even three versions. The texts are printed consecutively so that the reader can encounter the whole of each version as a poem in its own right while also enjoying the opportunity to read the poems against each other, almost as if the later version were a translation of the first. In the case of other poems in this selection it does not seem necessary to print the poem in its entirety in two versions, and it has not been feasible to do so. A compromise is required. As a result, the most interesting or significant alternatives from earlier versions are printed at the bottom of the relevant page though always in the form of whole lines or passages and not of isolated words. This is intended to facilitate comparison and to remind the reader of that process of choice, of definition, of making and remaking, by which Yeats arrived at his final version. In many cases the discarded version is markedly inferior, and it might be thought that to restore it to print is to do no service to Yeats. For example, 'He thinks of his Past Greatness when a Part of the Constellations of Heaven' originally ended: 'Although the rushes and the fowl of the air/ Cry of his love with their pitiful cries'. This conclusion was retained until 1922, when it became: 'O beast of the wilderness, bird of the air,/Must I endure your amorous cries?' The switch from statement to question, the stronger patterning, the firmer grammatical thrust, the translation of *pitiful* to *amorous*, all serve to effect a radical transformation from dying fall to anguished cry. The presence of the earlier conclusion helps us to focus more sharply on the perfectly achieved articulation of the 1922 version and on the long creative process out of which it emerged.

Even the printed record shows that Yeats's poems did not always click shut with that inevitable rightness which one might have deduced from their final, received and celebrated versions. The history of 'Leda and the Swan' is a striking demonstration; another less obvious example is provided by the careful shift in 'The Second Coming' from the conventional 'a waste of desert sand' to the more expressive compression of 'somewhere in sands of the desert'. On one occasion at least, a poem did not come into focus until it was detached from its original context. In its received version 'The Choice' is a terse eight-line reflection on the rival claims of life and art which articulates the problem with fierce intensity: 'The intellect of man is forced to choose/Perfection of the life, or of the work'. Originally this was published not as a self-enclosed poem but as a stanza in 'Coole Park and Ballylee, 1931'.

Yeats's struggle to find a shape and a form for his experience involved him in the difficulties of the poetic medium and in the recalcitrant material of life itself; it also implicated him in a cultural dilemma. He was born a subject of Queen Victoria, he received from 1910 a Civil List Pension, and he was even offered a knighthood by the British government during the First World War; yet he was by birth, by choice and by temperament an Irishman. One of his main objectives was not only to find an appropriate utterance for himself but to give a voice to Irishness. In the 1880s when Yeats was beginning his poetic career, the tradition of poetry written in the English language by Irishmen was thin and the poetry was often derivative or marginal. Irish poetry was not yet strong enough to attain its own identity or to claim its rights with sufficient assurance.

One temptation was to be charmingly provincial, to collaborate in the marginalising of the Irish imagination. This temptation is sharply articulated by James Joyce in his portrayal of the provincial ambitions of Little Chandler in the story 'A Little Cloud' in *Dubliners*. Chandler's unfulfilled and self-defeating desire is to escape from the restrictions of Dublin, where one can 'do nothing', and to establish himself as a poet in London, where he will be acknowledged by the English critics as 'one of the Celtic school by reason of the melancholy tone of his poems'. He even considers changing his name to make it more Irish-looking: 'perhaps it would be better to insert his mother's name before the surname: Thomas Malone; or better still: T. Malone Chandler'. William Butler Yeats was not unfamiliar with such temptations. Although his *Letters to the New Island* were self-consciously headed 'The Celt in London', he did recognise the importance of artistic integrity, and he largely resisted the easier course of sounding 'the Celtic note' merely to satisfy the ethnic preconceptions of the London reviewers. On the other hand he was careful to avoid that kind of cosmopolitanism which was essentially superficial or merely fashionable: 'I could not endure ... an international art, picking stories and symbols where it pleased.' He preferred to work towards the creation of 'a national literature that made Ireland beautiful in the memory, and yet had been freed from provincialism by an exacting criticism, a European pose'. It is one of Yeats's greatest achievements as a poet that he succeeded in keeping a balance so effectively that he opened the doors of possibility for the rich and confident expression of later Irish poetry, even in the case of those poets who resisted or resist his direct influence. Together with Joyce, Yeats made modern Irish poetry possible. Like Joyce, he set an example which was national without being nationalist. Like Joyce, though to a lesser extent, he was open to European influence; in particular he was indebted to the work of the *symbolistes*. Like Joyce, he applied to his work an exacting and critical eye.

The challenge was great and required titanic energies. In November 1892 Yeats told his readers: 'Here in Ireland the marble block is waiting for us almost untouched, and the statues will come as soon as we have come to use the chisel.' The sculptural analogy is in accord with Yeats's insistence on the coldness and hardness required of great poetry, and it looks forward to his late poem 'The Statues', where he claimed that 'We Irish' can resist the 'formless, spawning, fury' of 'this filthy modern tide' by paying proper homage to 'The lineaments of a plummet-measured face'. The emphasis here is on potential, on a new beginning. In 1907 Yeats recalled the heroic challenge in terms which intimated something rather different: 'We were to forge in Ireland a new sword on our old traditional anvil for that great battle that must in the end re-establish the old, confident joyous world.' Revisiting or revising this youthful commitment to a national ideal, Yeats also presented himself in retrospect as an ironical self-observer: all the while 'one part of me looked on, mischievous and mocking, and the other part spoke words which were more and more unreal'. Here again we encounter that acute awareness of self, that ability to stand judiciously and judicially outside the action of the moment which characterises so much of Yeats's poetry. The prevailing suggestion is of a heroism which involves a conclusive struggle to restore the values of a civilisation which have been lost. Compare the aim of Stephen Dedalus at the end of *A Portrait of the Artist as a Young Man*: 'to forge in the smithy of my soul the uncreated conscience of my race'. Stephen Dedalus and Joyce concentrate on making something new, while Yeats looks towards a disregarded past or a set of disinherited values. The forging of the sword may carry resonances of Cuchulain and the Fianna (and even perhaps of the Arthurian cycle or of Wagner's Siegfried, whose sword also features in *Ulysses*), yet the predominant allusion to the 'great battle' draws upon Irish peasant visions of an apocalyptic conflict which would 'break at last the power of their enemies'. In spite of his tendencies towards ironical qualification, Yeats did recognise a major cultural opportunity and an undertaking of national importance which was not to be shirked. And such an undertaking involved a calculated antagonism and resistance towards the prevailing values of contemporary English culture and contemporary English literature.

In particular Yeats resisted Matthew Arnold's authoritative claim that poetry should be 'a criticism of life'; instead he maintained that it should be a revelation of hidden life. This insistence on revelation rather than criticism was propelled by Yeats's distaste for the moralising which he associated with nineteenth-century English literature, especially in the symptomatic cases of Wordsworth, George Eliot and various influential interpreters of Shakespeare. Yeats aligned himself with 'a revolt against irrelevant descriptions of nature, the scientific and moral discursiveness of *In Memoriam* ... the political eloquence of Swinburne, the psychological curiosity of Browning, and the poetical diction of everybody'. He resisted the 'preoccupation of our art and literature with knowledge, with the surface of life, with the arbitrary, with mechanism'. Yeats's stand did not involve a simple rejection of what was English, since these corrupting and corrupted values were at work not only in England but in Ireland itself, which suffered from the cultural inferiority complex which often accompanies the political impotence of the colony. Joyce's *Ulysses* meticulously captures the impress of English culture on the Dublin of 1904: it records a city unmistakably Irish in its speech, its character and the ferment of its politics while permeated by English newspapers, English music-hall songs, English advertisements, English racing-results, by the debased currency of English everyday life as well as its coinage. According to Yeats, the consequence of this closeness to the English example was a culture and a literature which was second-hand and anachronistic: 'the cast off fashions, the cast off clothes, the cast off thoughts of some active centre of creative minds'. The Irish themselves decried their own distinctive culture, because they had learned to look at it through English eyes: 'Forms of emotion and thought which the future will recognise as peculiarly Irish ... are looked upon as un-Irish because of their novelty in a land that is so nearly conquered that it has all but nothing of its own.' It was imperative for the Irish writer to capture those forms of emotion and thought before 'English influence and the "union of hearts" made us as prosaic as our neighbours'.

As his use of the word *prosaic* suggests, Yeats was encouraged in this commitment by his own belief that, underneath the superficial coating of an imported culture, there was still an alternative set of values which could be identified specifically with Ireland and with the poetic imagination. The Irish exhibited an 'energy of thought about life itself' and in Ireland a poet could still turn for support to those 'who still care, I think, for the high thoughts and high feelings of poetry, if in a somewhat uncultivated fashion'. In the west of Ireland Yeats had discovered that there existed 'a people, a community bound together by imaginative possessions, by stories and poems which have grown out of its own life, and by a past of great passions which can still waken the heart to imaginative action'. In contrast the English had been deprived of their imaginative heritage; they were no longer 'a people' in Yeats's sense of the word, only a 'mob'. This strongly freighted comparative reading of the social and political history of Ireland and of England is given expression in Yeats's autobiographical novella *John Sherman*, when the displaced hero finds himself on a tow-path beside the Thames:

A faint mist half-covered away the houses and factory chimneys on the further side; beside him a band of osiers swayed softly, the deserted and full river lapping their stems. He looked on all these things with foreign eyes. He had no sense of possession. Indeed it seemed to him that everything in London was owned by too many to be owned by anyone.

To the Irish eye of the transplanted John Sherman, this English scene is both evocative and foreign. Yeats also allows Sherman an insight which coincides with his own strongly held belief that the inhabitants of London had been dispossessed and dislocated by the fragmenting and alienating tendencies of modern life. This loss of individuality had its roots in what Yeats interpreted as the cultural catastrophe of the seventeenth century. As he suggested elsewhere, the rise of Cromwell had marked a turning point in English history, when 'the old individual, poetical life went down, as it seems, for ever'.

In his claim that this poetical life had survived in Ireland, Yeats was much influenced by the fact that in certain parts of the country the oral tradition was still identifiably alive. Here 'maybe for the last time in Europe' the oral tradition was 'face to face with the world that reads and writes'. Gaelic poems and stories were made to be spoken and were still part of a world in which 'the common man has some share in imaginative art'. In contrast modern English literature was almost entirely the product of the printing-press, which influenced its character and even determined its nature, and was primarily directed towards a small, cultivated minority. With the passage of time, these formulations were modified, yet the central distinction between oral and written, and between English and Irish, continued to provide momentum for his own poetic and imaginative enterprises. An interest in folklore, in ballads and in the popular literary traditions of the countryside characterises not only the earlier phase of his career but also much of his later poetry, where the language and rhythms of speech are markedly more prominent than in the literary poems of his youth.

Yeats was aware of a particular responsibility towards the claims of the oral, which was threatened by the predominant tendencies of contemporary English culture. His own poetry is always the product of what he calls 'conscious, deliberate craft', yet it also transmits a powerful and recognisable sense of voice. As he put it in 1913 in a letter to his father: 'I have tried to make my work convincing with a speech so natural and dramatic that the hearer would feel the presence of a man thinking and feeling.' Or again: 'If a poem talks ... we have the passionate syntax, the impression of the man who speaks, the active man, no abstract poet.' In later years he insisted that he must 'write for the ear', so that he might be 'instantly understood as when an actor or folksinger stands before an audience'. In 1937 he claimed that he had spent his life 'clearing out of poetry every phrase written for the eye, and bringing all back to syntax, that is for ear alone'. This sense of 'personal utterance' is often accompanied and confirmed by a demeanour and a posture which might best be described as bardic. So there are the grand declarative gestures of his rhetoric. So there are the prophetic visions and pronouncements such as 'A terrible beauty is born' or 'The blood-dimmed tide is loosed' or 'Man is in love and loves what vanishes'. (Here Yeats is the inheritor both of the bardic faculty and of the Romantic tradition as transmitted by Shelley and Blake.) And above all there is a commitment to the word rather than the world, a conviction that words themselves are the conductors of great and potent energies.

Yeats's commitment to the potency of the word was also connected with his belief in the virtues of English as it was spoken in those parts of Ireland which had not yet been corrupted by the 'base idiom' of the newspapers, the dangerous generalisations of politics and the clichés of contemporary English discourse, of 'a speech exhausted from abstraction'. In the Elizabethan period Irish writers 'belonged to the old individual, poetical life, and spoke a language [Irish] in which it was all but impossible to think an abstract thought'. Irish speech in the English language drew much of its strength from the character of the Irish language which had influenced its syntax, its idiom and its linguistic character. By returning to the spoken word and even to the model of peasant speech, Yeats found an antidote and an alternative to the prevailing idiom. At times this drew him towards dialect, partly under the influence of J. M. Synge and of Lady Gregory: so he remembered that he had found himself 'continually testing both my verse and my prose by translating it into dialect'. This practice was so salutary and carried such a cultural charge that he used it to suggest the peculiar force of Ezra Pound's bracing and abrasive influence in helping him 'to get back to the definite and concrete away from modern abstractions'. To talk over a poem with Pound was 'like getting you to put a sentence into dialect'.

Yeats was strengthened in his commitment to these values

and these convictions by his need to resist the influence of contemporary England and of contemporary English literature. Unlike Joyce, who avoided England and preferred to integrate himself in the safely distanced perspectives of Europe, Yeats lived much of his life in London, which he described, not without irony perhaps, as 'the capitol of the enemy', where his curious spelling translates the centre of the British Empire into a suggestive Latin equivalent. He did not settle in Ireland until 1922, after the establishment of the Free State, when he became a Senator. For an Irishman and particularly an Irish writer to live in England might induce 'an unnatural condition of mind', though the uncomfortably intimate presence of England could also provide, as it did for eighteenth-century writers such as Swift, Goldsmith and Burke, 'the opposite that stung their thought into expression and made it lucid'. Yeats's Irishness was cultivated in an English environment which was rigorously excluded from his poetry. In particular he resisted the influences of London itself, which brought to a negative focus all the most destabilising and threatening tendencies not only of English life but of the modern city and the modern world. Such a tendency was not specifically Irish: in his resistance to the urban, which was located at the centre of the British Empire, Yeats was encouraged by the intellectual example of English writers such as Ruskin and Morris. His reaction is strikingly different from those of his friend (and, briefly, secretary) Ezra Pound and of T. S. Eliot, both of whom also discovered London with the eyes of a foreigner. Whereas both the American poets engaged with the city and its culture in their own imaginative work, Yeats excluded it from his poetry, though it exercised an influence on his search for the ideal city, whether in Renaissance Italy or in the Byzantium where 'religious aesthetic and practical life were one'. Yeats's distaste for London applied by extension to Dublin, which he had once identified as 'shabby England' because of its derivative culture. Dublin leaves its mark on *Responsibilities* (1914), where its 'gaunt houses', its 'obscure spite', its 'greasy till' and its mean and narrow-minded philistinism are set against 'the Muses' sterner laws', the paradoxical 'delirium of the brave' and the enlightened patronage which enriched the life of Urbino, Ferrara and Florence. Yet by this time Dublin was no longer a provincial English city but had developed a distinctive character of its own. By the time Yeats produced *The Green Helmet, Poems Written in Discouragement* and *Responsibilities*, he had observed the transformation of a 'well-mannered smooth-spoken city' into an 'unmannerly town', and he had marked a new impetus towards free discussion, which brought 'the passion for reality' as 'the accumulated hatred of years was suddenly transferred from England to Ireland'. 'Easter 1916' is, in one sense, a Dublin poem: it offers an ambivalent celebration of that revolutionary drama which had been enacted against a backdrop of 'grey/Eighteenth-century houses'. Yet here, as almost everywhere in Yeats, the modern city is not a central presence, though it is often the invisible antagonist. For Yeats it was antithetical to art and provided metaphors for repudiation: 'In this congested city we sleep, as it were, fifteen in a bed. Art is solitary man.' The contrast with Joyce is unavoidable: compare *The Tower* to *Ulysses*.

Yeats's hostility towards the modern city and his recourse to the ideals of the Renaissance or of Byzantium, of courtly Japan or of Ireland's heroic age, might suggest that his work was out of touch with the times. His concern with the ancient, the traditional, the mystical (as in the systematic configurations of *A Vision*) and the mythical might also seem to point in that direction. Yet, as Eliot observed in his review of *Ulysses*, the mythical method had already been 'adumbrated by Mr. Yeats, and of the need for which I believe Mr. Yeats to have been the first contemporary to be conscious'. This method was 'simply a way of controlling, of ordering, of giving a shape and a significance to the immense panorama of futility and anarchy which is contemporary history'. Yeats's commitment to a private code of eclectic values was a deliberately cultivated alternative to 'our life in cities, which deafens or kills the passive meditative life, and our education that enlarges the separated, self-moving mind', both of which 'have made our souls less sensitive'. He could be mannered or esoteric or archaistic, and his cultivation of aristocratic values did carry considerable political risks; yet his work represents a cumulative and coherent response to the spirit of the age which compels our attention.

The strength of Yeats's vision is based above all on his absolute commitment to the craft of poetry. In order to maintain this fidelity it was necessary to negotiate with the claims of the external world and in particular of public life. Although in his earlier years Yeats had identified himself as 'a Nationalist', he habitually resisted the simplifications of propaganda and of popular rhetoric. The older Yeats was much more open to the receipt of public affairs than his younger self; yet the events of Easter 1916, of the Troubles and the Civil War, and of post-war Europe, were registered almost less, perhaps, as external realities than as part of Yeats's own poetic and psychological life. The title of 'Meditations in Time of Civil War' indicates a reflective and distancing process; here as in 'Easter 1916' public events are placed and recorded but the prevailing perspective is a subjective one, and the conflicts are internalised.

Yeats himself provided a helpful guide to his own practice when he wrote in 'Anima Hominis' (1917): 'We make out of the quarrel with others, rhetoric, but of the quarrel with ourselves, poetry.' It was through his consistent attention to the dialectic within and the poetic means which he evolved to express it that Yeats maintained the vigour of his poetry. Unlike Pound or Eliot or Joyce he could not be classified as a modernist; he was neither as experimental nor as revolutionary as they were. Yet his poetry was constantly developing and changing, most significantly and most dramatically after he passed his fiftieth birthday. As early as 1906 he publicly admitted that for him a commitment to drama had involved 'the search for more of manful energy, more of cheerful acceptance of whatever arises out of the logic of events, and for clean outline, instead of those outlines of lyric poetry that are blurred with desire and vague regret'. His poetic diction was gradually transformed as he learned from his experience as a playwright, from life itself (and sometimes from contemporaries such as Pound) to replace the wavering organic rhythms and the embroideries of earlier work with a more naked muscularity of expression. The contrast between *The Wind Among the Reeds* and the Crazy Jane poems of the thirties could hardly be more striking. Thus, although Yeats was never a modernist, he was a modern. The physical and sexual frankness of his later poetry and its extraordinary blend of directness with 'magnanimities of sound' were both the result of a more liberated sense of poetic possibilities and the product of a lifelong commitment to the means of expression. Yeats is a compelling poetic presence not least because he assumed so many shapes in the long process of his poetic evolution.

A Note on the Text

The order of *Last Poems* is controversial and must remain problematic. Until recently the order and selection of poems universally followed was that established after Yeats's death by his widow and his publishers in *Last Poems and Plays* (1940). This edition combined thirty-five poems from *New Poems* and three from *On the Boiler* with those poems which had been printed in *Last Poems and Two Plays* (1939) under the imprint of the Cuala Press. After the appearance of *Collected Poems* in 1949 this conjunction of poems from three sources acquired canonical status, with significant consequences. *New Poems*, which had been published during Yeats's lifetime, was not accorded individual identity and did not feature among the named volumes which together constituted the corpus of Yeats's poetic achievement. *On the Boiler* was also omitted as a separate heading, but this was less surprising, since it was essentially a volume of prose which included three poems. The *Collected Poems* of 1949 also chose to ignore the sequence of those poems which had been published in *Last Poems and Two Plays* shortly after Yeats's death in 1939.

The present selection coincides with the practice of several of Yeats's most recent editors in breaking with this tradition by acknowledging the existence of *New Poems*, *On the Boiler* and *Last Poems and Two Plays* as separate volumes and by following the sequence of poems which they established. The ordering of the poems in *Last Poems and Two Plays* was, of course, posthumous, but, as Curtis Bradford has shown, it corresponds to a manuscript list prepared by Yeats and may therefore be assumed to embody his intentions. The effect of these changes is to produce a redistribution which significantly affects the resonance of individual poems and of the collection by altering the relationships between the constituent elements. *Last Poems* begins with 'The Gyres' and ends with 'Under Ben Bulben'. In *Last Poems and Two Plays* (which is followed here) 'Under Ben Bulben' is the first poem and the volume ends not with the poet's epitaph for himself but with the brief lyric 'Politics'. The main consequence of starting with 'Under Ben Bulben' is to imply that all the other poems are delivered from beyond the grave and represent a legacy to Yeats's successors, while the choice of 'Politics' as a conclusion introduces an insistence on the human and the physical which is characteristically Yeatsian, even while lamenting an old man's distance from the love which he celebrates. It is important to notice, though, that *Last Poems and Two Plays* did not end with 'Politics' but with two plays focused on last things: *The Death of Cuchulain* and *Purgatory*. No edition of the poetry can do justice to the complexity of this original volume.

In spite of this process of reordering, the editorial policy informing the present selection is essentially conservative, in keeping with the general aim of the series and the constraints imposed by copyright. The main initiative is the printing of alternative versions of a number of poems and the inclusion of a selection of variant readings, all from printed texts. There is no attempt to be comprehensive; the choices represent an editorial selection which is intended to illustrate the most significant and interesting elements in Yeats's revisionary process and the diversity of his textual history.

The main source for poems up to and including *The Winding Stair* is *Collected Poems* (1933). Exceptions are provided by 'The Phases of the Moon', 'Leda and the Swan' and 'All Souls' Night', which are based on the versions in *A Vision* (1937), as well as 'The Hero, the Girl and the Fool', which is based on the version in *The Tower* (1928). Poems from *A Full Moon in March* (1935), *New Poems* (1938) and *On the Boiler* (1939) are based on the texts which were established in those volumes. *Last Poems* presents more of a problem, since some of the poems did not appear until after Yeats's death, and there is considerable textual uncertainty, especially in matters of punctuation. My main sources are as follows: *Last Poems and Two Plays* (for 'Under Ben Bulben', 'The Black Tower' and 'Cuchulain Comforted'); *London Mercury*, March 1939 (for 'The Statues', 'News for the Delphic Oracle', 'Long-legged Fly' and 'A Bronze Head'); *London Mercury*, December 1938 (for 'John Kinsella's Lament for Mrs. Mary Moore' and 'High Talk'); *London Mercury*, January 1939 (for 'The Man and the Echo', 'The Circus Animals' Desertion' and 'Politics'). In a small number of cases, in these poems, as elsewhere in the edition, I have found it necessary to intervene very slightly in matters of spelling and punctuation. In punctuation I have looked for intelligibility rather than consistency and intervened only when it seemed unavoidable. In spelling I have aimed at consistency, almost exclusively in proper names; this does not apply in the case of hyphenated words, where Yeats's practice seems too diverse to be brought under a rule.

The publishers are grateful to the following for permission to reproduce copyright material: to A. P. Watt Ltd, on behalf of Michael B. Yeats, and Macmillan London Ltd for 'Reprisals'; to Oxford University Press and the Estate of W. B. Yeats for *Vision and Revision in Last Poems* by Jon Stallworthy (1969); to Grafton Books, a division of HarperCollins Publishers, for *The Letters of W. B. Yeats*, edited by Allan Wade (London, Hart-Davis, 1954); to the Morris Library (Special Collections), Southern Illinois University at Carbondale, and the Estate of W. B. Yeats for *Yeats at Work* by Curtis Bradford.

Love Song

◇◇◇◇

From the Gaelic

My love, we will go, we will go, I and you,
And away in the woods we will scatter the dew;
And the salmon behold, and the ousel too,
My love, we will hear, I and you, we will hear,
The calling afar of the doe and the deer.   5
And the bird in the branches will cry for us clear,
And the cuckoo unseen in his festival mood;
And death, oh my fair one, will never come near
In the bosom afar of the fragrant wood.

The Wanderings of Oisin

◇◇◇◇

Book III

Fled foam underneath us, and round us, a
    wandering and milky smoke,
High as the saddle-girth, covering away from our
    glances the tide;
And those that fled, and that followed, from the
    foam-pale distance broke;
The immortal desire of Immortals we saw in
    their faces, and sighed.

I mused on the chase with the Fenians, and Bran,
    Sceolan, Lomair,   5
And never a song sang Niamh, and over my
    finger-tips

Came now the sliding of tears and sweeping of
    mist-cold hair,
And now the warmth of sighs, and after the
    quiver of lips.

Were we days long or hours long in riding, when,
    rolled in a grisly peace,
An isle lay level before us, with dripping hazel
10   and oak?
And we stood on a sea's edge we saw not; for
    whiter than new-washed fleece
Fled foam underneath us, and round us, a
    wandering and milky smoke.

And we rode on the plains of the sea's edge; the
    sea's edge barren and grey,
Grey sand on the green of the grasses and over
    the dripping trees,
Dripping and doubling landward, as though they
15   would hasten away,
Like an army of old men longing for rest from
    the moan of the seas.

But the trees grew taller and closer, immense in
    their wrinkling bark;
Dropping; a murmurous dropping; old silence
    and that one sound;
For no live creatures lived there, no weasels
    moved in the dark:
Long sighs arose in our spirits, beneath us
20   bubbled the ground.

And the ears of the horse went sinking away in
    the hollow night,
For, as drift from a sailor slow drowning the
    gleams of the world and the sun,
Ceased on our hands and our faces, on hazel and
    oak leaf, the light,
And the stars were blotted above us, and the
    whole of the world was one.

Till the horse gave a whinny; for, cumbrous with
    stems of the hazel and oak,   25
A valley flowed down from his hoofs, and there
    in the long grass lay,
Under the starlight and shadow, a monstrous
    slumbering folk,
Their naked and gleaming bodies poured out and
    heaped in the way.

And by them were arrow and war-axe, arrow and
    shield and blade;
And dew-blanched horns, in whose hollow a child
    of three years old   30
Could sleep on a couch of rushes, and all
    inwrought and inlaid,
And more comely than man can make them with
    bronze and silver and gold.

And each of the huge white creatures was huger
    than fourscore men;
The tops of their ears were feathered, their hands
    were the claws of birds,
And, shaking the plumes of the grasses and the
    leaves of the mural glen,   35
The breathing came from those bodies, long
    warless, grown whiter than curds.

The wood was so spacious above them, that He
    who has stars for His flocks
Could fondle the leaves with His fingers, nor go
    from His dew-cumbered skies;
So long were they sleeping, the owls had builded
    their nests in their locks,
Filling the fibrous dimness with long generations
    of eyes.   40

And over the limbs and the valley the slow owls
    wandered and came,
Now in a place of star-fire, and now in a shadow-
    place wide;

And the chief of the huge white creatures, his
    knees in the soft star-flame,
Lay loose in a place of shadow: we drew the reins
    by his side.

Golden the nails of his bird-claws, flung loosely
45   along the dim ground;
In one was a branch soft-shining with bells more
    many than sighs
In midst of an old man's bosom; owls ruffling
    and pacing around
Sidled their bodies against him, filling the shade
    with their eyes.

And my gaze was thronged with the sleepers; no,
    not since the world began,
In realms where the handsome were many, nor in
50   glamours by demons flung,
Have faces alive with such beauty been known to
    the salt eye of man,
Yet weary with passions that faded when the
    sevenfold seas were young.

And I gazed on the bell-branch, sleep's forebear,
    far sung by the Sennachies.
I saw how those slumberers, grown weary, there
    camping in grasses deep,
Of wars with the wide world and pacing the
55   shores of the wandering seas,
Laid hands on the bell-branch and swayed it, and
    fed of unhuman sleep.

Snatching the horn of Niamh, I blew a long
    lingering note.
Came sound from those monstrous sleepers, a
    sound like the stirring of flies.
He, shaking the fold of his lips, and heaving the
    pillar of his throat,
Watched me with mournful wonder out of the
60   wells of his eyes.

4

I cried, 'Come out of the shadow, king of the
    nails of gold!
And tell of your goodly household and the goodly
    works of your hands,
That we may muse in the starlight and talk of
    the battles of old;
Your questioner, Oisin, is worthy, he comes from
    the Fenian lands.'

Half open his eyes were, and held me, dull with
    the smoke of their dreams;   65
His lips moved slowly in answer, no answer out
    of them came;
Then he swayed in his fingers the bell-branch,
    slow dropping a sound in faint streams
Softer than snow-flakes in April and piercing the
    marrow like flame.

Wrapt in the wave of that music, with weariness
    more than of earth,
The moil of my centuries filled me; and gone like
    a sea-covered stone   70
Were the memories of the whole of my sorrow
    and the memories of the whole of my mirth,
And a softness came from the starlight and filled
    me full to the bone.

In the roots of the grasses, the sorrels, I laid my
    body as low;
And the pearl-pale Niamh lay by me, her brow
    on the midst of my breast;
And the horse was gone in the distance, and years
    after years 'gan flow;   75
Square leaves of the ivy moved over us, binding
    us down to our rest.

And, man of the many white croziers, a century
    there I forgot
How the fetlocks drip blood in the battle, when
    the fallen on fallen lie rolled;

How the falconer follows the falcon in the weeds
    of the heron's plot,
And the name of the demon whose hammer made
80   Conchubar's sword-blade of old.

And, man of the many white croziers, a century
    there I forgot
That the spear-shaft is made out of ashwood, the
    shield out of osier and hide;
How the hammers spring on the anvil, on the
    spearhead's burning spot;
How the slow, blue-eyed oxen of Finn low sadly
    at evening tide.

But in dreams, mild man of the croziers, driving
85   the dust with their throngs,
Moved round me, of seamen or landsmen, all
    who are winter tales;
Came by me the kings of the Red Branch, with
    roaring of laughter and songs,
Or moved as they moved once, love-making or
    piercing the tempest with sails.

Came Blanaid, Mac Nessa, tall Fergus who
    feastward of old time slunk,
Cook Barach, the traitor; and warward, the spittle
90   on his beard never dry,
Dark Balor, as old as a forest, car-borne, his
    mighty head sunk
Helpless, men lifting the lids of his weary and
    death-making eye.

And by me, in soft red raiment, the Fenians
    moved in loud streams,
And Grania, walking and smiling, sewed with her
    needle of bone.
So lived I and lived not, so wrought I and
95   wrought not, with creatures of dreams,
In a long iron sleep, as a fish in the water goes
    dumb as a stone.

At times our slumber was lightened. When the
    sun was on silver or gold;
When brushed with the wings of the owls, in the
    dimness they love going by;
When a glow-worm was green on a grass-leaf,
    lured from his lair in the mould;
Half wakening, we lifted our eyelids, and gazed
    on the grass with a sigh.   100

So watched I when, man of the croziers, at the
    heel of a century fell,
Weak, in the midst of the meadow, from his
    miles in the midst of the air,
A starling like them that forgathered 'neath a
    moon waking white as a shell
When the Fenians made foray at morning with
    Bran, Sceolan, Lomair.

I awoke: the strange horse without summons out
    of the distance ran,   105
Thrusting his nose to my shoulder; he knew in
    his bosom deep
That once more moved in my bosom the ancient
    sadness of man,
And that I would leave the Immortals, their
    dimness, their dews dropping sleep.

O, had you seen beautiful Niamh grow white as
    the waters are white,
Lord of the croziers, you even had lifted your
    hands and wept: 110
But, the bird in my fingers, I mounted,
    remembering alone that delight
Of twilight and slumber were gone, and that
    hoofs impatiently stept.

I cried, 'O Niamh! O white one! if only a twelve-
    houred day,
I must gaze on the beard of Finn, and move
    where the old men and young

In the Fenians' dwellings of wattle lean on the
115   chessboards and play,
Ah, sweet to me now were even bald Conan's
    slanderous tongue!

'Like me were some galley forsaken far off in
    Meridian isle,
Remembering its long-oared companions, sails
    turning to threadbare rags;
No more to crawl on the seas with long oars mile
    after mile,
But to be amid shooting of flies and flowering
120   of rushes and flags.'

Their motionless eyeballs of spirits grown mild
    with mysterious thought,
Watched her those seamless faces from the
    valley's glimmering girth;
As she murmured, 'O wandering Oisin, the
    strength of the bell-branch is naught,
For there moves alive in your fingers the
    fluttering sadness of earth.

'Then go through the lands in the saddle and see
125   what the mortals do,
And softly come to your Niamh over the tops of
    the tide;
But weep for your Niamh, O Oisin, weep; for if
    only your shoe
Brush lightly as haymouse earth's pebbles, you
    will come no more to my side.

'O flaming lion of the world, O when will you
    turn to your rest?'
I saw from a distant saddle; from the earth she
130   made her moan:
'I would die like a small withered leaf in the
    autumn, for breast unto breast
We shall mingle no more, nor our gazes empty
    their sweetness lone

'In the isles of the farthest seas where only the
   spirits come.
Were the winds less soft than the breath of a
   pigeon who sleeps on her nest,
Nor lost in the star-fires and odours the sound
   of the sea's vague drum?   135
O flaming lion of the world, O when will you
   turn to your rest?'

The wailing grew distant; I rode by the woods of
   the wrinkling bark,
Where ever is murmurous dropping, old silence
   and that one sound;
For no live creatures live there, no weasels move
   in the dark;
In a reverie forgetful of all things, over the
   bubbling ground.   140

And I rode by the plains of the sea's edge, where
   all is barren and grey,
Grey sand on the green of the grasses and over
   the dripping trees,
Dripping and doubling landward, as though they
   would hasten away,
Like an army of old men longing for rest from
   the moan of the seas.

And the winds made the sands on the sea's edge
   turning and turning go,   145
As my mind made the names of the Fenians. Far
   from the hazel and oak,
I rode away on the surges, where, high as the
   saddle-bow,
Fled foam underneath me, and round me, a
   wandering and milky smoke.

Long fled the foam-flakes around me, the winds
   fled out of the vast,
Snatching the bird in secret; nor knew I,
   embosomed apart,   150

When they froze the cloth on my body like
    armour riveted fast,
For Remembrance, lifting her leanness, keened in
    the gates of my heart.

Till, fattening the winds of the morning, an
    odour of new-mown hay
Came, and my forehead fell low, and my tears
    like berries fell down;
Later a sound came, half lost in the sound of a
155   shore far away,
From the great grass-barnacle calling, and later
    the shore-weeds brown.

If I were as I once was, the strong hoofs crushing
    the sand and the shells,
Coming out of the sea as the dawn comes, a
    chaunt of love on my lips,
Not coughing, my head on my knees, and
    praying, and wroth with the bells,
I would leave no saint's head on his body from
160   Rachlin to Bera of ships.

Making way from the kindling surges, I rode on
    a bridle-path
Much wondering to see upon all hands, of wattles
    and woodwork made,
Your bell-mounted churches, and guardless the
    sacred cairn and the rath,
And a small and a feeble populace stooping with
    mattock and spade,

Or weeding or ploughing with faces a-shining
165   with much-toil wet;
While in this place and that place, with bodies
    unglorious, their chieftains stood,
Awaiting in patience the straw-death, croziered
    one, caught in your net:
Went the laughter of scorn from my mouth like
    the roaring of wind in a wood.

And because I went by them so huge and so
    speedy with eyes so bright,
Came after the hard gaze of youth, or an old man
    lifted his head: 170
And I rode and I rode, and I cried out, 'The
    Fenians hunt wolves in the night,
So sleep thee by daytime.' A voice cried, 'The
    Fenians a long time are dead.'

A whitebeard stood hushed on the pathway, the
    flesh of his face as dried grass,
And in folds round his eyes and his mouth, he
    sad as a child without milk
And the dreams of the islands were gone, and I
    knew how men sorrow and pass,   175
And their hound, and their horse, and their love,
    and their eyes that glimmer like silk.

And wrapping my face in my hair, I murmured,
    'In old age they ceased';
And my tears were larger than berries, and I
    murmured, 'Where white clouds lie spread
On Crevroe or broad Knockfefin, with many of
    old they feast
On the floors of the gods.' He cried, 'No, the
    gods a long time are dead.'   180

And lonely and longing for Niamh, I shivered
    and turned me about,
The heart in me longing to leap like a
    grasshopper into her heart;
I turned and rode to the westward, and followed
    the sea's old shout
Till I saw where Maeve lies sleeping till starlight
    and midnight part.

And there at the foot of the mountain, two
    carried a sack full of sand,   185
They bore it with staggering and sweating, but
    fell with their burden at length.

Leaning down from the gem-studded saddle, I
    flung it five yards with my hand,
With a sob for men waxing so weakly, a sob for
    the Fenians' old strength.

The rest you have heard of, O croziered man;
    how, when divided the girth,
I fell on the path, and the horse went away like
190   a summer fly;
And my years three hundred fell on me, and I
    rose, and walked on the earth,
A creeping old man, full of sleep, with the spittle
    on his beard never dry.

How the men of the sand-sack showed me a
    church with its belfry in air;
Sorry place, where for swing of the war-axe in
    my dim eyes the crozier gleams;
What place have Caoilte and Conan, and Bran,
195   Sceolan, Lomair?
Speak, you too are old with your memories, an
    old man surrounded with dreams.

S. *Patrick*. Where the flesh of the footsole
    clingeth on the burning stones is their place;
Where the demons whip them with wires on the
    burning stones of wide Hell,
Watching the blessèd ones move far off, and the
    smile on God's face,
Between them a gateway of brass, and the howl
200   of the angels who fell.

Oisin. Put the staff in my hands; for I go to the
    Fenians, O cleric, to chaunt
The war-songs that roused them of old; they will
    rise, making clouds with their breath,
Innumerable, singing, exultant; the clay
    underneath them shall pant,
And demons be broken in pieces, and trampled
    beneath them in death.

And demons afraid in their darkness; deep horror
    of eyes and of wings,   205
Afraid, their ears on the earth laid, shall listen
    and rise up and weep;
Hearing the shaking of shields and the quiver of
    stretched bowstrings,
Hearing Hell loud with a murmur, as shouting
    and mocking we sweep.

We will tear out the flaming stones, and batter
    the gateway of brass
And enter, and none sayeth 'No' when there
    enters the strongly armed guest;   210
Make clean as a broom cleans, and march on as
    oxen move over young grass;
Then feast, making converse of wars, and of old
    wounds, and turn to our rest.

S. Patrick. On the flaming stones, without
    refuge, the limbs of the Fenians are tost;
None war on the masters of Hell, who could
    break up the world in their rage;
But kneel and wear out the flags and pray for
    your soul that is lost   215
Through the demon love of its youth and its
    godless and passionate age.

Oisin. Ah me! to be shaken with coughing and
    broken with old age and pain,
Without laughter, a show unto children, alone
    with remembrance and fear;
All emptied of purple hours as a beggar's cloak
    in the rain,
As a hay-cock out on the flood, or a wolf sucked
    under a weir.   220

It were sad to gaze on the blessèd and no man I
    loved of old there;
I throw down the chain of small stones! when life
    in my body has ceased,

I will go to Caoilte, and Conan, and Bran,
    Sceolan, Lomair,
And dwell in the house of the Fenians, be they in
    flames or at feast.

lines 217–24   Ah me! to be old without succour, a show
        unto children, a stain,
    Without laughter, a coughing, alone with
        remembrance and fear,
    All emptied of purple hours as a beggar's
        cloak in the rain,
    As a grass seed crushed by a pebble, as a
        wolf sucked under a weir.

    I will pray no more with the smooth stones:
        when life in my body has ceased –
    For lonely to move 'mong the soft eyes of
        best ones a sad thing were –
    I will go to the house of the Fenians, be
        they in flames or at feast,
    To Fin, Caolte, and Conan, and Bran,
        Sgeolan, Lomair.

(first edition, 1889)

CROSSWAYS

❖❖❖❖❖

The Indian to His Love

❖❖❖

The island dreams under the dawn
And great boughs drop tranquillity;
The peahens dance on a smooth lawn,
A parrot sways upon a tree,
Raging at his own image in the enamelled sea.   5

Here we will moor our lonely ship
And wander ever with woven hands,
Murmuring softly lip to lip,
Along the grass, along the sands,
Murmuring how far away are the unquiet lands: 10

How we alone of mortals are
Hid under quiet boughs apart,
While our love grows an Indian star,
A meteor of the burning heart,
One with the tide that gleams, the wings that
   gleam and dart,   15

The heavy boughs, the burnished dove
That moans and sighs a hundred days:
How when we die our shades will rove,
When eve has hushed the feathered ways,
With vapoury footsole by the water's drowsy
   blaze.   20

An Indian Song

Oh wanderer in the southern weather,
    Our isle awaits us; on each lea
The pea-hens dance, in crimson feather
    A parrot swaying on a tree
5   Rages at his own image in the enamelled sea.

There dreamy Time lets fall his sickle
    And Life the sandals of her fleetness,
    And sleek young Joy is no more fickle,
    And Love is kindly and deceitless,
10   And all is over save the murmur and the sweetness.

There we will moor our lonely ship
    And wander ever with woven hands,
Murmuring softly, lip to lip,
    Along the grass, along the sands –
15   Murmuring how far away are all earth's feverish lands:

How we alone of mortals are
    Hid in the earth's most hidden part,
While grows our love an Indian star,
    A meteor of the burning heart,
20   One with the waves that softly round us laugh and dart;

One with the leaves; one with the dove
    That moans and sighs a hundred days;
– How when we die our shades will rove,
    Dropping at eve in coral bays
25   A vapoury footfall on the ocean's sleepy blaze.

(The Wanderings of Oisin, 1889)

Ephemera

❖❖❖❖

'Your eyes that once were never weary of mine
Are bowed in sorrow under pendulous lids,
Because our love is waning.'
               And then she:
'Although our love is waning, let us stand

By the lone border of the lake once more,   5
Together in that hour of gentleness
When the poor tired child, Passion, falls asleep.
How far away the stars seem, and how far
Is our first kiss, and ah, how old my heart!'

Pensive they paced along the faded leaves,   10
While slowly he whose hand held hers replied:
'Passion has often worn our wandering hearts.'

The woods were round them, and the yellow
    leaves
Fell like faint meteors in the gloom, and once
A rabbit old and lame limped down the path;   15
Autumn was over him: and now they stood
On the lone border of the lake once more:
Turning, he saw that she had thrust dead leaves
Gathered in silence, dewy as her eyes,
In bosom and hair.
                            'Ah, do not mourn,' he said, 20
'That we are tired, for other loves await us;
Hate on and love through unrepining hours.
Before us lies eternity; our souls
Are love, and a continual farewell.'

Ephemera

An Autumn Idyl

'Your eyes that once were never weary of mine
Lie now half hidden under pendulous lids,
Veined in a dreamy sorrow for their love
That wanes.' 'Ah, wistful voice,' replied the other,
'Though our sad love is fading, let us yet   5
Stand by the border of the lake once more,
Together in that hour of gentleness
When the poor tired child, passion, falls asleep.
How far away the stars seem, and how far
Is our first kiss, and ah, how old my heart!'   10
Pensive they paced along the faded leaves,

17

While slowly answered he whose hand held hers –
'Often has passion worn our wandering hearts,
Earth's aliens. Why so sorrowful? Our souls
15   Shall warm their lives at many a rustling flame.'

The woods were round them, and the yellow leaves
Fell like faint meteors in the gloom, and once
A rabbit old and lame limped down the path –
Autumn was over him – and now they stood
20   On the lone border of the sullen lake.
Turning, he saw that she had thrust dead leaves,
Gathered in silence, dewy as her eyes,
In bosom and hair.
                Then he: 'Let us not mourn
That we are tired, for other loves await us.
25   Hate on and love through unrepining hours.
Before us lies eternity; our souls
Are love, and a continual farewell.'

He spake once more and fondled with his lips
That word of the soul's peace – 'Eternity.'

30   The little waves that walked in evening whiteness,
Glimmering in her drooped eyes, saw her lips move
And whisper, 'The innumerable reeds
I know the word they cry, "Eternity!"
And sing from shore to shore, and every year
35   They pine away and yellow and wear out,
And ah, they know not, as they pine and cease,
Not they are the eternal – 'tis the cry.'

                        (*The Wanderings of Oisin*, 1889)

The Stolen Child

❖❖❖

Where dips the rocky highland
Of Sleuth Wood in the lake,
There lies a leafy island
Where flapping herons wake
5   The drowsy water-rats;

There we've hid our faery vats,
Full of berries
And of reddest stolen cherries.
Come away, O human child!
To the waters and the wild   10
With a faery, hand in hand,
For the world's more full of weeping than you can
   understand.

Where the wave of moonlight glosses
The dim grey sands with light,
Far off by furthest Rosses   15
We foot it all the night,
Weaving olden dances,
Mingling hands and mingling glances
Till the moon has taken flight;
To and fro we leap   20
And chase the frothy bubbles,
While the world is full of troubles
And is anxious in its sleep.
Come away, O human child!
To the waters and the wild   25
With a faery, hand in hand,
For the world's more full of weeping than you can
   understand.

Where the wandering water gushes
From the hills above Glen-Car,
In pools among the rushes   30
That scarce could bathe a star,
We seek for slumbering trout
And whispering in their ears
Give them unquiet dreams;
Leaning softly out   35
From ferns that drop their tears
Over the young streams.
Come away, O human child!
To the waters and the wild

40 *With a faery, hand in hand,*
For the world's more full of weeping than you can
    understand.

Away with us he's going,
The solemn-eyed:
He'll hear no more the lowing
45 Of the calves on the warm hillside
Or the kettle on the hob
Sing peace into his breast,
Or see the brown mice bob
Round and round the oatmeal-chest.
50 *For he comes, the human child!*
To the waters and the wild
With a faery, hand in hand,
From a world more full of weeping than he can
    understand.

Down by the Salley Gardens
❖❖❖

Down by the salley gardens my love and I did meet;
She passed the salley gardens with little snow-white feet.
She bid me take love easy, as the leaves grow on the tree;
But I, being young and foolish, with her would not agree.

5 In a field by the river my love and I did stand,
And on my leaning shoulder she laid her snow-white hand.
She bid me take life easy, as the grass grows on the weirs;
But I was young and foolish, and now am full of tears.

THE ROSE

To the Rose upon the Rood of Time

Red Rose, proud Rose, sad Rose of all my days!
Come near me, while I sing the ancient ways:
Cuchulain battling with the bitter tide;
The Druid, grey, wood-nurtured, quiet-eyed,
Who cast round Fergus dreams, and ruin untold;   5
And thine own sadness, whereof stars, grown old
In dancing silver-sandalled on the sea,
Sing in their high and lonely melody.
Come near, that no more blinded by man's fate,
I find under the boughs of love and hate,   10
In all poor foolish things that live a day,
Eternal beauty wandering on her way.

Come near, come near, come near – Ah, leave me still
A little space for the rose-breath to fill!
Lest I no more hear common things that crave;   15
The weak worm hiding down in its small cave,
The field-mouse running by me in the grass,
And heavy mortal hopes that toil and pass;
But seek alone to hear the strange things said
By God to the bright hearts of those long dead,   20
And learn to chaunt a tongue men do not know.
Come near; I would, before my time to go,
Sing of old Eire and the ancient ways:
Red Rose, proud Rose, sad Rose of all my days.

Fergus and the Druid

❖❖❖

Fergus. This whole day have I followed in the
    rocks,
    And you have changed and flowed from shape
      to shape,
    First as a raven on whose ancient wings
    Scarcely a feather lingered, then you seemed
5   A weasel moving on from stone to stone,
    And now at last you wear a human shape,
    A thin grey man half lost in gathering night.

Druid. What would you, king of the proud Red
    Branch kings?

Fergus. This would I say, most wise of living
    souls:
10   Young subtle Conchubar sat close by me
    When I gave judgment, and his words were
      wise,
    And what to me was burden without end,
    To him seemed easy, so I laid the crown
    Upon his head to cast away my sorrow.

Druid. What would you, king of the proud Red
15   Branch kings?

Fergus. A king and proud! and that is my despair.
    I feast amid my people on the hill,
    And pace the woods, and drive my chariot-
      wheels
    In the white border of the murmuring sea;
20   And still I feel the crown upon my head.

Druid. What would you, Fergus?

Fergus.   Be no more a king
    But learn the dreaming wisdom that is yours.

Druid. Look on my thin grey hair and hollow
    cheeks
    And on these hands that may not lift the
    sword,
    This body trembling like a wind-blown reed.   25
    No woman's loved me, no man sought my
    help.

Fergus. A king is but a foolish labourer
    Who wastes his blood to be another's dream.

Druid. Take, if you must, this little bag of
    dreams;
    Unloose the cord, and they will wrap you
    round.   30

Fergus. I see my life go drifting like a river
    From change to change; I have been many
    things –
    A green drop in the surge, a gleam of light
    Upon a sword, a fir-tree on a hill,
    An old slave grinding at a heavy quern,   35
    A king sitting upon a chair of gold –
    And all these things were wonderful and great;
    But now I have grown nothing, knowing all.
    Ah, Druid, Druid, how great webs of sorrow
    Lay hidden in the small slate-coloured thing!   40

lines 27–8   A wild and foolish labourer is a king
                To do and do and do and never dream.

lines 38–40   But now I have grown nothing, being all:
                The sorrows of the world bow down my head,
                And in my heart the daemons and the gods
                Wage an eternal battle, and I feel
                The pain of wounds, the labour of the spear,
                But have no share in loss or victory.

(*National Observer*, 21 May 1892)

Cuchulain's Fight with the Sea

A man came slowly from the setting sun,
To Emer, raddling raiment in her dun,
And said, 'I am that swineherd whom you bid
Go watch the road between the wood and tide,
5 But now I have no need to watch it more.'

Then Emer cast the web upon the floor,
And raising arms all raddled with the dye,
Parted her lips with a loud sudden cry.

That swineherd stared upon her face and said,
10 'No man alive, no man among the dead,
Has won the gold his cars of battle bring.'

'But if your master comes home triumphing
Why must you blench and shake from foot to
    crown?'

Thereon he shook the more and cast him down
15 Upon the web-heaped floor, and cried his word:
'With him is one sweet-throated like a bird.'

'You dare me to my face,' and thereupon
She smote with raddled fist, and where her son
Herded the cattle came with stumbling feet,
20 And cried with angry voice, 'It is not meet
To idle life away, a common herd.'

'I have long waited, mother, for that word:
But wherefore now?'

                'There is a man to die;
You have the heaviest arm under the sky.'

25 'Whether under its daylight or its stars
My father stands amid his battle-cars.'

'But you have grown to be the taller man.'

'Yet somewhere under starlight or the sun
My father stands.'

      'Aged, worn out with wars
On foot, on horseback or in battle-cars.'   30

'I only ask what way my journey lies,
For He who made you bitter made you wise.'

'The Red Branch camp in a great company
Between wood's rim and the horses of the sea.
Go there, and light a camp-fire at wood's rim;   35
But tell your name and lineage to him
Whose blade compels, and wait till they have found
Some feasting man that the same oath has bound.'

Among those feasting men Cuchulain dwelt,
And his young sweetheart close beside him knelt,   40
Stared on the mournful wonder of his eyes,
Even as Spring upon the ancient skies,
And pondered on the glory of his days;
And all around the harp-string told his praise,
And Conchubar, the Red Branch king of kings,   45
With his own fingers touched the brazen strings.

At last Cuchulain spake, 'Some man has made
His evening fire amid the leafy shade.
I have often heard him singing to and fro,
I have often heard the sweet sound of his bow.   50
Seek out what man he is.'

      One went and came.
'He bade me let all know he gives his name
At the sword-point, and waits till we have found
Some feasting man that the same oath has bound.'

Cuchulain cried, 'I am the only man   55
Of all this host so bound from childhood on.'

After short fighting in the leafy shade,
He spake to the young man, 'Is there no maid

Who loves you, no white arms to wrap you round,
60 Or do you long for the dim sleepy ground,
That you have come and dared me to my face?'

'The dooms of men are in God's hidden place.'

'Your head a while seemed like a woman's head
That I loved once.'

                Again the fighting sped,
65 But now the war-rage in Cuchulain woke,
And through that new blade's guard the old blade
    broke,
And pierced him.
                'Speak before your breath is done.'

'Cuchulain I, mighty Cuchulain's son.'

'I put you from your pain, I can no more.'

70 While day its burden on to evening bore,
With head bowed on his knees Cuchulain stayed;
Then Conchubar sent that sweet-throated maid,
And she, to win him, his grey hair caressed;
In vain her arms, in vain her soft white breast.
75 Then Conchubar, the subtlest of all men,
Ranking his Druids round him ten by ten,
Spake thus: 'Cuchulain will dwell there and brood
For three days more in dreadful quietude,
And then arise, and raving slay us all.
80 Chaunt in his ear delusions magical,
That he may fight the horses of the sea.'
The Druids took them to their mystery,
And chaunted for three days.

                  Cuchulain stirred,
Stared on the horses of the sea, and heard
85 The cars of battle and his own name cried;
And fought with the invulnerable tide.

lines 80–86 Go, cast on him delusions magical,
          That he may fight the waves of the loud sea.'

Near to Cuchullin, round a quicken tree,
The Druids chanted, swaying in their hands
Tall wands of alder and white quicken wands.

In three days' time he stood up with a moan,
And went down to the long sands alone,
For four days warred he with the bitter tide,
And the waves flowed above him and he died.

(*United Ireland*, 11 June 1892)

The Rose of the World

❖❖❖

Who dreamed that beauty passes like a dream?
For these red lips, with all their mournful pride,
Mournful that no new wonder may betide,
Troy passed away in one high funeral gleam,
And Usna's children died.   5

We and the labouring world are passing by:
Amid men's souls, that waver and give place
Like the pale waters in their wintry race,
Under the passing stars, foam of the sky,
Lives on this lonely face.   10

Bow down, archangels, in your dim abode:
Before you were, or any hearts to beat,
Weary and kind one lingered by His seat;
He made the world to be a grassy road
Before her wandering feet.   15

lines 7–8 Amid men's souls that day by day give place,
             More fleeting than the sea's foam-fickle face,

(*National Observer*, 2 January 1892)

27

A Faery Song

*Sung by the people of Faery over Diarmuid and Grania,
in their bridal sleep under a Cromlech*

We who are old, old and gay,
O so old!
Thousands of years, thousands of years,
If all were told:

5   Give to these children, new from the world,
Silence and love;
And the long dew-dropping hours of the night,
And the stars above:

Give to these children, new from the world,
10 Rest far from men.
Is anything better, anything better?
Tell us it then:

Us who are old, old and gay,
O so old!
15 Thousands of years, thousands of years,
If all were told.

The Lake Isle of Innisfree

I will arise and go now, and go to Innisfree,
And a small cabin build there, of clay and wattles
    made:
Nine bean-rows will I have there, a hive for the
    honey-bee,
And live alone in the bee-loud glade.

And I shall have some peace there, for peace comes
5   dropping slow,

Dropping from the veils of the morning to where
    the cricket sings;
There midnight's all a glimmer, and noon a purple
    glow,
And evening full of the linnet's wings.

I will arise and go now, for always night and day
I hear lake water lapping with low sounds by the
    shore;   10
While I stand on the roadway, or on the pavements
    grey,
I hear it in the deep heart's core.

The Sorrow of Love

❖❖❖❖

The brawling of a sparrow in the eaves,
The brilliant moon and all the milky sky,
And all that famous harmony of leaves,
Had blotted out man's image and his cry.

A girl arose that had red mournful lips   5
And seemed the greatness of the world in tears,
Doomed like Odysseus and the labouring ships
And proud as Priam murdered with his peers;

Arose, and on the instant clamorous eaves,
A climbing moon upon an empty sky,   10
And all that lamentation of the leaves,
Could but compose man's image and his cry.

The Sorrow of Love

The quarrel of the sparrows in the eaves,
    The full round moon and the star-laden sky,
And the loud song of the ever-singing leaves
    Had hid away earth's old and weary cry.

5   And then you came with those red mournful lips,
      And with you came the whole of the world's tears,
    And all the sorrows of her labouring ships,
      And all the burden of her myriad years.

    And now the sparrows warring in the eaves,
10   The crumbling moon, the white stars in the sky,
    And the loud chanting of the unquiet leaves,
      Are shaken with earth's old and weary cry.

        (*The Countess Kathleen and Various Legends and Lyrics*, 1892)

line 10   The curd-pale moon, the white stars in the sky,

        (*Poems*, 1895)

When You are Old
❖❖❖

When you are old and grey and full of sleep,
And nodding by the fire, take down this book,
And slowly read, and dream of the soft look
Your eyes had once, and of their shadows deep;

5 How many loved your moments of glad grace,
And loved your beauty with love false or true,
But one man loved the pilgrim soul in you,
And loved the sorrows of your changing face;

And bending down beside the glowing bars,
10 Murmur, a little sadly, how Love fled
And paced upon the mountains overhead
And hid his face amid a crowd of stars.

lines 10–12   Murmur, a little sad, 'From us fled Love.
          He paced upon the mountains far above,
          And hid his face amid a crowd of stars.'

        (*The Countess Kathleen and Various Legends and Lyrics*, 1892)

Who Goes with Fergus?

Who will go drive with Fergus now,
And pierce the deep wood's woven shade,
And dance upon the level shore?
Young man, lift up your russet brow,
And lift your tender eyelids, maid,   5
And brood on hopes and fear no more.

And no more turn aside and brood
Upon love's bitter mystery;
For Fergus rules the brazen cars,
And rules the shadows of the wood,   10
And the white breast of the dim sea
And all dishevelled wandering stars.

line 6   And brood on hopes and fears no more,

(The Countess Kathleen and Various Legends and Lyrics, 1892)

The Man who Dreamed of Faeryland

He stood among a crowd at Dromahair;
His heart hung all upon a silken dress,
And he had known at last some tenderness,
Before earth took him to her stony care;
But when a man poured fish into a pile,   5
It seemed they raised their little silver heads,
And sang what gold morning or evening sheds
Upon a woven world-forgotten isle
Where people love beside the ravelled seas;
That Time can never mar a lover's vows   10
Under that woven changeless roof of boughs:
The singing shook him out of his new ease.

He wandered by the sands of Lissadell;
His mind ran all on money cares and fears,
15 And he had known at last some prudent years
Before they heaped his grave under the hill;
But while he passed before a plashy place,
A lug-worm with its grey and muddy mouth
Sang that somewhere to north or west or south
20 There dwelt a gay, exulting, gentle race
Under the golden or the silver skies;
That if a dancer stayed his hungry foot
It seemed the sun and moon were in the fruit:
And at that singing he was no more wise.

25 He mused beside the well of Scanavin,
He mused upon his mockers: without fail
His sudden vengeance were a country tale,
When earthy night had drunk his body in;
But one small knot-grass growing by the pool
30 Sang where – unnecessary cruel voice –
Old silence bids its chosen race rejoice,
Whatever ravelled waters rise and fall
Or stormy silver fret the gold of day,
And midnight there enfold them like a fleece
35 And lover there by lover be at peace.
The tale drove his fine angry mood away.

He slept under the hill of Lugnagall;
And might have known at last unhaunted sleep
Under that cold and vapour-turbaned steep,
40 Now that the earth had taken man and all:
Did not the worms that spired about his bones
Proclaim with that unwearied, reedy cry
That God has laid His fingers on the sky,
That from those fingers glittering summer runs
45 Upon the dancer by the dreamless wave.
Why should those lovers that no lovers miss
Dream, until God burn Nature with a kiss?
The man has found no comfort in the grave.

THE MAN WHO DREAMED OF FAERYLAND

line 4   Before earth made of him her sleepy care;

lines 7–11   And sang how day a Druid twilight sheds
Upon a dim, green, well-beloved isle,
Where people love beside star-laden seas;
How Time may never mar their faery vows
Under the woven roofs of quicken boughs; –

lines 21–3   And how beneath those three times blessed skies
A Danaan fruitage makes a shower of moons,
And as it falls awakens leafy tunes; –

lines 28–48   Now that deep earth has drunk his body in;
But one small knot-grass growing by the rim
Told where – ah, little, all-unneeded voice! –
Old Silence bids a lonely folk rejoice,
And chaplet their calm brows with leafage dim,
And how, when fades the sea-strewn rose of day,
A gentle feeling wraps them like a fleece,
And all their trouble dies into its peace; –
The tale drove his fine angry mood away.

He slept under the hill of Lugnagall,
And might have known at last unhaunted sleep
Under that cold and vapour-turbaned steep,
Now that old earth had taken man and all:
Were not the worms that spired about his bones
A-telling with their low and reedy cry
Of how God leans His hands out of the sky,
To bless that isle with honey in His tones,
That none may feel the power of squall and wave,
And no one any leaf-crowned dancer miss
Until He burn up Nature with a kiss; –
The man has found no comfort in the grave.

(*National Observer*, 7 February 1891)

The Dedication to a Book of Stories
selected from the Irish Novelists
❖❖❖❖

There was a green branch hung with many a bell
When her own people ruled this tragic Eire;
And from its murmuring greenness, calm of Faery,
A Druid kindness, on all hearers fell.

5   It charmed away the merchant from his guile,
And turned the farmer's memory from his cattle,
And hushed in sleep the roaring ranks of battle:
And all grew friendly for a little while.

Ah, Exiles wandering over lands and seas,
10   And planning, plotting always that some morrow
May set a stone upon ancestral Sorrow!
I also bear a bell-branch full of ease.

I tore it from green boughs winds tore and tossed
Until the sap of summer had grown weary!
15   I tore it from the barren boughs of Eire,
That country where a man can be so crossed;

Can be so battered, badgered and destroyed
That he's a loveless man: gay bells bring laughter
That shakes a mouldering cobweb from the rafter;
20   And yet the saddest chimes are best enjoyed.

Gay bells or sad, they bring you memories
Of half-forgotten innocent old places:
We and our bitterness have left no traces
On Munster grass and Connemara skies.

Dedication

There was a green branch hung with many a bell
When her own people ruled in wave-worn Eri,

34

And from its murmuring greenness, calm of faery
– A Druid kindness – on all hearers fell.

It charmed away the merchant from his guile,   5
And turned the farmer's memory from his cattle,
And hushed in sleep the roaring ranks of battle,
For all who heard it dreamed a little while.

Ah, Exiles, wandering over many seas,
Spinning at all times Eri's good to-morrow,   10
Ah, world-wide Nation, always growing Sorrow,
I also bear a bell branch full of ease.

I tore it from green boughs winds tossed and hurled,
Green boughs of tossing always, weary, weary,
I tore it from the green boughs of old Eri,   15
The willow of the many-sorrowed world.

Ah, Exiles, wandering over many lands,
My bell branch murmurs: the gay bells bring laughter,
Leaping to shake a cobweb from the rafter;
The sad bells bow the forehead on the hands.   20

A honied ringing! under the new skies
They bring you memories of old village faces,
Cabins gone now, old well-sides, old dear places,
And men who loved the cause that never dies.

(Representative Irish Tales, 1891)

The Lamentation of the Old Pensioner
◆◆◆

Although I shelter from the rain
Under a broken tree,
My chair was nearest to the fire
In every company
That talked of love or politics,   5
Ere Time transfigured me.

35

Though lads are making pikes again
For some conspiracy,
And crazy rascals rage their fill
10   At human tyranny,
My contemplations are of Time
That has transfigured me.

There's not a woman turns her face
Upon a broken tree,
15   And yet the beauties that I loved
Are in my memory;
I spit into the face of Time
That has transfigured me.

The Old Pensioner

I had a chair at every hearth,
When no one turned to see
With 'Look at that old fellow there;
And who may he be?'
5   And therefore do I wander on,
And the fret is on me.

The road-side trees keep murmuring –
Ah, wherefore murmur ye
As in the old days long gone by,
10   Green oak and poplar tree!
The well-known faces are all gone,
And the fret is on me.

(*Scots Observer*, 15 November 1890)

lines 6, 12   And the fret lies on me.

(*The Countess Kathleen and Various Legends and Lyrics*, 1892)

The Two Trees

❖❖❖❖

Beloved, gaze in thine own heart,
The holy tree is growing there;
From joy the holy branches start,
And all the trembling flowers they bear.
The changing colours of its fruit   5
Have dowered the stars with merry light;
The surety of its hidden root
Has planted quiet in the night;
The shaking of its leafy head
Has given the waves their melody,   10
And made my lips and music wed,
Murmuring a wizard song for thee.
There the Loves a circle go,
The flaming circle of our days,
Gyring, spiring to and fro   15
In those great ignorant leafy ways;
Remembering all that shaken hair
And how the wingèd sandals dart,
Thine eyes grow full of tender care:
Beloved, gaze in thine own heart.   20

Gaze no more in the bitter glass
The demons, with their subtle guile,
Lift up before us when they pass,
Or only gaze a little while;
For there a fatal image grows   25
That the stormy night receives,
Roots half hidden under snows,
Broken boughs and blackened leaves.
For all things turn to barrenness
In the dim glass the demons hold,   30
The glass of outer weariness,
Made when God slept in times of old.
There, through the broken branches, go

The ravens of unresting thought;
35 Flying, crying, to and fro,
Cruel claw and hungry throat,
Or else they stand and sniff the wind,
And shake their ragged wings; alas!
Thy tender eyes grow all unkind:
40 Gaze no more in the bitter glass.

lines 13–20 There, through bewildered branches, go
Winged Loves borne on in gentle strife,
Tossing and tossing to and fro
The flaming circle of our life.
When looking on their shaken hair,
And dreaming how they dance and dart,
Thine eyes grow full of tender care: –
Beloved gaze in thine own heart.

lines 35–8 Peering and flying to and fro,
To see men's souls bartered and bought.
When they are heard upon the wind,
And when they shake their wings – alas!

(*The Countess Kathleen and Various Legends and Lyrics*, 1892)

To Ireland in the Coming Times
❖❖❖

Know, that I would accounted be
True brother of a company
That sang, to sweeten Ireland's wrong,
Ballad and story, rann and song;
5 *Nor be I any less of them,*
Because the red-rose-bordered hem
Of her, whose history began
Before God made the angelic clan,
Trails all about the written page.
10 *When Time began to rant and rage*
The measure of her flying feet
Made Ireland's heart begin to beat;

And Time bade all his candles flare
To light a measure here and there;
And may the thoughts of Ireland brood   15
Upon a measured quietude.

Nor may I less be counted one
With Davis, Mangan, Ferguson,
Because, to him who ponders well,
My rhymes more than their rhyming tell   20
Of things discovered in the deep,
Where only body's laid asleep.
For the elemental creatures go
About my table to and fro,
That hurry from unmeasured mind   25
To rant and rage in flood and wind;
Yet he who treads in measured ways
May surely barter gaze for gaze.
Man ever journeys on with them
After the red-rose-bordered hem.   30
Ah, faeries, dancing under the moon,
A Druid land, a Druid tune!

While still I may, I write for you
The love I lived, the dream I knew.
From our birthday, until we die,   35
Is but the winking of an eye;
And we, our singing and our love,
What measurer Time has lit above,
And all benighted things that go
About my table to and fro,   40
Are passing on to where may be,
In truth's consuming ecstasy,
No place for love and dream at all;
For God goes by with white footfall.
I cast my heart into my rhymes,   45
That you, in the dim coming times,
May know how my heart went with them
After the red-rose-bordered hem.

lines 10–28   For in the world's first blossoming age
The light fall of her flying feet
Made Ireland's heart begin to beat,
And still the starry candles flare
To help her light foot here and there,
And still the thoughts of Ireland brood,
Upon her holy quietude.

Nor may I less be counted one
With Davis, Mangan, Ferguson,
Because to him who ponders well
My rhymes more than their rhyming tell
Of the dim wisdoms old and deep,
That God gives unto man in sleep.
For round about my table go
The magical powers to and fro.
In flood and fire and clay and wind,
They huddle from man's pondering mind,
Yet he who treads in austere ways
May surely meet their ancient gaze.

(*The Countess Kathleen and Various Legends and Lyrics*, 1892)

[*The poet, Owen Hanrahan, under a bush of may*]

❖❖❖

The poet, Owen Hanrahan, under a bush of may
Calls down a curse on his own head because it
   withers grey;
Then on the speckled eagle cock of Ballygawley
   Hill
Because it is the oldest thing that knows of cark
   and ill;
And on the yew that has been green from the times
5   out of mind
By the Steep Place of the Strangers and the Gap
   of the Wind:

And on the great grey pike that broods in Castle
    Dargan Lake
Having in his long body a many a hook and ache;
Then curses he old Paddy Bruen of the Well of
    Bride
Because no hair is on his head and drowsiness
    inside.   10
Then Paddy's neighbour, Peter Hart, and Michael
    Gill, his friend,
Because their wandering histories are never at an
    end.
And then old Shemus Cullinan, shepherd of the
    Green Lands
Because he holds two crutches between his crooked
    hands;
Then calls a curse from the dark North upon old
    Paddy Doe,   15
Who plans to lay his withering head upon a breast
    of snow,
Who plans to wreck a singing voice and break a
    merry heart;
He bids a curse hang over him till breath and body
    part,
But he calls down a blessing on the blossom of the
    may
Because it comes in beauty, and in beauty blows
    away.   20

line 1   The poet, Red O'Sullivan, under a bush of May

lines 5–7   And on the leaning, wrinkling ash, that many an
        age hath stood
        Hollow and knarled and broken to North of
        Markree Wood;
        And on the great grey pike that dwells in Castle
        Dargan Lake,

line 9   Then curses he old Paudeen Strange, herdsman of
        Tubber Bride,

THE POET, OWEN HANRAHAN, UNDER A BUSH OF MAY

lines 11-14   Because their rambling histories, are never at an end.
               And then old Shemus Cullinan, cooper of Scanavin,
               Because he holds two crutches in his fingers long and thin;
               Then calls a curse of Druid power upon old Paudeen Doe,

line 17   A threefold curse of Druid power, clinging till breath
                  depart;

                                      (*National Observer*, 29 September 1894)

line 17   He calls a curse that shall be his until his breath depart;

                                              (*The Secret Rose*, 1897)

THE WIND AMONG THE REEDS

❖❖❖❖❖❖

The Hosting of the Sidhe

❖❖❖❖

The host is riding from Knocknarea
And over the grave of Clooth-na-Bare;
Caoilte tossing his burning hair,
And Niamh calling *Away, come away:*
Empty your heart of its mortal dream.   5
The winds awaken, the leaves whirl round,
Our cheeks are pale, our hair is unbound,
Our breasts are heaving, our eyes are agleam,
Our arms are waving, our lips are apart;
And if any gaze on our rushing band,   10
We come between him and the deed of his hand,
We come between him and the hope of his heart.
The host is rushing 'twixt night and day,
And where is there hope or deed as fair?
Caoilte tossing his burning hair,   15
And Niamh calling *Away, come away.*

lines 5–8   'And brood no more where the fire is bright
Filling thy heart with a mortal dream,
For breasts are heaving and eyes a-gleam;
Away, come away, to the dim twilight.

(*National Observer*, 7 October 1893)

The Everlasting Voices

❖❖❖❖

O sweet everlasting Voices, be still;
Go to the guards of the heavenly fold

43

And bid them wander obeying your will,
Flame under flame, till Time be no more;
5   Have you not heard that our hearts are old,
That you call in birds, in wind on the hill,
In shaken boughs, in tide on the shore?
O sweet everlasting Voices, be still.

Into the Twilight

✦✦✦✦

Out-worn heart, in a time out-worn,
Come clear of the nets of wrong and right;
Laugh, heart, again in the grey twilight,
Sigh, heart, again in the dew of the morn.

5   Your mother Eire is always young,
Dew ever shining and twilight grey;
Though hope fall from you and love decay,
Burning in fires of a slanderous tongue.

Come, heart, where hill is heaped upon hill:
10   For there the mystical brotherhood
Of sun and moon and hollow and wood
And river and stream work out their will;

And God stands winding His lonely horn,
And time and the world are ever in flight;
15   And love is less kind than the grey twilight,
And hope is less dear than the dew of the morn.

lines 9–12   Come, heart, where hill is heaped upon hill,
For there live the mystic brotherhood
Of the flood and flame, of the height and wood,
And laugh out their whimsey and work out their will.

(*National Observer*, 29 July 1893)

The Song of Wandering Aengus

I went out to the hazel wood,
Because a fire was in my head,
And cut and peeled a hazel wand,
And hooked a berry to a thread;
And when white moths were on the wing,   5
And moth-like stars were flickering out,
I dropped the berry in a stream
And caught a little silver trout.

When I had laid it on the floor
I went to blow the fire aflame,   10
But something rustled on the floor,
And some one called me by my name:
It had become a glimmering girl
With apple blossom in her hair
Who called me by my name and ran   15
And faded through the brightening air.

Though I am old with wandering
Through hollow lands and hilly lands,
I will find out where she has gone,
And kiss her lips and take her hands;   20
And walk among long dappled grass,
And pluck till time and times are done
The silver apples of the moon,
The golden apples of the sun.

The Song of the Old Mother

I rise in the dawn, and I kneel and blow
Till the seed of the fire flicker and glow;

And then I must scrub and bake and sweep
Till stars are beginning to blink and peep;
5 And the young lie long and dream in their bed
Of the matching of ribbons for bosom and head,
And their day goes over in idleness,
And they sigh if the wind but lift a tress:
While I must work because I am old,
10 And the seed of the fire gets feeble and cold.

The Lover mourns for the Loss of Love

◇◆◇◆

Pale brows, still hands and dim hair,
I had a beautiful friend
And dreamed that the old despair
Would end in love in the end:
5 She looked in my heart one day
And saw your image was there;
She has gone weeping away.

He mourns for the Change that has come upon him and his Beloved, and longs for the End of the World

◇◆◇◆

Do you not hear me calling, white deer with no
    horns?
I have been changed to a hound with one red ear;
I have been in the Path of Stones and the Wood of
    Thorns,

For somebody hid hatred and hope and desire and
    fear
Under my feet that they follow you night and day.   5
A man with a hazel wand came without sound;
He changed me suddenly; I was looking another
    way;
And now my calling is but the calling of a hound;
And Time and Birth and Change are hurrying by.
I would that the Boar without bristles had come
    from the West   10
And had rooted the sun and moon and stars out of
    the sky
And lay in the darkness, grunting, and turning to
    his rest.

He reproves the Curlew

◇◇◇

O curlew, cry no more in the air,
Or only to the water in the West;
Because your crying brings to my mind
Passion-dimmed eyes and long heavy hair
That was shaken out over my breast: 5
There is enough evil in the crying of wind.

He remembers Forgotten Beauty

◇◇◇

When my arms wrap you round I press
My heart upon the loveliness
That has long faded from the world;
The jewelled crowns that kings have hurled
In shadowy pools, when armies fled;   5

The love-tales wrought with silken thread
By dreaming ladies upon cloth
That has made fat the murderous moth;
The roses that of old time were
10   Woven by ladies in their hair,
The dew-cold lilies ladies bore
Through many a sacred corridor
Where such grey clouds of incense rose
That only God's eyes did not close:
15   For that pale breast and lingering hand
Come from a more dream-heavy land,
A more dream-heavy hour than this;
And when you sigh from kiss to kiss
I hear white Beauty sighing, too,
20   For hours when all must fade like dew,
But flame on flame, and deep on deep,
Throne over throne where in half sleep,
Their swords upon their iron knees,
Brood her high lonely mysteries.

line 10   Woven by ladies in their hair,
Before they drowned their lovers' eyes
In twilight shaken with low sighs;

lines 21–24   Till there be naught but throne on throne
Of seraphs, brooding, each alone,
A sword upon his iron knees,
On her most lonely mysteries.

(*Savoy*, July 1896)

To his Heart, bidding it have no Fear
❖❖❖❖

Be you still, be you still, trembling heart;
Remember the wisdom out of the old days:

Him who trembles before the flame and the flood,
And the winds that blow through the starry ways,
Let the starry winds and the flame and the flood   5
Cover over and hide, for he has no part
With the lonely, majestical multitude.

Windle-Straws

II
Out of the Old Days

Be you still, be you still, trembling heart;
   Remember the wisdom out of the old days:
     Who trembles before the flame and the flood,
   And the winds blowing through the starry ways,
     And blowing us evil and good;   5
     Let the starry winds and the flame and the flood
   Cover over and hide, for he has no part
     With the lonely, proud, winged multitude.

(*Savoy*, November 1896)

The Valley of the Black Pig
❖❖❖❖

The dews drop slowly and dreams gather: unknown
   spears
Suddenly hurtle before my dream-awakened eyes,
And then the clash of fallen horsemen and the cries
Of unknown perishing armies beat about my ears.
We who still labour by the cromlech on the shore,   5
The grey cairn on the hill, when day sinks drowned
   in dew,

Being weary of the world's empires, bow down to
   you,
Master of the still stars and of the flaming door.

The Secret Rose
◇◇◇

Far-off, most secret, and inviolate Rose,
Enfold me in my hour of hours; where those
Who sought thee in the Holy Sepulchre,
Or in the wine-vat, dwell beyond the stir
5   And tumult of defeated dreams; and deep
Among pale eyelids, heavy with the sleep
Men have named beauty. Thy great leaves enfold
The ancient beards, the helms of ruby and gold
Of the crownéd Magi; and the king whose eyes
10   Saw the Pierced Hands and Rood of elder rise
In Druid vapour and make the torches dim;
Till vain frenzy awoke and he died; and him
Who met Fand walking among flaming dew
By a grey shore where the wind never blew,
15   And lost the world and Emer for a kiss;
And him who drove the gods out of their liss,
And till a hundred morns had flowered red
Feasted, and wept the barrows of his dead;
And the proud dreaming king who flung the crown
20   And sorrow away, and calling bard and clown
Dwelt among wine-stained wanderers in deep
   woods;
And him who sold tillage, and house, and goods,
And sought through lands and islands numberless
   years,
Until he found, with laughter and with tears,
25   A woman of so shining loveliness
That men threshed corn at midnight by a tress,
A little stolen tress. I, too, await

The hour of thy great wind of love and hate.
When shall the stars be blown about the sky,
Like the sparks blown out of a smithy, and die?   30
Surely thine hour has come, thy great wind blows,
Far-off, most secret, and inviolate Rose?

The Travail of Passion

❖❖❖❖

When the flaming lute-thronged angelic door is wide;
When an immortal passion breathes in mortal clay;
Our hearts endure the scourge, the plaited thorns,
    the way
Crowded with bitter faces, the wounds in palm
    and side,
The vinegar-heavy sponge, the flowers by Kedron
    stream;   5
We will bend down and loosen our hair over you,
That it may drop faint perfume, and be heavy
    with dew,
Lilies of death-pale hope, roses of passionate
    dream.

lines 3–5   Our hearts endure the plaited thorn, the crowded way,
      The knotted scourge, the nail-pierced hands, the wounded
       side,
      The hissop-heavy sponge, the flowers by Kidron stream:

                     (*Savoy*, January 1896)

The Lover pleads with his Friend for Old Friends

❖❖❖❖

Though you are in your shining days,
Voices among the crowd

And new friends busy with your praise,
Be not unkind or proud,
5   But think about old friends the most:
Time's bitter flood will rise,
Your beauty perish and be lost
For all eyes but these eyes.

The Lover speaks to the Hearers of his Songs in Coming Days
❖❖❖❖

O women, kneeling by your altar-rails long hence,
When songs I wove for my beloved hide the prayer,
And smoke from this dead heart drifts through the
    violet air
And covers away the smoke of myrrh and
    frankincense;
5   Bend down and pray for all that sin I wove in song,
Till the Attorney for Lost Souls cry her sweet cry,
And call to my beloved and me: 'No longer fly
Amid the hovering, piteous, penitential throng.'

He wishes his Beloved were Dead
❖❖❖❖

Were you but lying cold and dead,
And lights were paling out of the West,
You would come hither, and bend your head,
And I would lay my head on your breast;
5   And you would murmur tender words,
Forgiving me, because you were dead:
Nor would you rise and hasten away,

Though you have the will of the wild birds,
But know your hair was bound and wound
About the stars and moon and sun: 10
O would, beloved, that you lay
Under the dock-leaves in the ground,
While lights were paling one by one.

line 13   While birds grew silent one by one.

(*Sketch*, 9 February 1898)

He wishes for the Cloths of Heaven

❖❖❖❖

Had I the heavens' embroidered cloths,
Enwrought with golden and silver light,
The blue and the dim and the dark cloths
Of night and light and the half-light,
I would spread the cloths under your feet: 5
But I, being poor, have only my dreams;
I have spread my dreams under your feet;
Tread softly because you tread on my dreams.

He thinks of his Past Greatness when a Part of the Constellations of Heaven

❖❖❖❖

I have drunk ale from the Country of the Young
And weep because I know all things now:
I have been a hazel-tree, and they hung
The Pilot Star and the Crooked Plough
Among my leaves in times out of mind: 5
I became a rush that horses tread:

I became a man, a hater of the wind,
Knowing one, out of all things, alone, that his head
May not lie on the breast nor his lips on the hair
10 Of the woman that he loves, until he dies.
O beast of the wilderness, bird of the air,
Must I endure your amorous cries?

lines 11–12 Although the rushes and the fowl of the air
Cry of his love with their pitiful cries.

(*Dome*, October 1898)

[*I walked among the seven woods of Coole*]
❖❖❖❖

I walked among the seven woods of Coole:
Shan-walla, where a willow-bordered pond
Gathers the wild duck from the winter dawn;
Shady Kyle-dortha; sunnier Kyle-na-no,
5 *Where many hundred squirrels are as happy*
As though they had been hidden by green boughs
Where old age cannot find them; Pairc-na-lee,
Where hazel and ash and privet blind the paths;
Dim Pairc-na-carraig, where the wild bees fling
10 *Their sudden fragrances on the green air;*
Dim Pairc-na-tarav, where enchanted eyes
Have seen immortal, mild, proud shadows walk;
Dim Inchy wood, that hides badger and fox
And marten-cat, and borders that old wood
15 *Wise Biddy Early called the wicked wood:*
Seven odours, seven murmurs, seven woods.
I had not eyes like those enchanted eyes,
Yet dreamed that beings happier than men
Moved round me in the shadows, and at night

My dreams were cloven by voices and by fires;   20
And the images I have woven in this story
Of Forgael and Dectora and the empty waters
Moved round me in the voices and the fires,
And more I may not write of, for they that cleave
The waters of sleep can make a chattering tongue   25
Heavy like stone, their wisdom being half silence.
How shall I name you, immortal, mild, proud
    shadows?
I only know that all we know comes from you,
And that you come from Eden on flying feet.
Is Eden far away, or do you hide   30
From human thought, as hares and mice and coneys
That run before the reaping-hook and lie
In the last ridge of the barley? Do our woods
And winds and ponds cover more quiet woods,
More shining winds, more star-glimmering ponds?   35
Is Eden out of time and out of space?
And do you gather about us when pale light
Shining on water and fallen among leaves,
And winds blowing from flowers, and whirr of feathers
And the green quiet, have uplifted the heart?   40

I have made this poem for you, that men may read it
Before they read of Forgael and Dectora,
As men in the old times, before the harps began,
Poured out wine for the high invisible ones.

September 1900

(From *The Shadowy Waters*, 1900)

In the Seven Woods
❖❖❖❖

I have heard the pigeons of the Seven Woods
Make their faint thunder, and the garden bees
Hum in the lime-tree flowers; and put away
The unavailing outcries and the old bitterness
5   That empty the heart. I have forgot awhile
Tara uprooted, and new commonness
Upon the throne and crying about the streets
And hanging its paper flowers from post to post,
Because it is alone of all things happy.
10 I am contented, for I know that Quiet
Wanders laughing and eating her wild heart
Among pigeons and bees, while that Great Archer,
Who but awaits His hour to shoot, still hangs
A cloudy quiver over Pairc-na-lee.

August 1902

The Folly of Being Comforted
❖❖❖❖

One that is ever kind said yesterday:
'Your well-belovèd's hair has threads of grey,
And little shadows come about her eyes;
Time can but make it easier to be wise
5   Though now it seems impossible, and so
All that you need is patience.'

Heart cries, 'No,

56

I have not a crumb of comfort, not a grain.
Time can but make her beauty over again:
Because of that great nobleness of hers
The fire that stirs about her, when she stirs,   10
Burns but more clearly. O she had not these ways
When all the wild summer was in her gaze.'

O heart! O heart! if she'd but turn her head,
You'd know the folly of being comforted.

lines 5–7   Though now it's hard, till trouble is at an end;
             And so be patient; be wise and patient friend.'
             But heart there is no comfort, not a grain;

(*Speaker*, 11 January 1902)

Adam's Curse
❖❖❖

We sat together at one summer's end,
That beautiful mild woman, your close friend,
And you and I, and talked of poetry.
I said, 'A line will take us hours maybe;
Yet if it does not seem a moment's thought,   5
Our stitching and unstitching has been naught.
Better go down upon your marrow-bones
And scrub a kitchen pavement, or break stones
Like an old pauper, in all kinds of weather;
For to articulate sweet sounds together   10
Is to work harder than all these, and yet
Be thought an idler by the noisy set
Of bankers, schoolmasters, and clergymen
The martyrs call the world.'

                  And thereupon
That beautiful mild woman for whose sake   15

There's many a one shall find out all heartache
On finding that her voice is sweet and low
Replied, 'To be born woman is to know –
Although they do not talk of it at school –
20 That we must labour to be beautiful.'

I said, 'It's certain there is no fine thing
Since Adam's fall but needs much labouring.
There have been lovers who thought love should be
So much compounded of high courtesy
25 That they would sigh and quote with learned looks
Precedents out of beautiful old books;
Yet now it seems an idle trade enough.'

We sat grown quiet at the name of love;
We saw the last embers of daylight die,
30 And in the trembling blue-green of the sky
A moon, worn as if it had been a shell
Washed by time's waters as they rose and fell
About the stars and broke in days and years.

I had a thought for no one's but your ears:
35 That you were beautiful, and that I strove
To love you in the old high way of love;
That it had all seemed happy, and yet we'd grown
As weary-hearted as that hollow moon.

lines 14–19   That woman then
Murmured with her young voice for whose mild sake
There's many a one shall find out all heartache
In finding that it's young and mild and low.
'There is one thing that all we women know
Although we never heard of it at school

(*Monthly Review*, December 1902)

Red Hanrahan's Song about Ireland

❖❖❖❖

The old brown thorn-trees break in two high over
    Cummen Strand,
Under a bitter black wind that blows from the left
    hand;
Our courage breaks like an old tree in a black wind
    and dies,
But we have hidden in our hearts the flame out of
    the eyes
Of Cathleen, the daughter of Houlihan.   5

The wind has bundled up the clouds high over
    Knocknarea,
And thrown the thunder on the stones for all that
    Maeve can say.
Angers that are like noisy clouds have set our hearts
    abeat;
But we have all bent low and low and kissed the
    quiet feet
Of Cathleen, the daughter of Houlihan.   10

The yellow pool has overflowed high up on Clooth-
    na–Bare,
For the wet winds are blowing out of the clinging
    air;
Like heavy flooded waters our bodies and our
    blood;
But purer than a tall candle before the Holy Rood
Is Cathleen, the daughter of Houlihan.   15

[Red Hanrahan's Song about Ireland]

Veering, fleeting, fickle, the winds of Knocknarea,
When in ragged vapour they mutter night and day,
Veering, fleeting, fickle, our loves and angers meet:
But we bend together and kiss the quiet feet
Of Kathleen-Ny-Hoolihan.   5

Weak and worn and weary the waves of Cummen Strand,
When the wind comes blowing across the hilly land;
Weak and worn and weary our courage droops and dies
But our hearts are lighted from the flame in the eyes
10 Of Kathleen-Ny-Hoolihan.

Dark and dull and earthy the stream of Drumahair
When the rain is pelting out of the wintry air;
Dark and dull and earthy our souls and bodies be:
But pure as a tall candle before the Trinity
15 Our Kathleen-Ny-Hoolihan.

(*National Observer*, 4 August 1894)

[*Red Hanrahan's Song about Ireland*]

O tufted reeds, bend low and low in pools on the Green
Land,
Under the bitter Black Winds blowing out of the left hand!
Like tufted reeds our courage droops in a Black Wind and
dies:
But we have hidden in our hearts the flame out of the eyes
5 Of Kathleen the Daughter of Hoolihan.

O tattered clouds of the world, call from the high Cairn of
Maive,
And shake down thunder on the stones because the Red
Winds rave!
Like tattered clouds of the world, passions call and our hearts
beat:
But we have all bent low and low, and kissed the quiet feet
10 Of Kathleen the Daughter of Hoolihan.

O heavy swollen waters, brim the Fall of the Oak trees,
For the Grey Winds are blowing up, out of the clinging seas!
Like heavy swollen waters are our bodies and our blood:
But purer than a tall candle before the Blessed Rood
15 Is Kathleen the Daughter of Hoolihan.

(*The Secret Rose*, 1897)

The Old Men Admiring Themselves
in the Water
❖❖❖❖

I heard the old, old men say,
'Everything alters,
And one by one we drop away.'
They had hands like claws, and their knees
Were twisted like the old thorn-trees   5
By the waters.
I heard the old, old men say,
'All that's beautiful drifts away
Like the waters.'

O Do Not Love Too Long
❖❖❖❖

Sweetheart, do not love too long:
I loved long and long,
And grew to be out of fashion
Like an old song.

All through the years of our youth   5
Neither could have known
Their own thought from the other's,
We were so much at one.

But O, in a minute she changed –
O do not love too long,   10
Or you will grow out of fashion
Like an old song.

[*The friends that have it I do wrong*]
❖❖❖

The friends that have it I do wrong
When ever I remake a song,
Should know what issue is at stake:
It is myself that I remake.

(From *Collected Works*, 1908)

From THE GREEN HELMET AND OTHER POEMS

❖❖❖❖❖❖

A Woman Homer Sung

❖❖❖❖

If any man drew near
When I was young,
I thought, 'He holds her dear,'
And shook with hate and fear.
But O! 'twas bitter wrong   5
If he could pass her by
With an indifferent eye.

Whereon I wrote and wrought,
And now, being grey,
I dream that I have brought   10
To such a pitch my thought
That coming time can say,
'He shadowed in a glass
What thing her body was.'

For she had fiery blood   15
When I was young,
And trod so sweetly proud
As 'twere upon a cloud,
A woman Homer sung,
That life and letters seem   20
But an heroic dream.

Words

I had this thought a while ago,
'My darling cannot understand
What I have done, or what would do
In this blind bitter land.'

5   And I grew weary of the sun
Until my thoughts cleared up again,
Remembering that the best I have done
Was done to make it plain;

That every year I have cried, 'At length
10   My darling understands it all,
Because I have come into my strength,
And words obey my call';

That had she done so who can say
What would have shaken from the sieve?
15   I might have thrown poor words away
And been content to live.

No Second Troy

Why should I blame her that she filled my days
With misery, or that she would of late
Have taught to ignorant men most violent ways,
Or hurled the little streets upon the great,
5   Had they but courage equal to desire?
What could have made her peaceful with a mind
That nobleness made simple as a fire,
With beauty like a tightened bow, a kind
That is not natural in an age like this,

Being high and solitary and most stern?   10
Why, what could she have done, being what she is?
Was there another Troy for her to burn?

Reconciliation
❖❖❖

Some may have blamed you that you took away
The verses that could move them on the day
When, the ears being deafened, the sight of the
    eyes blind
With lightning, you went from me, and I could
    find
Nothing to make a song about but kings,   5
Helmets, and swords, and half-forgotten things
That were like memories of you – but now
We'll out, for the world lives as long ago;
And while we're in our laughing, weeping fit,
Hurl helmets, crowns, and swords into the pit.   10
But, dear, cling close to me; since you were gone,
My barren thoughts have chilled me to the bone.

Against Unworthy Praise
❖❖❖

O heart, be at peace, because
Nor knave nor dolt can break
What's not for their applause,
Being for a woman's sake.
Enough if the work has seemed,   5
So did she your strength renew,
A dream that a lion had dreamed
Till the wilderness cried aloud,

A secret between you two,
10   Between the proud and the proud.

What, still you would have their praise!
But here's a haughtier text,
The labyrinth of her days
That her own strangeness perplexed;
15   And how what her dreaming gave
Earned slander, ingratitude,
From self-same dolt and knave;
Aye, and worse wrong than these.
Yet she, singing upon her road,
20   Half lion, half child, is at peace.

The Fascination of What's Difficult
❖❖❖

The fascination of what's difficult
Has dried the sap out of my veins, and rent
Spontaneous joy and natural content
Out of my heart. There's something ails our colt
5   That must, as if it had not holy blood
Nor on Olympus leaped from cloud to cloud,
Shiver under the lash, strain, sweat and jolt
As though it dragged road metal. My curse on plays
That have to be set up in fifty ways,
10   On the day's war with every knave and dolt,
Theatre business, management of men.
I swear before the dawn comes round again
I'll find the stable and pull out the bolt.

The Coming of Wisdom with Time

❖❖❖❖

Though leaves are many, the root is one;
Through all the lying days of my youth
I swayed my leaves and flowers in the sun;
Now I may wither into the truth.

On hearing that the Students of our New University have joined the Agitation against Immoral Literature

❖❖❖❖

Where, where but here have Pride and Truth,
That long to give themselves for wage,
To shake their wicked sides at youth
Restraining reckless middle-age?

The Mask

❖❖❖❖

'Put off that mask of burning gold
With emerald eyes.'
'O no, my dear, you make so bold
To find if hearts be wild and wise,
And yet not cold.'   5

'I would but find what's there to find,
Love or deceit.'

'It was the mask engaged your mind,
And after set your heart to beat,
10   Not what's behind.'

'But lest you are my enemy,
I must enquire.'
'O no, my dear, let all that be;
What matter, so there is but fire
15   In you, in me?'

Upon a House shaken by the Land Agitation

❖❖❖

How should the world be luckier if this house,
Where passion and precision have been one
Time out of mind, became too ruinous
To breed the lidless eye that loves the sun?
5 And the sweet laughing eagle thoughts that grow
Where wings have memory of wings, and all
That comes of the best knit to the best? Although
Mean roof-trees were the sturdier for its fall,
How should their luck run high enough to reach
10 The gifts that govern men, and after these
To gradual Time's last gift, a written speech
Wrought of high laughter, loveliness and ease?

At the Abbey Theatre
❖❖❖

(*Imitated from Ronsard*)

Dear Craoibhin Aoibhin, look into our case.
When we are high and airy hundreds say
That if we hold that flight they'll leave the place,
While those same hundreds mock another day
Because we have made our art of common things,   5
So bitterly, you'd dream they longed to look
All their lives through into some drift of wings.
You've dandled them and fed them from the book
And know them to the bone; impart to us –
We'll keep the secret – a new trick to please.   10
Is there a bridle for this Proteus
That turns and changes like his draughty seas?
Or is there none, most popular of men,
But when they mock us, that we mock again?

These are the Clouds
❖❖❖

These are the clouds about the fallen sun,
The majesty that shuts his burning eye:
The weak lay hand on what the strong has done,
Till that be tumbled that was lifted high
And discord follow upon unison,   5
And all things at one common level lie.
And therefore, friend, if your great race were run
And these things came, so much the more thereby
Have you made greatness your companion,
Although it be for children that you sigh: 10
These are the clouds about the fallen sun,
The majesty that shuts his burning eye.

At Galway Races

There where the course is,
Delight makes all of the one mind,
The riders upon the galloping horses,
The crowd that closes in behind:
5   We, too, had good attendance once,
Hearers and hearteners of the work;
Aye, horsemen for companions,
Before the merchant and the clerk
Breathed on the world with timid breath.
10   Sing on: somewhere at some new moon,
We'll learn that sleeping is not death,
Hearing the whole earth change its tune,
Its flesh being wild, and it again
Crying aloud as the racecourse is,
15   And we find hearteners among men
That ride upon horses.

All Things can Tempt Me

All things can tempt me from this craft of verse:
One time it was a woman's face, or worse –
The seeming needs of my fool-driven land;
Now nothing but comes readier to the hand
5   Than this accustomed toil. When I was young,
I had not given a penny for a song
Did not the poet sing it with such airs
That one believed he had a sword upstairs;
Yet would be now, could I but have my wish,
10   Colder and dumber and deafer than a fish.

Brown Penny

❖❖❖

I whispered, 'I am too young,'
And then, 'I am old enough';
Wherefore I threw a penny
To find out if I might love.
'Go and love, go and love, young man,   5
If the lady be young and fair.'
Ah, penny, brown penny, brown penny,
I am looped in the loops of her hair.

O love is the crooked thing,
There is nobody wise enough   10
To find out all that is in it,
For he would be thinking of love
Till the stars had run away
And the shadows eaten the moon.
Ah, penny, brown penny, brown penny,   15
One cannot begin it too soon.

RESPONSIBILITIES

◈◈◈◈◈◈

[*Pardon, old fathers, if you still remain*]

◈◈◈◈

Pardon, old fathers, if you still remain
Somewhere in ear-shot for the story's end,
Old Dublin merchant 'free of the ten and four'
Or trading out of Galway into Spain;
5   *Old country scholar, Robert Emmet's friend,*
A hundred-year-old memory to the poor;
Merchant and scholar who have left me blood
That has not passed through any huckster's loin,
Soldiers that gave, whatever die was cast:
10   *A Butler or an Armstrong that withstood*
Beside the brackish waters of the Boyne
James and his Irish when the Dutchman crossed;
Old merchant skipper that leaped overboard
After a ragged hat in Biscay Bay;
15   *You most of all, silent and fierce old man,*
Because the daily spectacle that stirred
My fancy, and set my boyish lips to say,
'Only the wasteful virtues earn the sun';
Pardon that for a barren passion's sake,
20   *Although I have come close on forty-nine,*
I have no child, I have nothing but a book,
Nothing but that to prove your blood and mine.

January 1914

line 7   Traders or soldiers who have left me blood

lines 9–13   Pardon, and you that did not weigh the cost,
               Old Butlers when you took to horse and stood

72

Till your bad master blenched and all was lost;
And merchant skipper that leaped overboard

(*Responsibilities: Poems and a Play*, 1914)

September 1913
❖❖❖

What need you, being come to sense,
But fumble in a greasy till
And add the halfpence to the pence
And prayer to shivering prayer, until
You have dried the marrow from the bone;   5
For men were born to pray and save:
Romantic Ireland's dead and gone,
It's with O'Leary in the grave.

Yet they were of a different kind,
The names that stilled your childish play,   10
They have gone about the world like wind,
But little time had they to pray
For whom the hangman's rope was spun,
And what, God help us, could they save?
Romantic Ireland's dead and gone,   15
It's with O'Leary in the grave.

Was it for this the wild geese spread
The grey wing upon every tide;
For this that all that blood was shed,
For this Edward Fitzgerald died,   20
And Robert Emmet and Wolfe Tone,
All that delirium of the brave?
Romantic Ireland's dead and gone,
It's with O'Leary in the grave.

Yet could we turn the years again,   25
And call those exiles as they were

In all their loneliness and pain,
You'd cry, 'Some woman's yellow hair
Has maddened every mother's son':
30 They weighed so lightly what they gave.
But let them be, they're dead and gone,
They're with O'Leary in the grave.

To a Friend whose Work has come to Nothing

❖❖❖❖

Now all the truth is out,
Be secret and take defeat
From any brazen throat,
For how can you compete,
5 Being honour bred, with one
Who, were it proved he lies,
Were neither shamed in his own
Nor in his neighbours' eyes?
Bred to a harder thing
10 Than Triumph, turn away
And like a laughing string
Whereon mad fingers play
Amid a place of stone,
Be secret and exult,
15 Because of all things known
That is most difficult.

Paudeen

❖❖❖❖

Indignant at the fumbling wits, the obscure spite
Of our old Paudeen in his shop, I stumbled blind

Among the stones and thorn-trees, under morning
   light;
Until a curlew cried and in the luminous wind
A curlew answered; and suddenly thereupon I
   thought   5
That on the lonely height where all are in God's
   eye,
There cannot be, confusion of our sound forgot,
A single soul that lacks a sweet crystalline cry.

line 5   A curlew answered and I was startled by the thought

                      (*Poems Written in Discouragement*, 1913)

To a Shade
❖❖❖❖

If you have revisited the town, thin Shade,
Whether to look upon your monument
(I wonder if the builder has been paid)
Or happier-thoughted when the day is spent
To drink of that salt breath out of the sea   5
When grey gulls flit about instead of men,
And the gaunt houses put on majesty:
Let these content you and be gone again;
For they are at their old tricks yet.
                         A man
Of your own passionate serving kind who had
   brought   10
In his full hands what, had they only known,
Had given their children's children loftier thought,
Sweeter emotion, working in their veins
Like gentle blood, has been driven from the place,
And insult heaped upon him for his pains,   15
And for his open-handedness, disgrace;

Your enemy, an old foul mouth, had set
The pack upon him.
                    Go, unquiet wanderer,
And gather the Glasnevin coverlet
20   About your head till the dust stops your ear,
The time for you to taste of that salt breath
And listen at the corners has not come;
You had enough of sorrow before death –
Away, away! You are safer in the tomb.

September 29, 1913

lines 17–19   An old foul mouth that once cried out on you
              Herding the pack.
                          Unquiet wanderer
              Draw the Glasnevin coverlet anew

(*Poems Written in Discouragement*, 1913)

Beggar to Beggar Cried

❖❖❖

'Time to put off the world and go somewhere
And find my health again in the sea air,'
Beggar to beggar cried, being frenzy-struck,
'And make my soul before my pate is bare.'

5   'And get a comfortable wife and house
To rid me of the devil in my shoes,'
Beggar to beggar cried, being frenzy-struck,
'And the worse devil that is between my thighs.'

'And though I'd marry with a comely lass,
10   She need not be too comely – let it pass,'
Beggar to beggar cried, being frenzy-struck,
'But there's a devil in a looking-glass.'

'Nor should she be too rich, because the rich
Are driven by wealth as beggars by the itch,'
Beggar to beggar cried, being frenzy-struck,   15
'And cannot have a humorous happy speech.'

'And there I'll grow respected at my ease,
And hear amid the garden's nightly peace,'
Beggar to beggar cried, being frenzy-struck,
'The wind-blown clamour of the barnacle-geese.'   20

Running to Paradise
◇◇◇◇

As I came over Windy Gap
They threw a halfpenny into my cap,
For I am running to Paradise;
And all that I need do is to wish
And somebody puts his hand in the dish   5
To throw me a bit of salted fish:
And there the king is but as the beggar.

My brother Mourteen is worn out
With skelping his big brawling lout,
And I am running to Paradise;   10
A poor life, do what he can,
And though he keep a dog and a gun,
A serving-maid and a serving-man:
And there the king is but as the beggar.

Poor men have grown to be rich men,   15
And rich men grown to be poor again,
And I am running to Paradise;
And many a darling wit's grown dull
That tossed a bare heel when at school,
Now it has filled an old sock full: 20
And there the king is but as the beggar.

The wind is old and still at play
While I must hurry upon my way,
For I am running to Paradise;
25   Yet never have I lit on a friend
To take my fancy like the wind
That nobody can buy or bind:
And there the king is but as the beggar.

I

The Witch

❖❖❖❖

Toil and grow rich,
What's that but to lie
With a foul witch
And after, drained dry,
5   To be brought
To the chamber where
Lies one long sought
With despair?

II

The Peacock

❖❖❖❖

What's riches to him
That has made a great peacock
With the pride of his eye?
The wind-beaten, stone-grey,
5   And desolate Three Rock
Would nourish his whim.
Live he or die

78

Amid wet rocks and heather,
His ghost will be gay
Adding feather to feather   10
For the pride of his eye.

The Mountain Tomb
❖❖❖❖

Pour wine and dance if manhood still have pride,
Bring roses if the rose be yet in bloom;
The cataract smokes upon the mountain side,
Our Father Rosicross is in his tomb.

Pull down the blinds, bring fiddle and clarionet   5
That there be no foot silent in the room
Nor mouth from kissing, nor from wine unwet;
Our Father Rosicross is in his tomb.

In vain, in vain; the cataract still cries;
The everlasting taper lights the gloom;   10
All wisdom shut into his onyx eyes,
Our Father Rosicross sleeps in his tomb.

I

To a Child Dancing in the Wind
❖❖❖❖

Dance there upon the shore;
What need have you to care
For wind or water's roar?
And tumble out your hair
That the salt drops have wet;   5
Being young you have not known

79

The fool's triumph, nor yet
Love lost as soon as won,
Nor the best labourer dead
10   And all the sheaves to bind.
What need have you to dread
The monstrous crying of wind?

II

Two Years Later
❖❖❖❖

Has no one said those daring
Kind eyes should be more learn'd?
Or warned you how despairing
The moths are when they are burned?
5   I could have warned you; but you are young,
So we speak a different tongue.

O you will take whatever's offered
And dream that all the world's a friend,
Suffer as your mother suffered,
10   Be as broken in the end.
But I am old and you are young,
And I speak a barbarous tongue.

A Memory of Youth
❖❖❖❖

The moments passed as at a play;
I had the wisdom love brings forth;
I had my share of mother-wit,
And yet for all that I could say,

And though I had her praise for it,   5
A cloud blown from the cut-throat north
Suddenly hid Love's moon away.

Believing every word I said,
I praised her body and her mind
Till pride had made her eyes grow bright,   10
And pleasure made her cheeks grow red,
And vanity her footfall light,
Yet we, for all that praise, could find
Nothing but darkness overhead.

We sat as silent as a stone,   15
We knew, though she'd not said a word,
That even the best of love must die,
And had been savagely undone
Were it not that Love upon the cry
Of a most ridiculous little bird   20
Tore from the clouds his marvellous moon.

lines 6–7   And she seemed happy as a king,
             Love's moon was withering away.

lines 15–16 I sat as silent as a stone
             And knew, though she'd not said a word,

line 21   Threw up in the air his marvellous moon.

(Poetry, December 1912)

Fallen Majesty
❖❖❖❖

Although crowds gathered once if she but showed
    her face,
And even old men's eyes grew dim, this hand
    alone,
Like some last courtier at a gypsy camping-place

Babbling of fallen majesty, records what's gone.

The lineaments, a heart that laughter has made
5   sweet,
These, these remain, but I record what's gone. A
     crowd
Will gather, and not know it walks the very street
Whereon a thing once walked that seemed a
     burning cloud.

lines 7–8 Will gather and not know that through its very street
     Once walked a thing that seemed, as it were, a
      burning cloud.

(*Poetry*, December 1912)

The Cold Heaven
◇◇◇◇

Suddenly I saw the cold and rook-delighting
     heaven
That seemed as though ice burned and was but
     the more ice,
And thereupon imagination and heart were driven
So wild that every casual thought of that and this
Vanished, and left but memories, that should be
5   out of season
With the hot blood of youth, of love crossed long
     ago;
And I took all the blame out of all sense and
     reason,
Until I cried and trembled and rocked to and fro,
Riddled with light. Ah! when the ghost begins to
     quicken,
10   Confusion of the death-bed over, is it sent
Out naked on the roads, as the books say, and
     stricken
By the injustice of the skies for punishment?

The Magi

Now as at all times I can see in the mind's eye,
In their stiff, painted clothes, the pale unsatisfied
   ones
Appear and disappear in the blue depth of the
   sky
With all their ancient faces like rain-beaten
   stones,
And all their helms of silver hovering side by
   side,   5
And all their eyes still fixed, hoping to find once
   more,
Being by Calvary's turbulence unsatisfied,
The uncontrollable mystery on the bestial floor.

A Coat

I made my song a coat
Covered with embroideries
Out of old mythologies
From heel to throat;
But the fools caught it,   5
Wore it in the world's eyes
As though they'd wrought it.
Song, let them take it,
For there's more enterprise
In walking naked.   10

[*A woman's beauty is like a white*]
❖❖❖

[*Song for the folding and unfolding of the cloth*]

First Musician.
A woman's beauty is like a white
Frail bird, like a white sea-bird alone
At daybreak after stormy night
Between two furrows upon the ploughed land:
5   A sudden storm, and it was thrown
Between dark furrows upon the ploughed land.
How many centuries spent
The sedentary soul
In toils of measurement
10   Beyond eagle or mole,
Beyond hearing or seeing,
Or Archimedes' guess,
To raise into being
That loveliness?

15   A strange, unserviceable thing,
A fragile, exquisite, pale shell,
That the vast troubled waters bring
To the loud sands before day has broken.
The storm arose and suddenly fell
20   Amid the dark before day had broken.
What death? what discipline?
What bonds no man could unbind,
Being imagined within
The labyrinth of the mind,
25   What pursuing or fleeing,
What wounds, what bloody press,
Dragged into being
This loveliness?

(*The Only Jealousy of Emer*, 1917–18)

THE WILD SWANS AT COOLE

The Wild Swans at Coole

The trees are in their autumn beauty,
The woodland paths are dry,
Under the October twilight the water
Mirrors a still sky;
Upon the brimming water among the stones   5
Are nine-and-fifty swans.

The nineteenth autumn has come upon me
Since I first made my count;
I saw, before I had well finished,
All suddenly mount   10
And scatter wheeling in great broken rings
Upon their clamorous wings.

I have looked upon those brilliant creatures,
And now my heart is sore.
All's changed since I, hearing at twilight,   15
The first time on this shore,
The bell-beat of their wings above my head,
Trod with a lighter tread.

Unwearied still, lover by lover,
They paddle in the cold   20
Companionable streams or climb the air;
Their hearts have not grown old;
Passion or conquest, wander where they will,
Attend upon them still.

But now they drift on the still water,   25
Mysterious, beautiful;

Among what rushes will they build,
By what lake's edge or pool
Delight men's eyes when I awake some day
30 To find they have flown away?

In Memory of Major Robert Gregory
❖❖❖❖

I

Now that we're almost settled in our house
I'll name the friends that cannot sup with us
Beside a fire of turf in th' ancient tower,
And having talked to some late hour
5 Climb up the narrow winding stair to bed:
Discoverers of forgotten truth
Or mere companions of my youth,
All, all are in my thoughts to-night being dead.

II

Always we'd have the new friend meet the old
10 And we are hurt if either friend seem cold,
And there is salt to lengthen out the smart
In the affections of our heart,
And quarrels are blown up upon that head;
But not a friend that I would bring
15 This night can set us quarrelling,
For all that come into my mind are dead.

III

Lionel Johnson comes the first to mind,
That loved his learning better than mankind,
Though courteous to the worst; much falling he
20 Brooded upon sanctity

86

Till all his Greek and Latin learning seemed
A long blast upon the horn that brought
A little nearer to his thought
A measureless consummation that he dreamed.

IV

And that enquiring man John Synge comes next, 25
That dying chose the living world for text
And never could have rested in the tomb
But that, long travelling, he had come
Towards nightfall upon certain set apart
In a most desolate stony place, 30
Towards nightfall upon a race
Passionate and simple like his heart.

V

And then I think of old George Pollexfen,
In muscular youth well known to Mayo men
For horsemanship at meets or at racecourses, 35
That could have shown how pure-bred horses
And solid men, for all their passion, live
But as the outrageous stars incline
By opposition, square and trine;
Having grown sluggish and contemplative. 40

VI

They were my close companions many a year,
A portion of my mind and life, as it were,
And now their breathless faces seem to look
Out of some old picture-book;
I am accustomed to their lack of breath, 45
But not that my dear friend's dear son,
Our Sidney and our perfect man,
Could share in that discourtesy of death.

VII

For all things the delighted eye now sees
50   Were loved by him: the old storm-broken trees
That cast their shadows upon road and bridge;
The tower set on the stream's edge;
The ford where drinking cattle make a stir
Nightly, and startled by that sound
55   The water-hen must change her ground;
He might have been your heartiest welcomer.

VIII

When with the Galway foxhounds he would ride
From Castle Taylor to the Roxborough side
Or Esserkelly plain, few kept his pace;
60   At Mooneen he had leaped a place
So perilous that half the astonished meet
Had shut their eyes; and where was it
He rode a race without a bit?
And yet his mind outran the horses' feet.

IX

65   We dreamed that a great painter had been born
To cold Clare rock and Galway rock and thorn,
To that stern colour and that delicate line
That are our secret discipline
Wherein the gazing heart doubles her might.
70   Soldier, scholar, horseman, he,
And yet he had the intensity
To have published all to be a world's delight.

X

What other could so well have counselled us
In all lovely intricacies of a house
75   As he that practised or that understood
All work in metal or in wood,

In moulded plaster or in carven stone?
Soldier, scholar, horseman, he,
And all he did done perfectly
As though he had but that one trade alone.   80

XI

Some burn damp faggots, others may consume
The entire combustible world in one small room
As though dried straw, and if we turn about
The bare chimney is gone black out
Because the work had finished in that flare.   85
Soldier, scholar, horseman, he,
As 'twere all life's epitome.
What made us dream that he could comb grey hair?

XII

I had thought, seeing how bitter is that wind
That shakes the shutter, to have brought to mind   90
All those that manhood tried, or childhood loved
Or boyish intellect approved,
With some appropriate commentary on each;
Until imagination brought
A fitter welcome; but a thought   95
Of that late death took all my heart for speech.

An Irish Airman Foresees his Death
❖❖❖

I know that I shall meet my fate
Somewhere among the clouds above;
Those that I fight I do not hate,
Those that I guard I do not love;
My country is Kiltartan Cross,   5
My countrymen Kiltartan's poor,

No likely end could bring them loss
Or leave them happier than before.
Nor law, nor duty bade me fight,
10   Nor public men, nor cheering crowds,
A lonely impulse of delight
Drove to this tumult in the clouds;
I balanced all, brought all to mind,
The years to come seemed waste of breath,
15   A waste of breath the years behind
In balance with this life, this death.

line 10   Nor public man, nor angry crowds

(*The Wild Swans at Coole*, 1919)

Men Improve with the Years
◇◇◇◇

I am worn out with dreams;
A weather-worn, marble triton
Among the streams;
And all day long I look
5   Upon this lady's beauty
As though I had found in a book
A pictured beauty,
Pleased to have filled the eyes
Or the discerning ears,
10   Delighted to be but wise,
For men improve with the years;
And yet, and yet,
Is this my dream, or the truth?
O would that we had met
15   When I had my burning youth!
But I grow old among dreams,
A weather-worn, marble triton
Among the streams.

The Collar-Bone of a Hare

✦✦✦✦

Would I could cast a sail on the water
Where many a king has gone
And many a king's daughter,
And alight at the comely trees and the lawn,
The playing upon pipes and the dancing,   5
And learn that the best thing is
To change my loves while dancing
And pay but a kiss for a kiss.

I would find by the edge of that water
The collar-bone of a hare   10
Worn thin by the lapping of water,
And pierce it through with a gimlet, and stare
At the old bitter world where they marry in
    churches,
And laugh over the untroubled water
At all who marry in churches,   15
Through the white thin bone of a hare.

Solomon to Sheba

✦✦✦✦

Sang Solomon to Sheba,
And kissed her dusky face,
'All day long from mid-day
We have talked in the one place,
All day long from shadowless noon   5
We have gone round and round
In the narrow theme of love
Like an old horse in a pound.'

To Solomon sang Sheba,

10 Planted on his knees,
  'If you had broached a matter
  That might the learned please,
  You had before the sun had thrown
  Our shadows on the ground
15 Discovered that my thoughts, not it,
  Are but a narrow pound.'

  Said Solomon to Sheba,
  And kissed her Arab eyes,
  'There's not a man or woman
20 Born under the skies
  Dare match in learning with us two,
  And all day long we have found
  There's not a thing but love can make
  The world a narrow pound.'

The Living Beauty

❖❖❖❖

  I bade, because the wick and oil are spent
  And frozen are the channels of the blood,
  My discontented heart to draw content
  From beauty that is cast out of a mould
5 In bronze, or that in dazzling marble appears,
  Appears, but when we have gone is gone again,
  Being more indifferent to our solitude
  Than 'twere an apparition. O heart, we are old;
  The living beauty is for younger men:
10 We cannot pay its tribute of wild tears.

lines 1–3 I'll say and maybe dream I have drawn content,
   Seeing that time has frozen up the blood
   The wick of youth being burned and the oil spent,

(*Little Review*, October 1918)

A Song

◆◆◆◆

I thought no more was needed
Youth to prolong
Than dumb-bell and foil
To keep the body young.
O who could have foretold   5
That the heart grows old?

Though I have many words,
What woman's satisfied,
I am no longer faint
Because at her side?   10
O who could have foretold
That the heart grows old?

I have not lost desire
But the heart that I had;
I thought 'twould burn my body   15
Laid on the death-bed,
For who could have foretold
That the heart grows old?

The Scholars

◆◆◆◆

Bald heads forgetful of their sins,
Old, learned, respectable bald heads
Edit and annotate the lines
That young men, tossing on their beds,
Rhymed out in love's despair   5
To flatter beauty's ignorant ear.

All shuffle there; all cough in ink;

All wear the carpet with their shoes;
All think what other people think;
10   All know the man their neighbour knows.
Lord, what would they say
Did their Catullus walk that way?

lines 7–10   They'll cough in ink to the world's end;
              Wear out the carpet with their shoes
              Earning respect; have no strange friend;
              If they have sinned nobody knows:

(*Catholic Anthology, 1914–15*, 1915)

Lines Written in Dejection
❖❖❖

When have I last looked on
The round green eyes and the long wavering bodies
Of the dark leopards of the moon?
All the wild witches, those most noble ladies,
5   For all their broom-sticks and their tears,
Their angry tears, are gone.
The holy centaurs of the hills are vanished;
I have nothing but the embittered sun;
Banished heroic mother moon and vanished,
10   And now that I have come to fifty years
I must endure the timid sun.

The Dawn
❖❖❖

I would be ignorant as the dawn
That has looked down
On that old queen measuring a town

With the pin of a brooch,
Or on the withered men that saw   5
From their pedantic Babylon
The careless planets in their courses,
The stars fade out where the moon comes,
And took their tablets and did sums;
I would be ignorant as the dawn   10
That merely stood, rocking the glittering coach
Above the cloudy shoulders of the horses;
I would be – for no knowledge is worth a straw –
Ignorant and wanton as the dawn.

On Woman
◇◇◇◇

May God be praised for woman
That gives up all her mind,
A man may find in no man
A friendship of her kind
That covers all he has brought   5
As with her flesh and bone,
Nor quarrels with a thought
Because it is not her own.

Though pedantry denies,
It's plain the Bible means   10
That Solomon grew wise
While talking with his queens,
Yet never could, although
They say he counted grass,
Count all the praises due   15
When Sheba was his lass,
When she the iron wrought, or
When from the smithy fire
It shuddered in the water:

20 Harshness of their desire
That made them stretch and yawn,
Pleasure that comes with sleep,
Shudder that made them one.
What else He give or keep
25 God grant me — no, not here,
For I am not so bold
To hope a thing so dear
Now I am growing old,
But when, if the tale's true,
30 The Pestle of the moon
That pounds up all anew
Brings me to birth again —
To find what once I had
And know what once I have known,
35 Until I am driven mad,
Sleep driven from my bed,
By tenderness and care,
Pity, an aching head,
Gnashing of teeth, despair;
40 And all because of some one
Perverse creature of chance,
And live like Solomon
That Sheba led a dance.

The Fisherman

❖❖❖❖

Although I can see him still,
The freckled man who goes
To a grey place on a hill
In grey Connemara clothes
5 At dawn to cast his flies,
It's long since I began
To call up to the eyes

This wise and simple man.
All day I'd looked in the face
What I had hoped 'twould be   10
To write for my own race
And the reality;
The living men that I hate,
The dead man that I loved,
The craven man in his seat,   15
The insolent unreproved,
And no knave brought to book
Who has won a drunken cheer,
The witty man and his joke
Aimed at the commonest ear,   20
The clever man who cries
The catch-cries of the clown,
The beating down of the wise
And great Art beaten down.

Maybe a twelvemonth since   25
Suddenly I began,
In scorn of this audience,
Imagining a man,
And his sun-freckled face,
And grey Connemara cloth,   30
Climbing up to a place
Where stone is dark under froth,
And the down-turn of his wrist
When the flies drop in the stream;
A man who does not exist,   35
A man who is but a dream;
And cried, 'Before I am old
I shall have written him one
Poem maybe as cold
And passionate as the dawn.'   40

97

Memory

❖❖❖

One had a lovely face,
And two or three had charm,
But charm and face were in vain
Because the mountain grass
5   Cannot but keep the form
Where the mountain hare has lain.

Her Praise

❖❖❖

She is foremost of those that I would hear
    praised.
I have gone about the house, gone up and down
As a man does who has published a new book,
Or a young girl dressed out in her new gown,
And though I have turned the talk by hook or
5   crook
Until her praise should be the uppermost theme,
A woman spoke of some new tale she had read,
A man confusedly in a half dream
As though some other name ran in his head.
She is foremost of those that I would hear
10   praised.
I will talk no more of books or the long war
But walk by the dry thorn until I have found
Some beggar sheltering from the wind, and there
Manage the talk until her name come round.
15   If there be rags enough he will know her name
And be well pleased remembering it, for in the
    old days,

Though she had young men's praise and old
    men's blame,
Among the poor both old and young gave her
    praise.

The People
❖❖❖❖

'What have I earned for all that work,' I said,
'For all that I have done at my own charge?
The daily spite of this unmannerly town,
Where who has served the most is most defamed,
The reputation of his lifetime lost   5
Between the night and morning. I might have
    lived,
And you know well how great the longing has
    been,
Where every day my footfall should have lit
In the green shadow of Ferrara wall;
Or climbed among the images of the past –   10
The unperturbed and courtly images –
Evening and morning, the steep street of Urbino
To where the duchess and her people talked
The stately midnight through until they stood
In their great window looking at the dawn;   15
I might have had no friend that could not mix
Courtesy and passion into one like those
That saw the wicks grow yellow in the dawn;
I might have used the one substantial right
My trade allows: chosen my company,   20
And chosen what scenery had pleased me best.'
Thereon my phoenix answered in reproof,
'The drunkards, pilferers of public funds,
All the dishonest crowd I had driven away,
When my luck changed and they dared meet my
    face,   25
Crawled from obscurity, and set upon me

Those I had served and some that I had fed;
Yet never have I, now nor any time,
Complained of the people.'

                All I could reply
Was: 'You, that have not lived in thought but
30   deed,
Can have the purity of a natural force,
But I, whose virtues are the definitions
Of the analytic mind, can neither close
The eye of the mind nor keep my tongue from
    speech.'
35 And yet, because my heart leaped at her words,
I was abashed, and now they come to mind
After nine years, I sink my head abashed.

A Thought from Propertius

❖❖❖

She might, so noble from head
To great shapely knees
The long flowing line,
Have walked to the altar
5   Through the holy images
At Pallas Athene's side,
Or been fit spoil for a centaur
Drunk with the unmixed wine.

A Deep-sworn Vow

❖❖❖

Others because you did not keep
That deep-sworn vow have been friends of mine;

Yet always when I look death in the face,
When I clamber to the heights of sleep,
Or when I grow excited with wine,   5
Suddenly I meet your face.

Presences
❖❖❖

This night has been so strange that it seemed
As if the hair stood up on my head.
From going-down of the sun I have dreamed
That women laughing, or timid or wild,
In rustle of lace or silken stuff,   5
Climbed up my creaking stair. They had read
All I had rhymed of that monstrous thing
Returned and yet unrequited love.
They stood in the door and stood between
My great wood lectern and the fire   10
Till I could hear their hearts beating:
One is a harlot, and one a child
That never looked upon man with desire,
And one, it may be, a queen.

On being asked for a War Poem
❖❖❖

I think it better that in times like these
A poet's mouth be silent, for in truth
We have no gift to set a statesman right;
He has had enough of meddling who can please
A young girl in the indolence of her youth,   5
Or an old man upon a winter's night.

lines 1–2   I think it better that at times like these
We poets keep our mouths shut, for in truth

(*Book of the Homeless*, 1916)

Upon a Dying Lady
❖❖❖

I
Her Courtesy

With the old kindness, the old distinguished
  grace,
She lies, her lovely piteous head amid dull red
  hair
Propped upon pillows, rouge on the pallor of her
  face.
She would not have us sad because she is lying
  there,
5 And when she meets our gaze her eyes are
  laughter-lit,
Her speech a wicked tale that we may vie with
  her,
Matching our broken-hearted wit against her wit,
Thinking of saints and of Petronius Arbiter.

II
Certain Artists bring her Dolls and Drawings

Bring where our Beauty lies
A new modelled doll, or drawing,
With a friend's or an enemy's
Features, or maybe showing
5 Her features when a tress
Of dull red hair was flowing
Over some silken dress

Cut in the Turkish fashion,
Or, it may be, like a boy's.
We have given the world our passion,   10
We have naught for death but toys.

III
She turns the Dolls' Faces to the Wall

Because to-day is some religious festival
They had a priest say Mass, and even the Japanese,
Heel up and weight on toe, must face the wall
– Pedant in passion, learned in old courtesies,
Vehement and witty she had seemed –; the
    Venetian lady   5
Who had seemed to glide to some intrigue in her
    red shoes,
Her domino, her panniered skirt copied from
    Longhi;
The meditative critic; all are on their toes,
Even our Beauty with her Turkish trousers on.
Because the priest must have like every dog his day   10
Or keep us all awake with baying at the moon,
We and our dolls being but the world were best
    away.

IV
The End of Day

She is playing like a child
And penance is the play,
Fantastical and wild
Because the end of day
Shows her that some one soon   5
Will come from the house, and say –
Though play is but half done –
'Come in and leave the play.'

V

Her Race

She has not grown uncivil
As narrow natures would
And called the pleasures evil
Happier days thought good;
5   She knows herself a woman,
No red and white of a face,
Or rank, raised from a common
Unreckonable race;
And how should her heart fail her
10   Or sickness break her will
With her dead brother's valour
For an example still?

VI

Her Courage

When her soul flies to the predestined dancing-
    place
(I have no speech but symbol, the pagan speech I
    made
Amid the dreams of youth) let her come face to
    face,
Amid that first astonishment, with Grania's shade,
5   All but the terrors of the woodland flight forgot
That made her Diarmuid dear, and some old
    cardinal
Pacing with half-closed eyelids in a sunny spot
Who had murmured of Giorgione at his latest
    breath —
Aye, and Achilles, Timor, Babar, Barhaim, all
Who have lived in joy and laughed into the face of
10   Death.

VII
Her Friends bring her a Christmas Tree

Pardon, great enemy,
Without an angry thought
We've carried in our tree,
And here and there have bought
Till all the boughs are gay,   5
And she may look from the bed
On pretty things that may
Please a fantastic head.
Give her a little grace,
What if a laughing eye   10
Have looked into your face?
It is about to die.

VI, line 4   While wondering still to be a shade, with Grania's
shade,

(*Little Review*, August 1917)

Ego Dominus Tuus
❖❖❖

Hic. On the grey sand beside the shallow stream
Under your old wind-beaten tower, where still
A lamp burns on beside the open book
That Michael Robartes left, you walk in the
    moon
And though you have passed the best of life,
    still trace,   5
Enthralled by the unconquerable delusion,
Magical shapes.

Ille.   By the help of an image
I call to my own opposite, summon all
That I have handled least, least looked upon.

10   *Hic*. And I would find myself and not an image.

     Ille. That is our modern hope, and by its light
       We have lit upon the gentle sensitive mind
       And lost the old nonchalance of the hand;
       Whether we have chosen chisel, pen or brush,
15   We are but critics, or but half create,
       Timid, entangled, empty and abashed,
       Lacking the countenance of our friends.

     Hic.   And yet
       The chief imagination of Christendom,
       Dante Alighieri, so utterly found himself
20   That he has made that hollow face of his
       More plain to the mind's eye than any face
       But that of Christ.

     Ille.   And did he find himself
       Or was the hunger that had made it hollow
       A hunger for the apple on the bough
25   Most out of reach? and is that spectral image
       The man that Lapo and that Guido knew?
       I think he fashioned from his opposite
       An image that might have been a stony face
       Staring upon a Bedouin's horse-hair roof
       From doored and windowed cliff, or half
30   upturned
       Among the coarse grass and the camel-dung.
       He set his chisel to the hardest stone.
       Being mocked by Guido for his lecherous life,
       Derided and deriding, driven out
35   To climb that stair and eat that bitter bread,
       He found the unpersuadable justice, he found
       The most exalted lady loved by a man.

     Hic. Yet surely there are men who have made their
         art
       Out of no tragic war, lovers of life,
40   Impulsive men that look for happiness
       And sing when they have found it.

Ille.   No, not sing,
  For those that love the world serve it in action,
  Grow rich, popular and full of influence,
  And should they paint or write, still it is action:
  The struggle of the fly in marmalade.   45
  The rhetorician would deceive his neighbours,
  The sentimentalist himself; while art
  Is but a vision of reality.
  What portion in the world can the artist have
  Who has awakened from the common dream   50
  But dissipation and despair?

Hic.   And yet
  No one denies to Keats love of the world;
  Remember his deliberate happiness.

Ille. His art is happy, but who knows his mind?
  I see a schoolboy when I think of him,   55
  With face and nose pressed to a sweet-shop
    window,
  For certainly he sank into his grave
  His senses and his heart unsatisfied,
  And made – being poor, ailing and ignorant,
  Shut out from all the luxury of the world,   60
  The coarse-bred son of a livery-stable keeper –
  Luxuriant song.

Hic.   Why should you leave the lamp
  Burning alone beside an open book,
  And trace these characters upon the sands?
  A style is found by sedentary toil   65
  And by the imitation of great masters.

Ille. Because I seek an image, not a book.
  Those men that in their writings are most wise
  Own nothing but their blind, stupefied hearts.
  I call to the mysterious one who yet   70
  Shall walk the wet sands by the edge of the
    stream
  And look most like me, being indeed my double,

And prove of all imaginable things
The most unlike, being my anti-self,
75   And, standing by these characters, disclose
All that I seek; and whisper it as though
He were afraid the birds, who cry aloud
Their momentary cries before it is dawn,
Would carry it away to blasphemous men.

The Phases of the Moon

❖❖❖❖

An old man cocked his ear upon a bridge:
He and his friend, their faces to the South,
Had trod the uneven road. Their boots were soiled,
Their Connemara cloth worn out of shape;
5   *They had kept a steady pace as though their beds,*
Despite a dwindling and late risen moon,
Were distant still. An old man cocked his ear.

Aherne. What made that sound?

Robartes.   A rat or water-hen
Splashed, or an otter slid into the stream.
10   We are on the bridge; that shadow is the tower,
And the light proves that he is reading still.
He has found, after the manner of his kind,
Mere images; chosen this place to live in
Because, it may be, of the candle-light
15   From the far tower where Milton's Platonist
Sat late, or Shelley's visionary prince:
The lonely light that Samuel Palmer engraved,
An image of mysterious wisdom won by toil;
And now he seeks in book or manuscript
20   What he shall never find.

Aherne.   Why should not you

Who know it all ring at his door, and speak
Just truth enough to show that his whole life
Will scarcely find for him a broken crust
Of all those truths that are your daily bread;
And when you have spoken take the roads again?   25

Robartes. He wrote of me in that extravagant style
　　He had learnt from Pater, and to round his tale
　　Said I was dead; and dead I choose to be.

Aherne. Sing me the changes of the moon once
　　　　more;
　　True song, though speech: 'mine author sung it
　　　　me.'   30

Robartes. Twenty-and-eight the phases of the
　　　　moon,
　　The full and the moon's dark and all the
　　　　crescents,
　　Twenty-and-eight, and yet but six-and-twenty
　　The cradles that a man must needs be rocked
　　　　in:
　　For there's no human life at the full or the dark.   35
　　From the first crescent to the half, the dream
　　But summons to adventure and the man
　　Is always happy like a bird or a beast;
　　But while the moon is rounding towards the full
　　He follows whatever whim's most difficult   40
　　Among whims not impossible, and though
　　　　scarred,
　　As with the cat-o'-nine-tails of the mind,
　　His body moulded from within his body
　　Grows comelier. Eleven pass, and then
　　Athena takes Achilles by the hair,   45
　　Hector is in the dust, Nietzsche is born,
　　Because the hero's crescent is the twelfth.
　　And yet, twice born, twice buried, grow he must,
　　Before the full moon, helpless as a worm.
　　The thirteenth moon but sets the soul at war   50

In its own being, and when that war's begun
There is no muscle in the arm; and after,
Under the frenzy of the fourteenth moon,
The soul begins to tremble into stillness,
55   To die into the labyrinth of itself!

Aherne. Sing out the song; sing to the end, and sing
The strange reward of all that discipline.

Robartes. All thought becomes an image and the
    soul
Becomes a body: that body and that soul
60   Too perfect at the full to lie in a cradle,
Too lonely for the traffic of the world:
Body and soul cast out and cast away
Beyond the visible world.

Aherne.   All dreams of the soul
End in a beautiful man's or woman's body.

65 *Robartes*. Have you not always known it?

Aherne.   The song will have it
That those that we have loved got their long
    fingers
From death, and wounds, or on Sinai's top,
Or from some bloody whip in their own hands.
They ran from cradle to cradle till at last
70   Their beauty dropped out of the loneliness
Of body and soul.

Robartes.   The lover's heart knows that.

Aherne. It must be that the terror in their eyes
Is memory or foreknowledge of the hour
When all is fed with light and heaven is bare.

Robartes. When the moon's full those creatures of
75   the full
Are met on the waste hills by country men
Who shudder and hurry by: body and soul
Estranged amid the strangeness of themselves,

Caught up in contemplation, the mind's eye
Fixed upon images that once were thought,   80
For perfected, completed, and immovable
Images can break the solitude
Of lovely, satisfied, indifferent eyes.

And thereupon with aged, high-pitched voice
Aherne laughed, thinking of the man within,   85
His sleepless candle and laborious pen.

Robartes. And after that the crumbling of the
    moon.
The soul remembering its loneliness
Shudders in many cradles; all is changed.
It would be the world's servant, and as it serves,   90
Choosing whatever task's most difficult
Among tasks not impossible, it takes
Upon the body and upon the soul
The coarseness of the drudge.

Aherne.   Before the full
It sought itself and afterwards the world.   95

Robartes. Because you are forgotten, half out of
    life,
And never wrote a book, your thought is clear.
Reformer, merchant, statesman, learned man,
Dutiful husband, honest wife by turn,
Cradle upon cradle, and all in flight and all   100
Deformed, because there is no deformity
But saves us from a dream.

Aherne.   And what of those
That the last servile crescent has set free?

Robartes. Because all dark, like those that are all
    light,
They are cast beyond the verge, and in a cloud,   105
Crying to one another like the bats;
And having no desire they cannot tell

What's good or bad, or what it is to triumph
At the perfection of one's own obedience;
110   And yet they speak what's blown into the mind;
Deformed beyond deformity, unformed,
Insipid as the dough before it is baked,
They change their bodies at a word.

Aherne.   And then?

Robartes. When all the dough has been so kneaded
        up
115   That it can take what form cook Nature fancies,
The first thin crescent is wheeled round once
        more.

Aherne. But the escape; the song's not finished yet.

Robartes. Hunchback and Saint and Fool are the
        last crescents.
The burning bow that once could shoot an arrow
120   Out of the up and down, the wagon-wheel
Of beauty's cruelty and wisdom's chatter –
Out of that raving tide – is drawn betwixt
Deformity of body and of mind.

Aherne. Were not our beds far off I'd ring the bell,
125   Stand under the rough roof-timbers of the hall
Beside the castle door, where all is stark
Austerity, a place set out for wisdom
That he will never find; I'd play a part;
He would never know me after all these years
130   But take me for some drunken country man;
I'd stand and mutter there until he caught
'Hunchback and Saint and Fool,' and that they
        came
Under the three last crescents of the moon,
And then I'd stagger out. He'd crack his wits
135   Day after day, yet never find the meaning.

*And then he laughed to think that what seemed
        hard*

Should be so simple – a bat rose from the hazels
And circled round him with its squeaky cry,
The light in the tower window was put out.

(A Vision, 1937)

The Double Vision of Michael Robartes
❖❖❖

I

On the grey rock of Cashel the mind's eye
Has called up the cold spirits that are born
When the old moon is vanished from the sky
And the new still hides her horn.

Under the blank eyes and fingers never still   5
The particular is pounded till it is man.
When had I my own will?
O not since life began.

Constrained, arraigned, baffled, bent and unbent
By these wire-jointed jaws and limbs of wood,   10
Themselves obedient,
Knowing not evil and good;

Obedient to some hidden magical breath.
They do not even feel, so abstract are they,
So dead beyond our death,   15
Triumph that we obey.

II

On the grey rock of Cashel I suddenly saw
A Sphinx with woman breast and lion paw,
A Buddha, hand at rest,
Hand lifted up that blest;   20

And right between these two a girl at play
That, it may be, had danced her life away,

For now being dead it seemed
That she of dancing dreamed.

25   Although I saw it all in the mind's eye
There can be nothing solider till I die;
I saw by the moon's light
Now at its fifteenth night.

One lashed her tail; her eyes lit by the moon
30   Gazed upon all things known, all things unknown,
In triumph of intellect
With motionless head erect.

That other's moonlit eyeballs never moved,
Being fixed on all things loved, all things unloved,
35   Yet little peace he had,
For those that love are sad.

O little did they care who danced between,
And little she by whom her dance was seen
So she had outdanced thought.
40   Body perfection brought,

For what but eye and ear silence the mind
With the minute particulars of mankind?
Mind moved yet seemed to stop
As 'twere a spinning-top.

45   In contemplation had those three so wrought
Upon a moment, and so stretched it out
That they, time overthrown,
Were dead yet flesh and bone.

III

I knew that I had seen, had seen at last
50   That girl my unremembering nights hold fast
Or else my dreams that fly
If I should rub an eye,

And yet in flying fling into my meat

A crazy juice that makes the pulses beat
As though I had been undone   55
By Homer's Paragon

Who never gave the burning town a thought;
To such a pitch of folly I am brought,
Being caught between the pull
Of the dark moon and the full,   60

The commonness of thought and images
That have the frenzy of our western seas.
Thereon I made my moan,
And after kissed a stone,

And after that arranged it in a song   65
Seeing that I, ignorant for so long,
Had been rewarded thus
In Cormac's ruined house.

Reprisals
❖❖❖❖

Some nineteen German planes, they say,
You had brought down before you died.
We called it a good death. Today
Can ghost or man be satisfied?
Although your last exciting year   5
Outweighed all other years, you said,
Though battle joy may be so dear
A memory, even to the dead,
It chases other thought away,
Yet rise from your Italian tomb,   10
Flit to Kiltartan cross and stay
Till certain second thoughts have come
Upon the cause you served, that we
Imagined such a fine affair:

15 Half-drunk or whole-mad soldiery
    Are murdering your tenants there.
    Men that revere your father yet
    Are shot at on the open plain.
    Where may new-married women sit
20 And suckle children now? Armed men
    May murder them in passing by
    Nor law nor parliament take heed.
    Then close your ears with dust and lie
    Among the other cheated dead.

(First published in *Rann: An Ulster Quarterly of Poetry*, Autumn 1948)

MICHAEL ROBARTES AND THE DANCER
❖❖❖❖❖

An Image from a Past Life
❖❖❖❖

He. Never until this night have I been stirred.
    The elaborate starlight throws a reflection
    On the dark stream,
    Till all the eddies gleam;
    And thereupon there comes that scream   5
    From terrified, invisible beast or bird:
    Image of poignant recollection.

She. An image of my heart that is smitten through
    Out of all likelihood, or reason,
    And when at last,   10
    Youth's bitterness being past,
    I had thought that all my days were cast
    Amid most lovely places; smitten as though
    It had not learned its lesson.

He. Why have you laid your hands upon my eyes?   15
    What can have suddenly alarmed you
    Whereon 'twere best
    My eyes should never rest?
    What is there but the slowly fading west,
    The river imaging the flashing skies,   20
    All that to this moment charmed you?

She. A sweetheart from another life floats there
    As though she had been forced to linger
    From vague distress
    Or arrogant loveliness,   25
    Merely to loosen out a tress

Among the starry eddies of her hair
Upon the paleness of a finger.

He. But why should you grow suddenly afraid
30 And start – I at your shoulder –
Imagining
That any night could bring
An image up, or anything
Even to eyes that beauty had driven mad,
35 But images to make me fonder?

She. Now she has thrown her arms above her head;
Whether she threw them up to flout me,
Or but to find,
Now that no fingers bind,
40 That her hair streams upon the wind,
I do not know, that know I am afraid
Of the hovering thing night brought me.

Under Saturn
❖❖❖❖

Do not because this day I have grown saturnine
Imagine that lost love, inseparable from my
    thought
Because I have no other youth, can make me pine;
For how should I forget the wisdom that you
    brought,
The comfort that you made? Although my wits
5   have gone
On a fantastic ride, my horse's flanks are spurred
By childish memories of an old cross Pollexfen,
And of a Middleton, whose name you never heard,
And of a red-haired Yeats whose looks, although
    he died
10 Before my time, seem like a vivid memory.
You heard that labouring man who had served my
    people. He said

Upon the open road, near to the Sligo quay –
No, no, not said, but cried it out – 'You have come
    again,
And surely after twenty years it was time to come.'
I am thinking of a child's vow sworn in vain   15
Never to leave that valley his fathers called their
    home.

November 1919

lines 2–5   Imagine that some lost love, unassailable
            Being a portion of my youth, can make me pine
            And so forget the comfort that no words can tell
            Your coming brought; though I acknowledge I have
               gone

(*Dial*, November 1920)

Easter 1916
❖❖❖❖

I have met them at close of day
Coming with vivid faces
From counter or desk among grey
Eighteenth-century houses.
I have passed with a nod of the head   5
Or polite meaningless words,
Or have lingered awhile and said
Polite meaningless words,
And thought before I had done
Of a mocking tale or a gibe   10
To please a companion
Around the fire at the club,
Being certain that they and I
But lived where motley is worn:
All changed, changed utterly: 15

A terrible beauty is born.

That woman's days were spent
In ignorant good-will,
Her nights in argument
20 Until her voice grew shrill.
What voice more sweet than hers
When, young and beautiful,
She rode to harriers?
This man had kept a school
25 And rode our wingèd horse;
This other his helper and friend
Was coming into his force;
He might have won fame in the end,
So sensitive his nature seemed,
30 So daring and sweet his thought.
This other man I had dreamed
A drunken, vainglorious lout.
He had done most bitter wrong
To some who are near my heart,
35 Yet I number him in the song;
He, too, has resigned his part
In the casual comedy;
He, too, has been changed in his turn,
Transformed utterly:
40 A terrible beauty is born.

Hearts with one purpose alone
Through summer and winter seem
Enchanted to a stone
To trouble the living stream.
45 The horse that comes from the road,
The rider, the birds that range
From cloud to tumbling cloud,
Minute by minute they change;
A shadow of cloud on the stream
50 Changes minute by minute;
A horse-hoof slides on the brim,

And a horse plashes within it;
The long-legged moor-hens dive,
And hens to moor-cocks call;
Minute by minute they live: 55
The stone's in the midst of all.

Too long a sacrifice
Can make a stone of the heart.
O when may it suffice?
That is Heaven's part, our part   60
To murmur name upon name,
As a mother names her child
When sleep at last has come
On limbs that had run wild.
What is it but nightfall?   65
No, no, not night but death;
Was it needless death after all?
For England may keep faith
For all that is done and said.
We know their dream; enough   70
To know they dreamed and are dead;
And what if excess of love
Bewildered them till they died?
I write it out in a verse –
MacDonagh and MacBride   75
And Connolly and Pearse
Now and in time to be,
Wherever green is worn,
Are changed, changed utterly:
A terrible beauty is born.   80

September 25, 1916

lines 17–25   That woman at while would be shrill
In aimless argument;
Had ignorant good will;
All that she got she spent,
Her charity had no bounds:
Sweet voiced and young and beautiful,

She had ridden well to hounds.
This man had managed a school
An our wingèd mettlesome horse.

(Easter, 1916, **1916**)

Sixteen Dead Men
❖❖❖❖

O but we talked at large before
The sixteen men were shot,
But who can talk of give and take,
What should be and what not
5 While those dead men are loitering there
To stir the boiling pot?

You say that we should still the land
Till Germany's overcome;
But who is there to argue that
10 Now Pearse is deaf and dumb?
And is their logic to outweigh
MacDonagh's bony thumb?

How could you dream they'd listen
That have an ear alone
15 For those new comrades they have found,
Lord Edward and Wolfe Tone,
Or meddle with our give and take
That converse bone to bone?

On a Political Prisoner
❖❖❖❖

She that but little patience knew,
From childhood on, had now so much

A grey gull lost its fear and flew
Down to her cell and there alit,
And there endured her fingers' touch   5
And from her fingers ate its bit.

Did she in touching that lone wing
Recall the years before her mind
Became a bitter, an abstract thing,
Her thought some popular enmity: 10
Blind and leader of the blind
Drinking the foul ditch where they lie?

When long ago I saw her ride
Under Ben Bulben to the meet,
The beauty of her country-side   15
With all youth's lonely wildness stirred,
She seemed to have grown clean and sweet
Like any rock-bred, sea-borne bird:

Sea-borne, or balanced on the air
When first it sprang out of the nest   20
Upon some lofty rock to stare
Upon the cloudy canopy,
While under its storm-beaten breast
Cried out the hollows of the sea.

The Leaders of the Crowd

They must to keep their certainty accuse
All that are different of a base intent;
Pull down established honour; hawk for news
Whatever their loose fantasy invent
And murmur it with bated breath, as though   5
The abounding gutter had been Helicon
Or calumny a song. How can they know

123

Truth flourishes where the student's lamp has
   shone,
And there alone, that have no solitude?
10 So the crowd come they care not what may come.
They have loud music, hope every day renewed
And heartier loves; that lamp is from the tomb.

The Second Coming
❖❖❖

Turning and turning in the widening gyre
The falcon cannot hear the falconer;
Things fall apart; the centre cannot hold;
Mere anarchy is loosed upon the world,
5 The blood-dimmed tide is loosed, and everywhere
The ceremony of innocence is drowned;
The best lack all conviction, while the worst
Are full of passionate intensity.
Surely some revelation is at hand;
10 Surely the Second Coming is at hand.
The Second Coming! Hardly are those words out
When a vast image out of *Spiritus Mundi*
Troubles my sight: somewhere in sands of the
   desert
A shape with lion body and the head of a man,
15 A gaze blank and pitiless as the sun,
Is moving its slow thighs, while all about it
Reel shadows of the indignant desert birds.
The darkness drops again; but now I know
That twenty centuries of stony sleep
20 Were vexed to nightmare by a rocking cradle,
And what rough beast, its hour come round at last,
Slouches towards Bethlehem to be born?

line 13 Troubles my sight: a waste of desert sand;
line 17 Wind shadows of the indignant desert birds.
(*Dial*, November 1920)

A Prayer for my Daughter
❖❖❖

Once more the storm is howling, and half hid
Under this cradle-hood and coverlid
My child sleeps on. There is no obstacle
But Gregory's wood and one bare hill
Whereby the haystack- and roof-levelling wind,   5
Bred on the Atlantic, can be stayed;
And for an hour I have walked and prayed
Because of the great gloom that is in my mind.

I have walked and prayed for this young child an
    hour
And heard the sea-wind scream upon the tower,   10
And under the arches of the bridge, and scream
In the elms above the flooded stream;
Imagining in excited reverie
That the future years had come,
Dancing to a frenzied drum,   15
Out of the murderous innocence of the sea.

May she be granted beauty and yet not
Beauty to make a stranger's eye distraught,
Or hers before a looking-glass, for such,
Being made beautiful overmuch,   20
Consider beauty a sufficient end,
Lose natural kindness and maybe
The heart-revealing intimacy
That chooses right, and never find a friend.

Helen being chosen found life flat and dull   25
And later had much trouble from a fool,
While that great Queen, that rose out of the spray,
Being fatherless could have her way
Yet chose a bandy-leggèd smith for man.
It's certain that fine women eat   30
A crazy salad with their meat
Whereby the Horn of Plenty is undone.

In courtesy I'd have her chiefly learned;
Hearts are not had as a gift but hearts are earned
35 By those that are not entirely beautiful;
Yet many, that have played the fool
For beauty's very self, has charm made wise,
And many a poor man that has roved,
Loved and thought himself beloved,
40 From a glad kindness cannot take his eyes.

May she become a flourishing hidden tree
That all her thoughts may like the linnet be,
And have no business but dispensing round
Their magnanimities of sound,
45 Nor but in merriment begin a chase,
Nor but in merriment a quarrel.
O may she live like some green laurel
Rooted in one dear perpetual place.

My mind, because the minds that I have loved,
50 The sort of beauty that I have approved,
Prosper but little, has dried up of late,
Yet knows that to be choked with hate
May well be of all evil chances chief.
If there's no hatred in a mind
55 Assault and battery of the wind
Can never tear the linnet from the leaf.

An intellectual hatred is the worst,
So let her think opinions are accursed.
Have I not seen the loveliest woman born
60 Out of the mouth of Plenty's horn,
Because of her opinionated mind
Barter that horn and every good
By quiet natures understood
For an old bellows full of angry wind?

65 Considering that, all hatred driven hence,
The soul recovers radical innocence
And learns at last that it is self-delighting,

Self-appeasing, self-affrighting,
And that its own sweet will is Heaven's will;
She can, though every face should scowl   70
And every windy quarter howl
Or every bellows burst, be happy still.

And may her bridegroom bring her to a house
Where all's accustomed, ceremonious;
For arrogance and hatred are the wares   75
Peddled in the thoroughfares.
How but in custom and in ceremony
Are innocence and beauty born?
Ceremony's a name for the rich horn,
And custom for the spreading laurel tree.   80

June 1919

THE TOWER

❖❖❖❖❖❖

Sailing to Byzantium

❖❖❖❖

I

That is no country for old men. The young
In one another's arms, birds in the trees
– Those dying generations – at their song,
The salmon-falls, the mackerel-crowded seas,
5   Fish, flesh, or fowl, commend all summer long
Whatever is begotten, born, and dies.
Caught in that sensual music all neglect
Monuments of unageing intellect.

II

An aged man is but a paltry thing,
10   A tattered coat upon a stick, unless
Soul clap its hands and sing, and louder sing
For every tatter in its mortal dress,
Nor is there singing school but studying
Monuments of its own magnificence;
15   And therefore I have sailed the seas and come
To the holy city of Byzantium.

III

O sages standing in God's holy fire
As in the gold mosaic of a wall,
Come from the holy fire, perne in a gyre,
20   And be the singing-masters of my soul.

Consume my heart away; sick with desire
And fastened to a dying animal
It knows not what it is; and gather me
Into the artifice of eternity.

IV

Once out of nature I shall never take   25
My bodily form from any natural thing,
But such a form as Grecian goldsmiths make
Of hammered gold and gold enamelling
To keep a drowsy Emperor awake;
Or set upon a golden bough to sing   30
To lords and ladies of Byzantium
Of what is past, or passing, or to come.

                                    1927

The Tower
◆◆◆◆

I

What shall I do with this absurdity –
O heart, O troubled heart – this caricature,
Decrepit age that has been tied to me
As to a dog's tail?
                    Never had I more
Excited, passionate, fantastical   5
Imagination, nor an ear and eye
That more expected the impossible –
No, not in boyhood when with rod and fly,
Or the humbler worm, I climbed Ben Bulben's
     back
And had the livelong summer day to spend.   10
It seems that I must bid the Muse go pack,

Choose Plato and Plotinus for a friend
Until imagination, ear and eye,
Can be content with argument and deal
15 In abstract things; or be derided by
A sort of battered kettle at the heel.

II

I pace upon the battlements and stare
On the foundations of a house, or where
Tree, like a sooty finger, starts from the earth;
20 And send imagination forth
Under the day's declining beam, and call
Images and memories
From ruin or from ancient trees,
For I would ask a question of them all.

25 Beyond that ridge lived Mrs. French, and once
When every silver candlestick or sconce
Lit up the dark mahogany and the wine,
A serving-man, that could divine
That most respected lady's every wish,
30 Ran and with the garden shears
Clipped an insolent farmer's ears
And brought them in a little covered dish.

Some few remembered still when I was young
A peasant girl commended by a song,
35 Who'd lived somewhere upon that rocky place,
And praised the colour of her face,
And had the greater joy in praising her,
Remembering that, if walked she there,
Farmers jostled at the fair
40 So great a glory did the song confer.

And certain men, being maddened by those
    rhymes,
Or else by toasting her a score of times,
Rose from the table and declared it right

To test their fancy by their sight;
But they mistook the brightness of the moon   45
For the prosaic light of day —
Music had driven their wits astray —
And one was drowned in the great bog of Cloone.

Strange, but the man who made the song was blind;
Yet, now I have considered it, I find   50
That nothing strange; the tragedy began
With Homer that was a blind man,
And Helen has all living hearts betrayed.
O may the moon and sunlight seem
One inextricable beam,   55
For if I triumph I must make men mad.

And I myself created Hanrahan
And drove him drunk or sober through the dawn
From somewhere in the neighbouring cottages.
Caught by an old man's juggleries   60
He stumbled, tumbled, fumbled to and fro
And had but broken knees for hire
And horrible splendour of desire;
I thought it all out twenty years ago:

Good fellows shuffled cards in an old bawn;   65
And when that ancient ruffian's turn was on
He so bewitched the cards under his thumb
That all but the one card became
A pack of hounds and not a pack of cards,
And that he changed into a hare.   70
Hanrahan rose in frenzy there
And followed up those baying creatures towards —

O towards I have forgotten what — enough!
I must recall a man that neither love
Nor music nor an enemy's clipped ear   75
Could, he was so harried, cheer;
A figure that has grown so fabulous
There's not a neighbour left to say

When he finished his dog's day:
80   An ancient bankrupt master of this house.

Before that ruin came, for centuries,
Rough men-at-arms, cross-gartered to the knees
Or shod in iron, climbed the narrow stairs,
And certain men-at-arms there were
85   Whose images, in the Great Memory stored,
Come with loud cry and panting breast
To break upon a sleeper's rest
While their great wooden dice beat on the board.

As I would question all, come all who can;
90   Come old, necessitous, half-mounted man;
And bring beauty's blind rambling celebrant;
The red man the juggler sent
Through God-forsaken meadows; Mrs. French,
Gifted with so fine an ear;
95   The man drowned in a bog's mire,
When mocking Muses chose the country wench.

Did all old men and women, rich and poor,
Who trod upon these rocks or passed this door,
Whether in public or in secret rage
100   As I do now against old age?
But I have found an answer in those eyes
That are impatient to be gone;
Go therefore; but leave Hanrahan,
For I need all his mighty memories.

105   Old lecher with a love on every wind,
Bring up out of that deep considering mind
All that you have discovered in the grave,
For it is certain that you have
Reckoned up every unforeknown, unseeing
110   Plunge, lured by a softening eye,
Or by a touch or a sigh,
Into the labyrinth of another's being;

Does the imagination dwell the most

Upon a woman won or woman lost?
If on the lost, admit you turned aside   115
From a great labyrinth out of pride,
Cowardice, some silly over-subtle thought
Or anything called conscience once;
And that if memory recur, the sun's
Under eclipse and the day blotted out.   120

III

It is time that I wrote my will;
I choose upstanding men
That climb the streams until
The fountain leap, and at dawn
Drop their cast at the side   125
Of dripping stone; I declare
They shall inherit my pride,
The pride of people that were
Bound neither to Cause nor to State,
Neither to slaves that were spat on,   130
Nor to the tyrants that spat,
The people of Burke and of Grattan
That gave, though free to refuse –
Pride, like that of the morn,
When the headlong light is loose,   135
Or that of the fabulous horn,
Or that of the sudden shower
When all streams are dry,
Or that of the hour
When the swan must fix his eye   140
Upon a fading gleam,
Float out upon a long
Last reach of glittering stream
And there sing his last song.
And I declare my faith: 145
I mock Plotinus' thought
And cry in Plato's teeth,
Death and life were not

Till man made up the whole,
150 Made lock, stock and barrel
Out of his bitter soul,
Aye, sun and moon and star, all,
And further add to that
That, being dead, we rise,
155 Dream and so create
Translunar Paradise.
I have prepared my peace
With learned Italian things
And the proud stones of Greece,
160 Poet's imaginings
And memories of love,
Memories of the words of women,
All those things whereof
Man makes a superhuman
165 Mirror-resembling dream.

As at the loophole there
The daws chatter and scream,
And drop twigs layer upon layer.
When they have mounted up,
170 The mother bird will rest
On their hollow top,
And so warm her wild nest.

I leave both faith and pride
To young upstanding men
175 Climbing the mountain-side,
That under bursting dawn
They may drop a fly;
Being of that metal made
Till it was broken by
180 This sedentary trade.

Now shall I make my soul,
Compelling it to study
In a learned school
Till the wreck of body,

Slow decay of blood,   185
Testy delirium
Or dull decrepitude,
Or what worse evil come –
The death of friends, or death
Of every brilliant eye   190
That made a catch in the breath –
Seem but the clouds of the sky
When the horizon fades;
Or a bird's sleepy cry
Among the deepening shades.

                                              1926

Meditations in Time of Civil War
❖❖❖❖

I
Ancestral Houses

Surely among a rich man's flowering lawns,
Amid the rustle of his planted hills,
Life overflows without ambitious pains;
And rains down life until the basin spills,
And mounts more dizzy high the more it rains   5
As though to choose whatever shape it wills
And never stoop to a mechanical
Or servile shape, at others' beck and call.

Mere dreams, mere dreams! Yet Homer had not sung
Had he not found it certain beyond dreams   10
That out of life's own self-delight had sprung
The abounding glittering jet; though now it seems
As if some marvellous empty sea-shell flung
Out of the obscure dark of the rich streams,
And not a fountain, were the symbol which   15
Shadows the inherited glory of the rich.

Some violent bitter man, some powerful man

Called architect and artist in, that they,
Bitter and violent men, might rear in stone
20 The sweetness that all longed for night and day,
The gentleness none there had ever known;
But when the master's buried mice can play,
And maybe the great-grandson of that house,
For all its bronze and marble, 's but a mouse.

25 O what if gardens where the peacock strays
With delicate feet upon old terraces,
Or else all Juno from an urn displays
Before the indifferent garden deities;
O what if levelled lawns and gravelled ways
30 Where slippered Contemplation finds his ease
And Childhood a delight for every sense,
But take our greatness with our violence?

What if the glory of escutcheoned doors,
And buildings that a haughtier age designed,
35 The pacing to and fro on polished floors
Amid great chambers and long galleries, lined
With famous portraits of our ancestors;
What if those things the greatest of mankind
Consider most to magnify, or to bless,
40 But take our greatness with our bitterness?

II
My House

An ancient bridge, and a more ancient tower,
A farmhouse that is sheltered by its wall,
An acre of stony ground,
Where the symbolic rose can break in flower,
5 Old ragged elms, old thorns innumerable,
The sound of the rain or sound
Of every wind that blows;
The stilted water-hen
Crossing stream again
10 Scared by the splashing of a dozen cows;

A winding stair, a chamber arched with stone,
A grey stone fireplace with an open hearth,
A candle and written page.
Il Penseroso's Platonist toiled on
In some like chamber, shadowing forth   15
How the daemonic rage
Imagined everything.
Benighted travellers
From markets and from fairs
Have seen his midnight candle glimmering.   20

Two men have founded here. A man-at-arms
Gathered a score of horse and spent his days
In this tumultuous spot,
Where through long wars and sudden night alarms
His dwindling score and he seemed castaways   25
Forgetting and forgot;
And I, that after me
My bodily heirs may find,
To exalt a lonely mind,
Befitting emblems of adversity.   30

III
My Table

Two heavy trestles, and a board
Where Sato's gift, a changeless sword,
By pen and paper lies,
That it may moralise
My days out of their aimlessness.   5
A bit of an embroidered dress
Covers its wooden sheath.
Chaucer had not drawn breath
When it was forged. In Sato's house,
Curved like new moon, moon-luminous,   10
It lay five hundred years.
Yet if no change appears
No moon; only an aching heart

Conceives a changeless work of art.
15 Our learned men have urged
That when and where 'twas forged
A marvellous accomplishment,
In painting or in pottery, went
From father unto son
20 And through the centuries ran
And seemed unchanging like the sword.
Soul's beauty being most adored,
Men and their business took
The soul's unchanging look;
25 For the most rich inheritor,
Knowing that none could pass Heaven's door
That loved inferior art,
Had such an aching heart
That he, although a country's talk
30 For silken clothes and stately walk,
Had waking wits; it seemed
Juno's peacock screamed.

IV

My Descendants

Having inherited a vigorous mind
From my old fathers, I must nourish dreams
And leave a woman and a man behind
As vigorous of mind, and yet it seems
5 Life scarce can cast a fragrance on the wind,
Scarce spread a glory to the morning beams,
But the torn petals strew the garden plot;
And there's but common greenness after that.

And what if my descendants lose the flower
10 Through natural declension of the soul,
Through too much business with the passing hour,
Through too much play, or marriage with a fool?
May this laborious stair and this stark tower
Become a roofless ruin that the owl

May build in the cracked masonry and cry   15
Her desolation to the desolate sky.

The Primum Mobile that fashioned us
Has made the very owls in circles move;
And I, that count myself most prosperous,
Seeing that love and friendship are enough,   20
For an old neighbour's friendship chose the house
And decked and altered it for a girl's love,
And know whatever flourish and decline
These stones remain their monument and mine.

V
The Road at my Door

An affable Irregular,
A heavily-built Falstaffian man,
Comes cracking jokes of civil war
As though to die by gunshot were
The finest play under the sun.   5

A brown Lieutenant and his men,
Half dressed in national uniform,
Stand at my door, and I complain
Of the foul weather, hail and rain,
A pear-tree broken by the storm.   10

I count those feathered balls of soot
The moor-hen guides upon the stream,
To silence the envy in my thought;
And turn towards my chamber, caught
In the cold snows of a dream.   15

VI
The Stare's Nest by my Window

The bees build in the crevices
Of loosening masonry, and there
The mother birds bring grubs and flies.
My wall is loosening; honey-bees,
Come build in the empty house of the stare.   5

We are closed in, and the key is turned
On our uncertainty; somewhere
A man is killed, or a house burned,
Yet no clear fact to be discerned:
10   Come build in the empty house of the stare.

A barricade of stone or of wood;
Some fourteen days of civil war;
Last night they trundled down the road
That dead young soldier in his blood:
15   Come build in the empty house of the stare.

We had fed the heart on fantasies,
The heart's grown brutal from the fare;
More substance in our enmities
Than in our love; O honey-bees,
20   Come build in the empty house of the stare.

VII

I see Phantoms of Hatred and of the Heart's Fullness and of the Coming Emptiness

I climb to the tower-top and lean upon broken
    stone,
A mist that is like blown snow is sweeping over all,
Valley, river, and elms, under the light of a moon
That seems unlike itself, that seems unchangeable,
5 A glittering sword out of the east. A puff of wind
And those white glimmering fragments of the mist
    sweep by.
Frenzies bewilder, reveries perturb the mind;
Monstrous familiar images swim to the mind's eye.

'Vengeance upon the murderers,' the cry goes up,
'Vengeance for Jacques Molay.' In cloud-pale rags,
10   or in lace,
The rage-driven, rage-tormented, and rage-hungry
    troop,
Trooper belabouring trooper, biting at arm or at
    face,

Plunges towards nothing, arms and fingers
    spreading wide
For the embrace of nothing; and I, my wits astray
Because of all that senseless tumult, all but cried   15
For vengeance on the murderers of Jacques Molay.

Their legs long, delicate and slender, aquamarine
    their eyes,
Magical unicorns bear ladies on their backs.
The ladies close their musing eyes. No prophecies,
Remembered out of Babylonian almanacs,   20
Have closed the ladies' eyes, their minds are but a
    pool
Where even longing drowns under its own excess;
Nothing but stillness can remain when hearts are
    full
Of their own sweetness, bodies of their loveliness.

The cloud-pale unicorns, the eyes of aquamarine,   25
The quivering half-closed eyelids, the rags of cloud
    or of lace,
Or eyes that rage has brightened, arms it has made
    lean,
Give place to an indifferent multitude, give place
To brazen hawks. Nor self-delighting reverie,
Nor hate of what's to come, nor pity for what's
    gone,   30
Nothing but grip of claw, and the eye's
    complacency,
The innumerable clanging wings that have put out
    the moon.

I turn away and shut the door, and on the stair
Wonder how many times I could have proved
    my worth
In something that all others understand or share;   35
But O! ambitious heart, had such a proof drawn
    forth
A company of friends, a conscience set at ease,

It had but made us pine the more. The abstract joy,
The half-read wisdom of daemonic images,
40 Suffice the ageing man as once the growing boy.

1923

II, lines 21 ff. The river rises, and it sinks again;
One hears the rumble of it far below
Under its rocky hole.
What Median, Persian, Babylonian,
In reverie, or in vision, saw
Symbols of the soul,
Mind from mind has caught:
The subterranean streams,
Tower where a candle gleams,
A suffering passion and a labouring thought?

(*Dial*, January 1923)

Nineteen Hundred and Nineteen
❖❖❖

I

Many ingenious lovely things are gone
That seemed sheer miracle to the multitude,
Protected from the circle of the moon
That pitches common things about. There stood
5 Amid the ornamental bronze and stone
An ancient image made of olive wood –
And gone are Phidias' famous ivories
And all the golden grasshoppers and bees.

We too had many pretty toys when young:
10 A law indifferent to blame or praise,
To bribe or threat; habits that made old wrong
Melt down, as it were wax in the sun's rays;
Public opinion ripening for so long
We thought it would outlive all future days.

O what fine thought we had because we thought   15
That the worst rogues and rascals had died out.

All teeth were drawn, all ancient tricks unlearned,
And a great army but a showy thing;
What matter that no cannon had been turned
Into a ploughshare? Parliament and king   20
Thought that unless a little powder burned
The trumpeters might burst with trumpeting
And yet it lack all glory; and perchance
The guardsmen's drowsy chargers would not
    prance.

Now days are dragon-ridden, the nightmare   25
Rides upon sleep: a drunken soldiery
Can leave the mother, murdered at her door,
To crawl in her own blood, and go scot-free;
The night can sweat with terror as before
We pieced our thoughts into philosophy,   30
And planned to bring the world under a rule,
Who are but weasels fighting in a hole.

He who can read the signs nor sink unmanned
Into the half-deceit of some intoxicant
From shallow wits; who knows no work can stand,   35
Whether health, wealth or peace of mind were
    spent
On master-work of intellect or hand,
No honour leave its mighty monument,
Has but one comfort left: all triumph would
But break upon his ghostly solitude.   40

But is there any comfort to be found?
Man is in love and loves what vanishes,
What more is there to say? That country round
None dared admit, if such a thought were his,
Incendiary or bigot could be found   45
To burn that stump on the Acropolis,
Or break in bits the famous ivories
Or traffic in the grasshoppers or bees.

II

When Loie Fuller's Chinese dancers enwound
50   A shining web, a floating ribbon of cloth,
It seemed that a dragon of air
Had fallen among dancers, had whirled them round
Or hurried them off on its own furious path;
So the Platonic Year
55   Whirls out new right and wrong,
Whirls in the old instead;
All men are dancers and their tread
Goes to the barbarous clangour of a gong.

III

Some moralist or mythological poet
60   Compares the solitary soul to a swan;
I am satisfied with that,
Satisfied if a troubled mirror show it,
Before that brief gleam of its life be gone,
An image of its state;
65   The wings half spread for flight,
The breast thrust out in pride
Whether to play, or to ride
Those winds that clamour of approaching night.

A man in his own secret meditation
70   Is lost amid the labyrinth that he has made
In art or politics;
Some Platonist affirms that in the station
Where we should cast off body and trade
The ancient habit sticks,
75   And that if our works could
But vanish with our breath
That were a lucky death,
For triumph can but mar our solitude.

The swan has leaped into the desolate heaven:
80   That image can bring wildness, bring a rage

To end all things, to end
What my laborious life imagined, even
The half-imagined, the half-written page;
O but we dreamed to mend
Whatever mischief seemed   85
To afflict mankind, but now
That winds of winter blow
Learn that we were crack-pated when we dreamed.

IV

We, who seven years ago
Talked of honour and of truth,   90
Shriek with pleasure if we show
The weasel's twist, the weasel's tooth.

V

Come let us mock at the great
That had such burdens on the mind
And toiled so hard and late   95
To leave some monument behind,
Nor thought of the levelling wind.

Come let us mock at the wise;
With all those calendars whereon
They fixed old aching eyes,   100
They never saw how seasons run,
And now but gape at the sun.

Come let us mock at the good
That fancied goodness might be gay,
And sick of solitude   105
Might proclaim a holiday:
Wind shrieked — and where are they?

Mock mockers after that
That would not lift a hand maybe
To help good, wise or great   110

To bar that foul storm out, for we
Traffic in mockery.

VI

Violence upon the roads: violence of horses;
Some few have handsome riders, are garlanded
115 On delicate sensitive ear or tossing mane,
But wearied running round and round in their
      courses
All break and vanish, and evil gathers head:
Herodias' daughters have returned again,
A sudden blast of dusty wind and after
120 Thunder of feet, tumult of images,
Their purpose in the labyrinth of the wind;
And should some crazy hand dare touch a daughter
All turn with amorous cries, or angry cries,
According to the wind, for all are blind.
125 But now wind drops, dust settles; thereupon
There lurches past, his great eyes without thought
Under the shadow of stupid straw-pale locks,
That insolent fiend Robert Artisson
To whom the love-lorn Lady Kyteler brought
130 Bronzed peacock feathers, red combs of her cocks.

1919

I, lines 3–4   Above the murderous treachery of the moon,
                Or all that wayward ebb and flow. There stood

I, lines 41–3   And other comfort were a bitter wound:
                To be in love and love what vanishes.
                Greeks were but lovers; all that country round

(*Dial*, September 1921)

The Wheel

✦✦✦✦

Through winter-time we call on spring,
And through the spring on summer call,
And when abounding hedges ring
Declare that winter's best of all;
And after that there's nothing good   5
Because the spring-time has not come –
Nor know that what disturbs our blood
Is but its longing for the tomb.

The New Faces

✦✦✦✦

If you, that have grown old, were the first dead,
Neither catalpa tree nor scented lime
Should hear my living feet, nor would I tread
Where we wrought that shall break the teeth of
    Time.
Let the new faces play what tricks they will   5
In the old rooms; night can outbalance day,
Our shadows rove the garden gravel still,
The living seem more shadowy than they.

Two Songs from a Play

✦✦✦✦

I

I saw a staring virgin stand
Where holy Dionysus died,

And tear the heart out of his side,
And lay the heart upon her hand
5   And bear that beating heart away;
And then did all the Muses sing
Of Magnus Annus at the spring,
As though God's death were but a play.

Another Troy must rise and set,
10   Another lineage feed the crow,
Another Argo's painted prow
Drive to a flashier bauble yet.
The Roman Empire stood appalled:
It dropped the reins of peace and war
15   When that fierce virgin and her Star
Out of the fabulous darkness called.

II

In pity for man's darkening thought
He walked that room and issued thence
In Galilean turbulence;
20   The Babylonian starlight brought
A fabulous, formless darkness in;
Odour of blood when Christ was slain
Made all Platonic tolerance vain
And vain all Doric discipline.

25   Everything that man esteems
Endures a moment or a day.
Love's pleasure drives his love away,
The painter's brush consumes his dreams;
The herald's cry, the soldier's tread
30   Exhaust his glory and his might:
Whatever flames upon the night
Man's own resinous heart has fed.

Fragments

❖❖❖

I

Locke sank into a swoon;
The Garden died;
God took the spinning-jenny
Out of his side.

II

Where got I that truth?   5
Out of a medium's mouth,
Out of nothing it came,
Out of the forest loam,
Out of dark night where lay
The crowns of Nineveh.   10

Leda and the Swan

❖❖❖

A sudden blow: the great wings beating still
Above the staggering girl, her thighs caressed
By the dark webs, her nape caught in his bill,
He holds her helpless breast upon his breast.

How can those terrified vague fingers push   5
The feathered glory from her loosening thighs,
And how can body, laid in that white rush,
But feel the strange heart beating where it lies?

A shudder in the loins engenders there
The broken wall, the burning roof and tower   10
And Agamemnon dead.
                              Being so caught up,

So mastered by the brute blood of the air,
Did she put on his knowledge with his power
Before the indifferent beak could let her drop?

1923
(*A Vision*, 1937)

lines *1–4*   A rush, a sudden wheel, and hovering still
The bird descends, and her frail thighs are pressed.
By the webbed toes, and that all-powerful bill
Has laid her helpless face upon his breast.

lines *6–8*   The feathered glory from her loosening thighs!
All the stretched body's laid on the white rush
And feels the strange heart beating where it lies;

(*Dial*, June 1924)

line *6*   The feathered glory from her loosening thighs?

(*The Tower*, 1928)

On a Picture of a Black Centaur by Edmund Dulac

❖❖❖❖

Your hooves have stamped at the black margin of
   the wood,
Even where horrible green parrots call and swing.
My works are all stamped down into the sultry
   mud.
I knew that horse-play, knew it for a murderous
   thing.
What wholesome sun has ripened is wholesome
5   food to eat,
And that alone; yet I, being driven half insane
Because of some green wing, gathered old mummy
   wheat
In the mad abstract dark and ground it grain by
   grain
And after baked it slowly in an oven; but now

I bring full-flavoured wine out of a barrel found   10
Where seven Ephesian topers slept and never knew
When Alexander's empire passed, they slept so
    sound.
Stretch out your limbs and sleep a long Saturnian
    sleep;
I have loved you better than my soul for all my
    words,
And there is none so fit to keep a watch and keep   15
Unwearied eyes upon those horrible green birds.

Among School Children
❖❖❖❖

I

I walk through the long schoolroom questioning;
A kind old nun in a white hood replies;
The children learn to cipher and to sing,
To study reading books and histories,
To cut and sew, be neat in everything   5
In the best modern way – the children's eyes
In momentary wonder stare upon
A sixty-year-old smiling public man.

II

I dream of a Ledaean body, bent
Above a sinking fire, a tale that she   10
Told of a harsh reproof, or trivial event
That changed some childish day to tragedy –
Told, and it seemed that our two natures blent
Into a sphere from youthful sympathy,
Or else, to alter Plato's parable,   15
Into the yolk and white of the one shell.

III

And thinking of that fit of grief or rage
I look upon one child or t'other there
And wonder if she stood so at that age –
20   For even daughters of the swan can share
Something of every paddler's heritage –
And had that colour upon cheek or hair,
And thereupon my heart is driven wild:
She stands before me as a living child.

IV

25   Her present image floats into the mind –
Did Quattrocento finger fashion it
Hollow of cheek as though it drank the wind
And took a mess of shadows for its meat?
And I though never of Ledaean kind
30   Had pretty plumage once – enough of that,
Better to smile on all that smile, and show
There is a comfortable kind of old scarecrow.

V

What youthful mother, a shape upon her lap
Honey of generation had betrayed,
35   And that must sleep, shriek, struggle to escape
As recollection or the drug decide,
Would think her son, did she but see that shape
With sixty or more winters on its head,
A compensation for the pang of his birth,
40   Or the uncertainty of his setting forth?

VI

Plato thought nature but a spume that plays
Upon a ghostly paradigm of things;
Solider Aristotle played the taws
Upon the bottom of a king of kings;

World-famous golden-thighed Pythagoras   45
Fingered upon a fiddle-stick or strings
What a star sang and careless Muses heard:
Old clothes upon old sticks to scare a bird.

VII

Both nuns and mothers worship images,
But those the candles light are not as those   50
That animate a mother's reveries,
But keep a marble or a bronze repose.
And yet they too break hearts – O Presences
That passion, piety or affection knows,
And that all heavenly glory symbolise –   55
O self-born mockers of man's enterprise;

VIII

Labour is blossoming or dancing where
The body is not bruised to pleasure soul,
Nor beauty born out of its own despair,
Nor blear-eyed wisdom out of midnight oil.   60
O chestnut-tree, great rooted blossomer,
Are you the leaf, the blossom or the bole?
O body swayed to music, O brightening glance,
How can we know the dancer from the dance?

line 4   To study reading books and history

(*Dial*, August 1927)

The Hero, the Girl, and the Fool
❖❖❖❖

The Girl. I rage at my own image in the glass,
  That's so unlike myself that when you praise it
  It is as though you praised another, or even
  Mocked me with praise of my mere opposite;
  And when I wake towards morn I dread myself   5
  For the heart cries that what deception wins

Cruelty must keep; therefore be warned and go
If you have seen that image and not the woman.

The Hero. I have raged at my own strength because
you have loved it.

The Girl. If you are no more strength than I am
10   beauty
I had better find a convent and turn nun;
A nun at least has all men's reverence
And needs no cruelty.

The Hero.   I have heard one say
That men have reverence for their holiness
And not themselves.

15 *The Girl.*   Say on and say
That only God has loved us for ourselves,
But what care I that long for a man's love?

The Fool by the Roadside. When my days that have
From cradle run to grave
20 From grave to cradle run instead;
When thoughts that a fool
Has wound upon a spool
Are but loose thread, are but loose thread;

When cradle and spool are past
25 And I mere shade at last
Coagulate of stuff
Transparent like the wind,
I think that I may find
A faithful love, a faithful love.

                             (*The Tower*, 1928)

      line 18   When all works that have

                           (*Collected Poems*, 1933)

In *Collected Poems*, 1933, lines 18–29 only were printed as 'The Fool by the
Roadside'.

Cuchulain the Girl and the Fool

The Girl. I am jealous of the look men turn on you
    For all men love your worth; and I must rage
    At my own image in the looking-glass
    That's so unlike myself that when you praise it
    It is as though you praise another, or even   5
    Mock me with praise of my mere opposite;
    And when I wake towards morn I dread myself
    For the heart cries that what deception wins
    My cruelty must keep; and so begone
    If you have seen that image and not my worth.   10

Cuchulain. All men have praised my strength but not my
    worth.

The Girl. If you are no more strength than I am beauty
    I will find out some cavern in the hills
    And live among the ancient holy men,
    For they at least have all men's reverence   15
    And have no need of cruelty to keep
    What no deception won.

Cuchulain.   I have heard them say
    That men have reverence for their holiness
    And not their worth.

The Girl.   God loves us for our worth;
    But what care I that long for a man's love.   20

The Fool by the Roadside. When my days that have
    From cradle run to grave
    From grave to cradle run instead;
    When thoughts that a fool
    Has wound upon a spool
    Are but loose thread, are but loose thread.   25

    When cradle and spool are past
    And I mere shade at last
    Coagulate of stuff
    Transparent like the wind,   30
    I think that I may find
    A faithful love, a faithful love.

(*Seven Poems and a Fragment*, 1922)

All Souls' Night

❖❖❖❖

Epilogue to 'A Vision'

Midnight has come, and the great Christ Church
   Bell
And many a lesser bell sound through the room;
And it is All Souls' Night,
And two long glasses brimmed with muscatel
5 Bubble upon the table. A ghost may come;
For it is a ghost's right,
His element is so fine
Being sharpened by his death,
To drink from the wine-breath
10 While our gross palates drink from the whole wine.

I need some mind that, if the cannon sound
From every quarter of the world, can stay
Wound in mind's pondering
As mummies in the mummy-cloth are wound;
15 Because I have a marvellous thing to say,
A certain marvellous thing
None but the living mock,
Though not for sober ear;
It may be all that hear
20 Should laugh and weep an hour upon the clock.

Horton's the first I call. He loved strange thought
And knew that sweet extremity of pride
That's called platonic love,
And that to such a pitch of passion wrought
25 Nothing could bring him, when his lady died,
Anodyne for his love.
Words were but wasted breath;
One dear hope had he:
The inclemency

Of that or the next winter would be death.   30

Two thoughts were so mixed up I could not tell
Whether of her or God he thought the most,
But think that his mind's eye,
When upward turned, on one sole image fell;
And that a slight companionable ghost,   35
Wild with divinity,
Had so lit up the whole
Immense miraculous house
The Bible promised us,
It seemed a gold-fish swimming in a bowl.   40

On Florence Emery I call the next,
Who finding the first wrinkles on a face
Admired and beautiful,
And by foreknowledge of the future vexed;
Diminished beauty, multiplied commonplace;   45
Preferred to teach a school
Away from neighbour or friend,
Among dark skins, and there
Permit foul years to wear
Hidden from eyesight to the unnoticed end.   50

Before that end much had she ravelled out
From a discourse in figurative speech
By some learned Indian
On the soul's journey. How it is whirled about,
Wherever the orbit of the moon can reach,   55
Until it plunge into the sun;
And there, free and yet fast,
Being both Chance and Choice,
Forget its broken toys
And sink into its own delight at last.   60

I call MacGregor Mathers from his grave,
For in my first hard springtime we were friends,
Although of late estranged.
I thought him half a lunatic, half knave,
And told him so, but friendship never ends;   65

And what if mind seem changed,
And it seem changed with the mind,
When thoughts rise up unbid
On generous things that he did
70 And I grow half contented to be blind!

He had much industry at setting out,
Much boisterous courage, before loneliness
Had driven him crazed;
For meditations upon unknown thought
75 Make human intercourse grow less and less;
They are neither paid nor praised.
But he'd object to the host,
The glass because my glass;
A ghost-lover he was
80 And may have grown more arrogant being a ghost.

But names are nothing. What matter who it be,
So that his elements have grown so fine
The fume of muscatel
Can give his sharpened palate ecstasy
85 No living man can drink from the whole wine.
I have mummy truths to tell
Whereat the living mock,
Though not for sober ear,
For maybe all that hear
90 Should laugh and weep an hour upon the clock.

Such thought – such thought have I that hold it
   tight
Till meditation master all its parts,
Nothing can stay my glance
Until that glance run in the world's despite
To where the damned have howled away their
95   hearts,
And where the blessed dance;
Such thought, that in it bound
I need no other thing,

Wound in mind's wandering
As mummies in the mummy-cloth are wound.   100

Oxford, 1920

(*A Vision*, 1937)

lines 44–5   And knowing that the future would be vexed
With 'minished beauty, multiplied commonplace,

line 61   And I call up MacGregor from the grave

(*New Republic*, 9 March 1921)

THE WINDING STAIR AND OTHER POEMS

In Memory of Eva Gore-Booth and Con Markiewicz

The light of evening, Lissadell,
Great windows open to the south,
Two girls in silk kimonos, both
Beautiful, one a gazelle.
5 But a raving autumn shears
Blossom from the summer's wreath;
The older is condemned to death,
Pardoned, drags out lonely years
Conspiring among the ignorant.
10 I know not what the younger dreams –
Some vague Utopia – and she seems,
When withered old and skeleton-gaunt,
An image of such politics.
Many a time I think to seek
15 One or the other out and speak
Of that old Georgian mansion, mix
Pictures of the mind, recall
That table and the talk of youth,
Two girls in silk kimonos, both
20 Beautiful, one a gazelle.

Dear shadows, now you know it all,
All the folly of a fight
With a common wrong or right.
The innocent and the beautiful
Have no enemy but time;   25
Arise and bid me strike a match
And strike another till time catch;
Should the conflagration climb,
Run till all the sages know.
We the great gazebo built,   30
They convicted us of guilt;
Bid me strike a match and blow.

October 1927

Death
❖❖❖❖

Nor dread nor hope attend
A dying animal;
A man awaits his end
Dreading and hoping all;
Many times he died,   5
Many times rose again.
A great man in his pride
Confronting murderous men
Casts derision upon
Supersession of breath;   10
He knows death to the bone –
Man has created death.

A Dialogue of Self and Soul
❖❖❖

I

My Soul. I summon to the winding ancient stair;
 Set all your mind upon the steep ascent,
 Upon the broken, crumbling battlement,
 Upon the breathless starlit air,
5 Upon the star that marks the hidden pole;
 Fix every wandering thought upon
 That quarter where all thought is done:
 Who can distinguish darkness from the soul?

My Self. The consecrated blade upon my knees
10 Is Sato's ancient blade, still as it was,
 Still razor-keen, still like a looking-glass
 Unspotted by the centuries;
 That flowering, silken, old embroidery, torn
 From some court-lady's dress and round
15 The wooden scabbard bound and wound,
 Can, tattered, still protect, faded adorn.

My Soul. Why should the imagination of a man
 Long past his prime remember things that are
 Emblematical of love and war?
20 Think of ancestral night that can,
 If but imagination scorn the earth
 And intellect is wandering
 To this and that and t'other thing,
 Deliver from the crime of death and birth.

My Self. Montashigi, third of his family,
25 fashioned it
 Five hundred years ago, about it lie
 Flowers from I know not what embroidery –
 Heart's purple – and all these I set
 For emblems of the day against the tower

Emblematical of the night, 30
And claim as by a soldier's right
A charter to commit the crime once more.

My Soul. Such fullness in that quarter overflows
And falls into the basin of the mind
That man is stricken deaf and dumb and blind, 35
For intellect no longer knows
Is from the *Ought*, or *Knower* from the *Known* –
That is to say, ascends to Heaven;
Only the dead can be forgiven;
But when I think of that my tongue's a stone. 40

II

My Self. A living man is blind and drinks his drop.
What matter if the ditches are impure?
What matter if I live it all once more?
Endure that toil of growing up;
The ignominy of boyhood; the distress 45
Of boyhood changing into man;
The unfinished man and his pain
Brought face to face with his own clumsiness;

The finished man among his enemies? –
How in the name of Heaven can he escape 50
That defiling and disfigured shape
The mirror of malicious eyes
Casts upon his eyes until at last
He thinks that shape must be his shape?
And what's the good of an escape 55
If honour finds him in the wintry blast?

I am content to live it all again
And yet again, if it be life to pitch
Into the frog-spawn of a blind man's ditch,
A blind man battering blind men; 60
Or into that most fecund ditch of all,
The folly that man does

Or must suffer if he woos
A proud woman not kindred of his soul.

65 I am content to follow to its source
Every event in action or in thought;
Measure the lot; forgive myself the lot!
When such as I cast out remorse
So great a sweetness flows into the breast
70 We must laugh and we must sing,
We are blest by everything,
Everything we look upon is blest.

Blood and the Moon
❖❖❖

I

Blessed be this place,
More blessed still this tower;
A bloody, arrogant power
Rose out of the race
5 Uttering, mastering it,
Rose like these walls from these
Storm-beaten cottages –
In mockery I have set
A powerful emblem up,
10 And sing it rhyme upon rhyme
In mockery of a time
Half dead at the top.

II

Alexandria's was a beacon tower, and Babylon's
An image of the moving heavens, a log-book of
the sun's journey and the moon's;
And Shelley had his towers, thought's crowned
15 powers he called them once.

I declare this tower is my symbol; I declare
This winding, gyring, spiring treadmill of a stair
  is my ancestral stair;
That Goldsmith and the Dean, Berkeley and Burke
  have travelled there.

Swift beating on his breast in sibylline frenzy blind
Because the heart in his blood-sodden breast had
  dragged him down into mankind,   20
Goldsmith deliberately sipping at the honey-pot of
  his mind,

And haughtier-headed Burke that proved the State
  a tree,
That this unconquerable labyrinth of the birds,
  century after century,
Cast but dead leaves to mathematical equality;

And God-appointed Berkeley that proved all
  things a dream,   25
That this pragmatical, preposterous pig of a world,
  its farrow that so solid seem,
Must vanish on the instant if the mind but change
  its theme;

Saeva Indignatio and the labourer's hire,
The strength that gives our blood and state
  magnanimity of its own desire;
Everything that is not God consumed with
  intellectual fire.   30

III

The purity of the unclouded moon
Has flung its arrowy shaft upon the floor.
Seven centuries have passed and it is pure,
The blood of innocence has left no stain.
There, on blood-saturated ground, have stood   35
Soldier, assassin, executioner,
Whether for daily pittance or in blind fear

Or out of abstract hatred, and shed blood,
But could not cast a single jet thereon.
40 Odour of blood on the ancestral stair!
And we that have shed none must gather there
And clamour in drunken frenzy for the moon.

IV

Upon the dusty, glittering windows cling,
And seem to cling upon the moonlit skies,
45 Tortoiseshell butterflies, peacock butterflies,
A couple of night-moths are on the wing.
Is every modern nation like the tower,
Half dead at the top? No matter what I said,
For wisdom is the property of the dead,
50 A something incompatible with life; and power,
Like everything that has the stain of blood,
A property of the living; but no stain
Can come upon the visage of the moon
When it has looked in glory from a cloud.

Oil and Blood
❖❖❖

In tombs of gold and lapis lazuli
Bodies of holy men and women exude
Miraculous oil, odour of violet.

But under heavy loads of trampled clay
5 Lie bodies of the vampires full of blood;
Their shrouds are bloody and their lips are wet.

The Nineteenth Century and After

❖❖❖❖

Though the great song return no more
There's keen delight in what we have:
The rattle of pebbles on the shore
Under the receding wave.

The Seven Sages

❖❖❖❖

The First. My great-grandfather spoke to Edmund
　　Burke
　In Grattan's house.

The Second.　　　　　　My great-grandfather shared
　A pot-house bench with Oliver Goldsmith once.

The Third. My great-grandfather's father talked
　　of the music,
　Drank tar-water with the Bishop of Cloyne.　　　　5

The Fourth. But mine saw Stella once.

The Fifth.　　　　　　Whence came our thought?

The Sixth. From four great minds that hated
　　Whiggery.

The Fifth. Burke was a Whig.

The Sixth.　　　　　　　Whether they knew or not,
　Goldsmith and Burke, Swift and the Bishop of
　　Cloyne
　All hated Whiggery; but what is Whiggery?　　　10
　A levelling, rancorous, rational sort of mind
　That never looked out of the eye of a saint
　Or out of drunkard's eye.

The Seventh.   All's Whiggery now,
 But we old men are massed against the world.

The First. American colonies, Ireland, France and
15 India
 Harried, and Burke's great melody against it.

The Second. Oliver Goldsmith sang what he had
  seen,
 Roads full of beggars, cattle in the fields,
 But never saw the trefoil stained with blood,
 The avenging leaf those fields raised up against
20 it.

The Fourth. The tomb of Swift wears it away.

The Third.   A voice
 Soft as the rustle of a reed from Cloyne
 That gathers volume; now a thunder-clap.

The Sixth. What schooling had these four?

The Seventh.   They walked the roads
25 Mimicking what they heard, as children mimic;
 They understood that wisdom comes of beggary.

The Crazed Moon
❖❖❖

  Crazed through much child-bearing
  The moon is staggering in the sky;
  Moon-struck by the despairing
  Glances of her wandering eye
5 We grope, and grope in vain,
  For children born of her pain.

  Children dazed or dead!
  When she in all her virginal pride
  First trod on the mountain's head

What stir ran through the countryside   10
Where every foot obeyed her glance!
What manhood led the dance!

Fly-catchers of the moon,
Our hands are blenched, our fingers seem
But slender needles of bone;   15
Blenched by that malicious dream
They are spread wide that each
May rend what comes in reach.

Coole Park, 1929
❖❖❖

I meditate upon a swallow's flight,
Upon an aged woman and her house,
A sycamore and lime tree lost in night
Although that western cloud is luminous,
Great works constructed there in nature's spite   5
For scholars and for poets after us,
Thoughts long knitted into a single thought,
A dance-like glory that those walls begot.

There Hyde before he had beaten into prose
That noble blade the Muses buckled on,   10
There one that ruffled in a manly pose
For all his timid heart, there that slow man,
That meditative man, John Synge, and those
Impetuous men, Shawe-Taylor and Hugh Lane,
Found pride established in humility,   15
A scene well set and excellent company.

They came like swallows and like swallows went,
And yet a woman's powerful character
Could keep a swallow to its first intent;
And half a dozen in formation there,   20
That seemed to whirl upon a compass-point,

Found certainty upon the dreaming air,
The intellectual sweetness of those lines
That cut through time or cross it withershins.

25   Here, traveller, scholar, poet, take your stand
When all those rooms and passages are gone,
When nettles wave upon a shapeless mound
And saplings root among the broken stone,
And dedicate – eyes bent upon the ground,
30   Back turned upon the brightness of the sun
And all the sensuality of the shade –
A moment's memory to that laurelled head.

Coole Park and Ballylee, 1931
◆◆◆◆

Under my window-ledge the waters race,
Otters below and moor-hens on the top,
Run for a mile undimmed in Heaven's face
Then darkening through 'dark' Raftery's 'cellar'
    drop,
5   Run underground, rise in a rocky place
In Coole demesne, and there to finish up
Spread to a lake and drop into a hole.
What's water but the generated soul?

Upon the border of that lake's a wood
10   Now all dry sticks under a wintry sun,
And in a copse of beeches there I stood,
For Nature's pulled her tragic buskin on
And all the rant's a mirror of my mood:
At sudden thunder of the mounting swan
15   I turned about and looked where branches break
The glittering reaches of the flooded lake.

Another emblem there! That stormy white
But seems a concentration of the sky;

And, like the soul, it sails into the sight
And in the morning's gone, no man knows why;   20
And is so lovely that it sets to right
What knowledge or its lack had set awry,
So arrogantly pure, a child might think
It can be murdered with a spot of ink.

Sound of a stick upon the floor, a sound   25
From somebody that toils from chair to chair;
Beloved books that famous hands have bound,
Old marble heads, old pictures everywhere;
Great rooms where travelled men and children
   found
Content or joy; a last inheritor   30
Where none has reigned that lacked a name and
   fame
Or out of folly into folly came.

A spot whereon the founders lived and died
Seemed once more dear than life; ancestral trees,
Or gardens rich in memory glorified   35
Marriages, alliances and families,
And every bride's ambition satisfied.
Where fashion or mere fantasy decrees
Man shifts about – all that great glory spent –
Like some poor Arab tribesman and his tent.   40

We were the last romantics – chose for theme
Traditional sanctity and loveliness;
Whatever's written in what poets name
The book of the people; whatever most can bless
The mind of man or elevate a rhyme;   45
But all is changed, that high horse riderless,
Though mounted in that saddle Homer rode
Where the swan drifts upon a darkening flood.

lines 41 ff.   The intellect of man is forced to choose
            Perfection of the life, or of the work,
            And if it take the second must refuse
            A heavenly mansion, raging in the dark,

And when the story's finished, what's the news?
In luck or out the toil has left its mark:
That old perplexity an empty purse,
Or the day's vanity, the night's remorse.

(*Words for Music Perhaps and Other Poems*, 1932,
and separately as 'The Choice' in
The Winding Stair and Other Poems, 1933, and afterwards)

At Algeciras – A Meditation upon Death
❖❖❖❖

The heron-billed pale cattle-birds
That feed on some foul parasite
Of the Moroccan flocks and herds
Cross the narrow Straits to light
5   In the rich midnight of the garden trees
Till the dawn break upon those mingled seas.

Often at evening when a boy
Would I carry to a friend –
Hoping more substantial joy
10 Did an older mind commend –
Not such as are in Newton's metaphor,
But actual shells of Rosses' level shore.

Greater glory in the sun,
An evening chill upon the air,
15 Bid imagination run
Much on the Great Questioner;
What He can question, what if questioned I
Can with a fitting confidence reply.

November 1928

lines 5–6   In Algeciras gardens, and there rest
Until the morning break as on a dark breast.

(*A Packet for Ezra Pound*, 1929)

Byzantium
❖❖❖❖

The unpurged images of day recede;
The Emperor's drunken soldiery are abed;
Night resonance recedes, night-walkers' song
After great cathedral gong;
A starlit or a moonlit dome disdains   5
All that man is,
All mere complexities,
The fury and the mire of human veins.

Before me floats an image, man or shade,
Shade more than man, more image than a shade;   10
For Hades' bobbin bound in mummy-cloth
May unwind the winding path;
A mouth that has no moisture and no breath
Breathless mouths may summon;
I hail the superhuman;   15
I call it death-in-life and life-in-death.

Miracle, bird or golden handiwork,
More miracle than bird or handiwork,
Planted on the star-lit golden bough,
Can like the cocks of Hades crow,   20
Or, by the moon embittered, scorn aloud
In glory of changeless metal
Common bird or petal
And all complexities of mire or blood.

At midnight on the Emperor's pavement flit   15
Flames that no faggot feeds, nor steel has lit,
Nor storm disturbs, flames begotten of flame,
Where blood-begotten spirits come
And all complexities of fury leave,
Dying into a dance,   30
An agony of trance,
An agony of flame that cannot singe a sleeve.

Astraddle on the dolphin's mire and blood,
Spirit after spirit! The smithies break the flood,
35 The golden smithies of the Emperor!
Marbles of the dancing floor
Break bitter furies of complexity,
Those images that yet
Fresh images beget,
40 That dolphin-torn, that gong-tormented sea.

1930

The Mother of God

❖❖❖❖

The threefold terror of love; a fallen flare
Through the hollow of an ear;
Wings beating about the room;
The terror of all terrors that I bore
5   The Heavens in my womb.

Had I not found content among the shows
Every common woman knows,
Chimney corner, garden walk,
Or rocky cistern where we tread the clothes
10 And gather all the talk?

What is this flesh I purchased with my pains,
This fallen star my milk sustains,
This love that makes my heart's blood stop
Or strikes a sudden chill into my bones
15 And bids my hair stand up?

Vacillation
◆◆◆

I

Between extremities
Man runs his course;
A brand, or flaming breath,
Comes to destroy
All those antinomies   5
Of day and night;
The body calls it death,
The heart remorse.
But if these be right
What is joy?   10

II

A tree there is that from its topmost bough
Is half all glittering flame and half all green
Abounding foliage moistened with the dew;
And half is half and yet is all the scene;
And half and half consume what they renew,   15
And he that Attis' image hangs between
That staring fury and the blind lush leaf
May know not what he knows, but knows not grief.

III

Get all the gold and silver that you can,
Satisfy ambition, or animate   20
The trivial days and ram them with the sun,
And yet upon these maxims meditate:
All women dote upon an idle man
Although their children need a rich estate;
No man has ever lived that had enough   25
Of children's gratitude or woman's love.

No longer in Lethean foliage caught

Begin the preparation for your death
And from the fortieth winter by that thought
30 Test every work of intellect or faith,
And everything that your own hands have wrought,
And call those works extravagance of breath
That are not suited for such men as come
Proud, open-eyed and laughing to the tomb.

IV

35 My fiftieth year had come and gone,
I sat, a solitary man,
In a crowded London shop,
An open book and empty cup
On the marble table-top.

40 While on the shop and street I gazed
My body of a sudden blazed;
And twenty minutes more or less
It seemed, so great my happiness,
That I was blessèd and could bless.

V

45 Although the summer sunlight gild
Cloudy leafage of the sky,
Or wintry moonlight sink the field
In storm-scattered intricacy,
I cannot look thereon,
50 Responsibility so weighs me down.

Things said or done long years ago,
Or things I did not do or say
But thought that I might say or do,
Weigh me down, and not a day
55 But something is recalled,
My conscience or my vanity appalled.

VI

A rivery field spread out below,

An odour of the new-mown hay
In his nostrils, the great lord of Chou
Cried, casting off the mountain snow,   60
'Let all things pass away.'

Wheels by milk-white asses drawn
Where Babylon or Nineveh
Rose; some conqueror drew rein
And cried to battle-weary men,   65
'Let all things pass away.'

From man's blood-sodden heart are sprung
Those branches of the night and day
Where the gaudy moon is hung.
What's the meaning of all song?   70
'Let all things pass away.'

VII

The Soul. Seek out reality, leave things that seem.

The Heart. What, be a singer born and lack a
    theme?

The Soul. Isaiah's coal, what more can man desire?

The Heart. Struck dumb in the simplicity of fire!   75

The Soul. Look on that fire, salvation walks within.

The Heart. What theme had Homer but original
    sin?

VIII

Must we part, Von Hügel, though much alike, for
    we
Accept the miracles of the saints and honour
    sanctity?
The body of Saint Teresa lies undecayed in tomb,   80
Bathed in miraculous oil, sweet odours from it
    come,

Healing from its lettered slab. Those self-same
    hands perchance
Eternalised the body of a modern saint that once
Had scooped out Pharaoh's mummy. I – though
    heart might find relief
Did I become a Christian man and choose for my
85   belief
What seems most welcome in the tomb – play a
    predestined part.
Homer is my example and his unchristened heart.
The lion and the honeycomb, what has Scripture
    said?
So get you gone, Von Hügel, though with blessings
    on your head.

                              1932

The Results of Thought
❖❖❖

    Acquaintance; companion;
    One dear brilliant woman;
    The best-endowed, the elect,
    All by their youth undone,
5   All, all, by that inhuman
    Bitter glory wrecked.

    But I have straightened out
    Ruin, wreck and wrack;
    I toiled long years and at length
10   Came to so deep a thought
    I can summon back
    All their wholesome strength.

    What images are these
    That turn dull-eyed away,
15   Or shift Time's filthy load,

Straighten aged knees,
Hesitate or stay?
What heads shake or nod?

August 1931

Remorse for Intemperate Speech
❖❖❖❖

I ranted to the knave and fool,
But outgrew that school,
Would transform the part,
Fit audience found, but cannot rule
My fanatic [1] heart.   5

I sought my betters: though in each
Fine manners, liberal speech,
Turn hatred into sport,
Nothing said or done can reach
My fanatic heart.   10

Out of Ireland have we come.
Great hatred, little room,
Maimed us at the start.
I carry from my mother's womb
A fanatic heart.   15

August 28, 1931

[1] I pronounce 'fanatic' in what is, I suppose, the older and more Irish way, so that the last line of each stanza contains but two beats.

Words for Music Perhaps
❖❖❖❖

I
Crazy Jane and the Bishop

Bring me to the blasted oak
That I, midnight upon the stroke,
(*All find safety in the tomb.*)
May call down curses on his head
5   Because of my dear Jack that's dead.
Coxcomb was the least he said:
The solid man and the coxcomb.

Nor was he Bishop when his ban
Banished Jack the Journeyman,
10   (*All find safety in the tomb.*)
Nor so much as parish priest,
Yet he, an old book in his fist,
Cried that we lived like beast and beast:
The solid man and the coxcomb.

15   The Bishop has a skin, God knows,
Wrinkled like the foot of a goose,
(*All find safety in the tomb.*)
Nor can he hide in holy black
The heron's hunch upon his back,
20   But a birch-tree stood my Jack:
The solid man and the coxcomb.

Jack had my virginity,
And bids me to the oak, for he
(*All find safety in the tomb.*)
25   Wanders out into the night
And there is shelter under it,
But should that other come, I spit:
The solid man and the coxcomb.

III
Crazy Jane on the Day of Judgment

'Love is all
Unsatisfied
That cannot take the whole
Body and soul';
And that is what Jane said.　　　　5

'Take the sour
If you take me,
I can scoff and lour
And scold for an hour.'
'That's certainly the case,' said he.　　10

'Naked I lay,
The grass my bed;
Naked and hidden away,
That black day';
And that is what Jane said.　　　　15

'What can be shown?
What true love be?
All could be known or shown
If Time were but gone.'
'That's certainly the case,' said he.　　20

IV
Crazy Jane and Jack the Journeyman

I know, although when looks meet
I tremble to the bone,
The more I leave the door unlatched
The sooner love is gone,
For love is but a skein unwound　　　5
Between the dark and dawn.

A lonely ghost the ghost is
That to God shall come;
I – love's skein upon the ground,
My body in the tomb –　　　　10

Shall leap into the light lost
In my mother's womb.

But were I left to lie alone
In an empty bed,
15 The skein so bound us ghost to ghost
When he turned his head
Passing on the road that night,
Mine would walk, being dead.

V

Crazy Jane on God

That lover of a night
Came when he would,
Went in the dawning light
Whether I would or no;
5   Men come, men go;
All things remain in God.

Banners choke the sky;
Men-at-arms tread;
Armoured horses neigh
10 Where the great battle was
In the narrow pass:
All things remain in God.

Before their eyes a house
That from childhood stood
15 Uninhabited, ruinous,
Suddenly lit up
From door to top:
All things remain in God.

I had wild Jack for a lover;
20 Though like a road
That men pass over
My body makes no moan
But sings on:
All things remain in God.

VI
Crazy Jane talks with the Bishop

I met the Bishop on the road
And much said he and I.
'Those breasts are flat and fallen now,
Those veins must soon be dry;
Live in a heavenly mansion,   5
Not in some foul sty.'

'Fair and foul are near of kin,
And fair needs foul,' I cried.
'My friends are gone, but that's a truth
Nor grave nor bed denied,   10
Learned in bodily lowliness
And in the heart's pride.

'A woman can be proud and stiff
When on love intent;
But Love has pitched his mansion in   15
The place of excrement;
For nothing can be sole or whole
That has not been rent.'

VII
Crazy Jane Grown Old looks at the Dancers

I found that ivory image there
Dancing with her chosen youth,
But when he wound her coal-black hair
As though to strangle her, no scream
Or bodily movement did I dare,   5
Eyes under eyelids did so gleam;
Love is like the lion's tooth.

When she, and though some said she played
I said that she had danced heart's truth,
Drew a knife to strike him dead,   10
I could but leave him to his fate;
For no matter what is said

They had all that had their hate;
Love is like the lion's tooth.

15 Did he die or did she die?
Seemed to die or died they both?
God be with the times when I
Cared not a thraneen for what chanced
So that I had the limbs to try
20 Such a dance as there was danced –
Love is like the lion's tooth.

X
Her Anxiety

Earth in beauty dressed
Awaits returning spring.
All true love must die,
Alter at the best
5 Into some lesser thing.
Prove that I lie.

Such body lovers have,
Such exacting breath,
That they touch or sigh.
10 Every touch they give,
Love is nearer death.
Prove that I lie.

XVII
After Long Silence

Speech after long silence; it is right,
All other lovers being estranged or dead,
Unfriendly lamplight hid under its shade,
The curtains drawn upon unfriendly night,
5 That we descant and yet again descant
Upon the supreme theme of Art and Song:
Bodily decrepitude is wisdom; young
We loved each other and were ignorant.

184

XXV
The Delphic Oracle upon Plotinus

Behold that great Plotinus swim,
Buffeted by such seas;
Bland Rhadamanthus beckons him,
But the Golden Race looks dim,
Salt blood blocks his eyes.   5

Scattered on the level grass
Or winding through the grove
Plato there and Minos pass,
There stately Pythagoras
And all the choir of Love.   10

August 19, 1931

A Woman Young and Old
❖❖❖❖

VIII
Her Vision in the Wood

Dry timber under that rich foliage,
At wine-dark midnight in the sacred wood,
Too old for a man's love I stood in rage
Imagining men. Imagining that I could
A greater with a lesser pang assuage   5
Or but to find if withered vein ran blood,
I tore my body that its wine might cover
Whatever could recall the lip of lover.

And after that I held my fingers up,
Stared at the wine-dark nail, or dark that ran 10
Down every withered finger from the top;
But the dark changed to red, and torches shone,
And deafening music shook the leaves; a troop
Shouldered a litter with a wounded man,

15 Or smote upon the string and to the sound
Sang of the beast that gave the fatal wound.

All stately women moving to a song
With loosened hair or foreheads grief-distraught,
It seemed a Quattrocento painter's throng,
20 A thoughtless image of Mantegna's thought –
Why should they think that are for ever young?
Till suddenly in grief's contagion caught,
I stared upon his blood-bedabbled breast
And sang my malediction with the rest.

That thing all blood and mire, that beast-torn
25   wreck,
Half turned and fixed a glazing eye on mine,
And, though love's bitter-sweet had all come back,
Those bodies from a picture or a coin
Nor saw my body fall nor heard it shriek,
30 Nor knew, drunken with singing as with wine,
That they had brought no fabulous symbol there
But my heart's victim and its torturer.

IX

A Last Confession

What lively lad most pleasured me
Of all that with me lay?
I answer that I gave my soul
And loved in misery,
5   But had great pleasure with a lad
That I loved bodily.

Flinging from his arms I laughed
To think his passion such
He fancied that I gave a soul
10   Did but our bodies touch,
And laughed upon his breast to think
Beast gave beast as much.

I gave what other women gave

186

That stepped out of their clothes,
But when this soul, its body off,   15
Naked to naked goes,
He it has found shall find therein
What none other knows,

And give his own and take his own
And rule in his own right;   20
And though it loved in misery
Close and cling so tight,
There's not a bird of day that dare
Extinguish that delight.

From A FULL MOON IN MARCH

Parnell's Funeral

I

Under the Great Comedian's tomb the crowd.
A bundle of tempestuous cloud is blown
About the sky; where that is clear of cloud
Brightness remains; a brighter star shoots down;
5 What shudders run through all that animal blood?
What is this sacrifice? Can someone there
Recall the Cretan barb that pierced a star?

Rich foliage that the starlight glittered through,
A frenzied crowd, and where the branches sprang
10 A beautiful seated boy; a sacred bow;
A woman, and an arrow on a string;
A pierced boy, image of a star laid low.
That woman, the Great Mother imaging,
Cut out his heart. Some master of design
15 Stamped boy and tree upon Sicilian coin.

An age is the reversal of an age:
When strangers murdered Emmet, Fitzgerald,
    Tone,
We lived like men that watch a painted stage.
What matter for the scene, the scene once gone:
20 It had not touched our lives. But popular rage,
Hysterica passio dragged this quarry down.
None shared our guilt; nor did we play a part
Upon a painted stage when we devoured his heart.

Come, fix upon me that accusing eye.
I thirst for accusation. All that was sung,   25
All that was said in Ireland is a lie
Bred out of the contagion of the throng,
Saving the rhyme rats hear before they die.
Leave nothing but the nothings that belong
To this bare soul, let all men judge that can   30
Whether it be an animal or a man.

II

The rest I pass, one sentence I unsay.
Had de Valéra eaten Parnell's heart
No loose-lipped demagogue had won the day,
No civil rancour torn the land apart.   35

Had Cosgrave eaten Parnell's heart, the land's
Imagination had been satisfied,
Or lacking that, government in such hands,
O'Higgins its sole statesman had not died.

Had even O'Duffy – but I name no more –   40
Their school a crowd, his master solitude;
Through Jonathan Swift's dark grove he passed,
    and there
Plucked bitter wisdom that enriched his blood.

A Prayer for Old Age
❖❖❖

God guard me from those thoughts men think
In the mind alone;
He that sings a lasting song
Thinks in a marrow-bone;

From all that makes a wise old man   5

That can be praised of all;
O what am I that I should not seem
For the song's sake a fool?

I pray – for fashion's word is out
And prayer comes round again –
That I may seem, though I die old,
A foolish, passionate man.

Supernatural Songs
❖❖❖

I

Ribh at the Tomb of Baile and Aillinn

Because you have found me in the pitch-dark night
With open book you ask me what I do.
Mark and digest my tale, carry it afar
To those that never saw this tonsured head
Nor heard this voice that ninety years have cracked.
Of Baile and Aillinn you need not speak,
All know their tale, all know what leaf and twig,
What juncture of the apple and the yew,
Surmount their bones; but speak what none have
    heard.

The miracle that gave them such a death
Transfigured to pure substance what had once
Been bone and sinew; when such bodies join
There is no touching here, nor touching there,
Nor straining joy, but whole is joined to whole;
For the intercourse of angels is a light
Where for its moment both seem lost, consumed.

Here in the pitch-dark atmosphere above

The trembling of the apple and the yew,
Here on the anniversary of their death,
The anniversary of their first embrace,   20
Those lovers, purified by tragedy,
Hurry into each other's arms; these eyes,
By water, herb and solitary prayer
Made aquiline, are open to that light.
Though somewhat broken by the leaves, that light   25
Lies in a circle on the grass; therein
I turn the pages of my holy book.

V

Ribh considers Christian Love insufficient

Why should I seek for love or study it?
It is of God and passes human wit;
I study hatred with great diligence,
For that's a passion in my own control,
A sort of besom that can clear the soul   5
Of everything that is not mind or sense.

Why do I hate man, woman or event?
That is a light my jealous soul has sent.
From terror and deception freed it can
Discover impurities, can show at last   10
How soul may walk when all such things are past,
How soul could walk before such things began.

Then my delivered soul herself shall learn
A darker knowledge and in hatred turn
From every thought of God mankind has had.   15
Thought is a garment and the soul's a bride
That cannot in that trash and tinsel hide:
Hatred of God may bring the soul to God.

At stroke of midnight soul cannot endure
A bodily or mental furniture.   20
What can she take until her Master give!
Where can she look until He make the show!

What can she know until He bid her know!
How can she live till in her blood He live!

line 18   In hating God she may creep close to God.
(*Poetry*, December 1934)

VIII
Whence had they come?

Eternity is passion, girl or boy
Cry at the onset of their sexual joy
'For ever and for ever'; then awake
Ignorant what Dramatis Personae spake;
5   A passion-driven exultant man sings out
Sentences that he has never thought;
The Flagellant lashes those submissive loins
Ignorant what that dramatist enjoins,
What master made the lash. Whence had they
    come,
10   The hand and lash that beat down frigid Rome?
What sacred drama through her body heaved
When world-transforming Charlemagne was
    conceived?

XII
Meru

Civilisation is hooped together, brought
Under a rule, under the semblance of peace
By manifold illusion; but man's life is thought,
And he, despite his terror, cannot cease
5   Ravening through century after century,
Ravening, raging, and uprooting that he may come
Into the desolation of reality:
Egypt and Greece good-bye, and good-bye, Rome!
Hermits upon Mount Meru or Everest,
10   Caverned in night under the drifted snow,
Or where that snow and winter's dreadful blast

Beat down upon their naked bodies, know
That day brings round the night, that before dawn
His glory and his monuments are gone.

The Gyres
✦✦✦✦

The gyres! the gyres! Old Rocky Face, look forth;
Things thought too long can be no longer thought,
For beauty dies of beauty, worth of worth,
And ancient lineaments are blotted out.
5   Irrational streams of blood are staining earth;
Empedocles has thrown all things about;
Hector is dead and there's a light in Troy;
We that look on but laugh in tragic joy.

What matter though numb nightmare ride on top,
10 And blood and mire the sensitive body stain?
What matter? Heave no sigh, let no tear drop,
A greater, a more gracious time has gone;
For painted forms or boxes of make-up
In ancient tombs I sighed, but not again;
15 What matter? Out of Cavern comes a voice,
And all it knows is that one word 'Rejoice!'

Conduct and work grow coarse, and coarse the soul,
What matter? Those that Rocky Face holds dear,
Lovers of horses and of women, shall,
20 From marble of a broken sepulchre,
Or dark betwixt the polecat and the owl,
Or any rich, dark nothing disinter
The workman, noble and saint, and all things run
On that unfashionable gyre again.

Lapis Lazuli

◆◆◆

(*For Harry Clifton*)

I have heard that hysterical women say
They are sick of the palette and fiddle-bow,
Of poets that are always gay,
For everybody knows or else should know
That if nothing drastic is done   5
Aeroplane and Zeppelin will come out,
Pitch like King Billy bomb-balls in
Until the town lie beaten flat.

All perform their tragic play,
There struts Hamlet, there is Lear,   10
That's Ophelia, that Cordelia;
Yet they, should the last scene be there,
The great stage curtain about to drop,
If worthy their prominent part in the play,
Do not break up their lines to weep.   15
They know that Hamlet and Lear are gay;
Gaiety transfiguring all that dread.
All men have aimed at, found and lost;
Black out; Heaven blazing into the head:
Tragedy wrought to its uttermost.   20
Though Hamlet rambles and Lear rages,
And all the drop-scenes drop at once
Upon a hundred thousand stages,
It cannot grow by an inch or an ounce.

On their own feet they came, or on shipboard,   25
Camel-back, horse-back, ass-back, mule-back,
Old civilisations put to the sword.
Then they and their wisdom went to rack:
No handiwork of Callimachus,
Who handled marble as if it were bronze,   30
Made draperies that seemed to rise

When sea-wind swept the corner, stands;
His long lamp-chimney shaped like the stem
Of a slender palm, stood but a day;
35 All things fall and are built again,
And those that build them again are gay.

Two Chinamen, behind them a third,
Are carved in lapis lazuli,
Over them flies a long-legged bird,
40 A symbol of longevity;
The third, doubtless a serving-man,
Carries a musical instrument.

Every discoloration of the stone,
Every accidental crack or dent,
45 Seems a water-course or an avalanche,
Or lofty slope where it still snows
Though doubtless plum or cherry-branch
Sweetens the little half-way house
Those Chinamen climb towards, and I
50 Delight to imagine them seated there;
There on the mountain and the sky,
On all the tragic scene they stare.
One asks for mournful melodies;
Accomplished fingers begin to play.
55 Their eyes mid many wrinkles, their eyes,
Their ancient, glittering eyes, are gay.

The Lady's First Song

◆◆◆

I turn round
Like a dumb beast in a show,
Neither know what I am
Nor where I go,
5 My language beaten

Into one name;
I am in love
And that is my shame.
What hurts the soul
My soul adores,   10
No better than a beast
Upon all fours.

The Lady's Second Song
◇◇◇◇

What sort of man is coming
To lie between your feet?
What matter, we are but women.
Wash; make your body sweet;
I have cupboards of dried fragrance,   5
I can strew the sheet.
          The Lord have mercy upon us.

He shall love my soul as though
Body were not at all,
He shall love your body   10
Untroubled by the soul,
Love cram love's two divisions
Yet keep his substance whole.
          The Lord have mercy upon us.

Soul must learn a love that is   15
Proper to my breast,
Limbs a love in common
With every noble beast.
If soul may look and body touch,
Which is the more blest?   20
          The Lord have mercy upon us.

An Acre of Grass
❖❖❖

Picture and book remain,
An acre of green grass
For air and exercise,
Now strength of body goes;
5   Midnight, an old house
Where nothing stirs but a mouse.

My temptation is quiet.
· Here at life's end
Neither loose imagination,
10   Nor the mill of the mind
Consuming its rag and bone,
Can make the truth known.

Grant me an old man's frenzy,
Myself must I remake
15   Till I am Timon and Lear
Or that William Blake
Who beat upon the wall
Till Truth obeyed his call;

A mind Michael Angelo knew
20   That can pierce the clouds,
Or inspired by frenzy
Shake the dead in their shrouds;
Forgotten else by mankind,
An old man's eagle mind.

What Then?
❖❖❖

His chosen comrades thought at school
He must grow a famous man;

He thought the same and lived by rule,
All his twenties crammed with toil;
'What then?' sang Plato's ghost, 'what then?'   5

Everything he wrote was read,
After certain years he won
Sufficient money for his need,
Friends that have been friends indeed;
'What then?' sang Plato's ghost, 'what then?'   10

All his happier dreams came true –
A small old house, wife, daughter, son,
Grounds where plum and cabbage grew,
Poets and Wits about him drew;
'What then?' sang Plato's ghost, 'what then?'   15

'The work is done,' grown old he thought,
'According to my boyish plan;
Let the fools rage, I swerved in nought,
Something to perfection brought';
But louder sang that ghost, 'What then?'   20

Beautiful Lofty Things
❖❖❖❖

Beautiful lofty things: O'Leary's noble head;
My father upon the Abbey stage, before him a
    raging crowd:
'This Land of Saints,' and then as the applause
    died out,
'Of plaster Saints'; his beautiful mischievous head
    thrown back.
Standish O'Grady supporting himself between the
    tables   5
Speaking to a drunken audience high nonsensical
    words;

199

Augusta Gregory seated at her great ormolu table,
Her eightieth winter approaching: 'Yesterday he
    threatened my life.
I told him that nightly from six to seven I sat at
    this table,
The blinds drawn up'; Maud Gonne at Howth
10   station waiting a train,
Pallas Athene in that straight back and arrogant
    head:
All the Olympians; a thing never known again.

A Crazed Girl

❖❖❖

That crazed girl improvising her music,
Her poetry, dancing upon the shore,
Her soul in division from itself
Climbing, falling she knew not where,
5   Hiding amid the cargo of a steamship,
Her knee-cap broken, that girl I declare
A beautiful lofty thing, or a thing
Heroically lost, heroically found.

No matter what disaster occurred
10   She stood in desperate music wound,
Wound, wound, and she made in her triumph
Where the bales and the baskets lay
No common intelligible sound
But sang, 'O sea-starved, hungry sea.'

The Curse of Cromwell

❖❖❖

You ask what I have found, and far and wide I go:
Nothing but Cromwell's house and Cromwell's
    murderous crew,
The lovers and the dancers are beaten into the clay,
And the tall men and the swordsmen and the
    horsemen, where are they?
And there is an old beggar wandering in his pride,   5
His fathers served their fathers before Christ was
    crucified.
                O what of that, O what of that,
                What is there left to say?

All neighbourly content and easy talk are gone,
But there's no good complaining, for money's rant
    is on.   10
He that's mounting up must on his neighbour
    mount,
And we and all the Muses are things of no account.
They have schooling of their own, but I pass their
    schooling by,
What can they know that we know that know the
    time to die?
                O what of that, O what of that,   15
                What is there left to say?

But there's another knowledge that my heart
    destroys,
As the fox in the old fable destroyed the Spartan
    boy's,
Because it proves that things both can and cannot
    be;
That the swordsmen and the ladies can still keep
    company,   20
Can pay the poet for a verse and hear the fiddle
    sound,

That I am still their servant though all are
    underground.
            O what of that, O what of that,
            What is there left to say?

25   I came on a great house in the middle of the night,
    Its open lighted doorway and its windows all alight,
    And all my friends were there and made me
        welcome too;
    But I woke in an old ruin that the winds howled
        through;
    And when I pay attention I must out and walk
    Among the dogs and horses that understand my
30   talk.
            O what of that, O what of that,
            What is there left to say?

The Great Day

❖❖❖❖

Hurrah for revolution and more cannon-shot;
A beggar upon horseback lashes a beggar on foot;
Hurrah for revolution and cannon come again,
The beggars have changed places, but the lash goes on.

Parnell

❖❖❖❖

Parnell came down the road, he said to a cheering
    man:
'Ireland shall get her freedom and you still break
    stone.'

The Spur

❖❖❖❖

You think it horrible that lust and rage
Should dance attention upon my old age;
They were not such a plague when I was young;
What else have I to spur me into song?

line 2   Should dance attendance upon my old age;

(New Poems, 1938)

The Municipal Gallery Revisited

❖❖❖❖

I

Around me the images of thirty years;
An ambush; pilgrims at the water-side;
Casement upon trial, half hidden by the bars,
Guarded; Griffith staring in hysterical pride;
Kevin O'Higgins' countenance that wears   5
A gentle questioning look that cannot hide
A soul incapable of remorse or rest;
A revolutionary soldier kneeling to be blessed;

II

An Abbot or Archbishop with an upraised hand
Blessing the Tricolour. 'This is not,' I say,   10
'The dead Ireland of my youth, but an Ireland
The poets have imagined, terrible and gay.'
Before a woman's portrait suddenly I stand;
Beautiful and gentle in her Venetian way.
I met her all but fifty years ago   15
For twenty minutes in some studio.

III

Heart-smitten with emotion I sink down,
My heart recovering with covered eyes;
Wherever I had looked I had looked upon
20   My permanent or impermanent images:
Augusta Gregory's son; her sister's son,
Hugh Lane, 'onlie begetter' of all these;
Hazel Lavery living and dying, that tale
As though some ballad-singer had sung it all;

IV

25   Mancini's portrait of Augusta Gregory,
'Greatest since Rembrandt,' according to John
    Synge;
A great ebullient portrait certainly;
But where is the brush that could show anything
Of all that pride and that humility?
30   And I am in despair that time may bring
Approved patterns of women or of men
But not that selfsame excellence again.

V

My mediaeval knees lack health until they bend,
But in that woman, in that household where
35   Honour had lived so long, all lacking found.
Childless I thought, 'My children may find here
Deep-rooted things,' but never foresaw its end,
And now that end has come I have not wept;
No fox can foul the lair the badger swept –

VI

40   (An image out of Spenser and the common tongue).
John Synge, I and Augusta Gregory, thought
All that we did, all that we said or sang
Must come from contact with the soil, from that

Contact everything Antaeus-like grew strong.
We three alone in modern times had brought   45
Everything down to that sole test again,
Dream of the noble and the beggar-man.

VII

And here's John Synge himself, that rooted man,
'Forgetting human words,' a grave deep face.
You that would judge me, do not judge alone   50
This book or that, come to this hallowed place
Where my friends' portraits hang and look thereon;
Ireland's history in their lineaments trace;
Think where man's glory most begins and ends,
And say my glory was I had such friends.   55

lines 5–6 Kevin O'Higgins, and that look he wears,
Distracted gentleness that cannot hide

lines 35–8 Honour had lived so long, their health I found.
Childless, I thought, 'my children may learn here
What deep roots are,' and never foresaw the end
Of all that scholarly generations had held dear;
But now that end has come I have not wept;

line 48 And here's John Synge, a meditative man,

(*A Speech and Two Poems*, 1937)

Are You Content?
❖❖❖❖

I call on those that call me son,
Grandson, or great-grandson,
On uncles, aunts, great-uncles or great-aunts
To judge what I have done.
Have I, that put it into words,
Spoilt what old loins have sent?

Eyes spiritualised by death can judge,
I cannot, but I am not content.

He that in Sligo at Drumcliff
10   Set up the old stone Cross,
That red-headed rector in County Down,
A good man on a horse,
Sandymount Corbets, that notable man
Old William Pollexfen,
15   The smuggler Middleton, Butlers far back,
Half legendary men.

Infirm and aged I might stay
In some good company,
I who have always hated work,
20   Smiling at the sea,
Or demonstrate in my own life
What Robert Browning meant
By an old hunter talking with Gods;
But I am not content.

From ON THE BOILER

Why should not Old Men be Mad?

Why should not old men be mad?
Some have known a likely lad
That had a sound fly fisher's wrist
Turn to a drunken journalist;
A girl that knew all Dante once   5
Live to bear children to a dunce;
A Helen of social welfare dream,
Climb on a wagonette to scream.
Some think it a matter of course that chance
Should starve good men and bad advance,   10
That if their neighbours figured plain,
As though upon a lighted screen,
No single story would they find
Of an unbroken happy mind,
A finish worthy of the start.   15
Young men know nothing of this sort,
Observant old men know it well;
And when they know what old books tell,
And that no better can be had,
Know why an old man should be mad.   20

Crazy Jane on the Mountain

I am tired of cursing the Bishop,
(Said Crazy Jane)
Nine books or nine hats

Would not make him a man.
5   I have found something worse
To meditate on.
A King had some beautiful cousins
But where are they gone?
Battered to death in a cellar,
10   And he stuck to his throne.
Last night I lay on the mountain,
(Said Crazy Jane)
There in a two-horsed carriage
That on two wheels ran
15   Great bladdered Emer sat,
Her violent man
Cuchulain, sat at her side;
Thereupon,
Propped upon my two knees,
20   I kissed a stone;
I lay stretched out in the dirt
And I cried tears down.

LAST POEMS

❖❖❖❖❖❖

Under Ben Bulben

❖❖❖❖

I

Swear by what the sages spoke
Round the Mareotic Lake
That the Witch of Atlas knew,
Spoke and set the cocks a–crow.

Swear by those horsemen, by those women,   5
Complexion and form prove superhuman,
That pale, long visaged company
That air in immortality
Completeness of their passions won;
Now they ride the wintry dawn   10
Where Ben Bulben sets the scene.

Here's the gist of what they mean.

II

Many times man lives and dies
Between his two eternities,
That of race and that of soul,   15
And ancient Ireland knew it all.
Whether man die in his bed
Or the rifle knocks him dead,
A brief parting from those dear
Is the worst man has to fear.   20
Though grave–diggers' toil is long,

Sharp their spades, their muscles strong,
They but thrust their buried men
Back in the human mind again.

III

25 You that Mitchel's prayer have heard,
'Send war in our time, O Lord!'
Know that when all words are said
And a man is fighting mad,
Something drops from eyes long blind,
30 He completes his partial mind,
For an instant stands at ease,
Laughs aloud, his heart at peace.
Even the wisest man grows tense
With some sort of violence
35 Before he can accomplish fate,
Know his work or choose his mate.

IV

Poet and sculptor, do the work,
Nor let the modish painter shirk
What his great forefathers did,
40 Bring the soul of man to God,
Make him fill the cradles right.

Measurement began our might:
Forms a stark Egyptian thought,
Forms that gentler Phidias wrought.
45 Michael Angelo left a proof
On the Sistine Chapel roof,
Where but half-awakened Adam
Can disturb globe-trotting Madam
Till her bowels are in heat,
50 Proof that there's a purpose set
Before the secret working mind:
Profane perfection of mankind.

Quattrocento put in paint,
On backgrounds for a God or Saint,
Gardens where a soul's at ease;   55
Where everything that meets the eye,
Flowers and grass and cloudless sky,
Resemble forms that are or seem
When sleepers wake and yet still dream,
And when it's vanished still declare,   60
With only bed and bedstead there,
That heavens had opened.
                            Gyres run on;
When that greater dream had gone
Calvert and Wilson, Blake and Claude,
Prepared a rest for the people of God,   65
Palmer's phrase, but after that
Confusion fell upon our thought.

V

Irish poets, learn your trade,
Sing whatever is well made,
Scorn the sort now growing up   70
All out of shape from toe to top,
Their unremembering hearts and heads
Base-born products of base beds.
Sing the peasantry, and then
Hard-riding country gentlemen,   75
The holiness of monks, and after
Porter-drinkers' randy laughter;
Sing the lords and ladies gay
That were beaten into the clay
Through seven heroic centuries;   80
Cast your mind on other days
That we in coming days may be
Still the indomitable Irishry.

VI

Under bare Ben Bulben's head
85   In Drumcliff churchyard Yeats is laid.
An ancestor was rector there
Long years ago, a church stands near,
By the road an ancient cross.
No marble, no conventional phrase;
90   On limestone quarried near the spot
By his command these words are cut:

> *Cast a cold eye*
> *On life, on death.*
> *Horseman, pass by!*

September 4, 1938

The Black Tower
❖❖❖

Say that the men of the old black tower
Though they but feed as the goatherd feeds,
Their money spent, their wine gone sour,
Lack nothing that a soldier needs,
5   That all are oath-bound men;
Those banners come not in.

There in the tomb stand the dead upright,
But winds come up from the shore,
They shake when the winds roar,
10   *Old bones upon the mountain shake.*

Those banners come to bribe or threaten,
Or whisper that a man's a fool
Who, when his own right king's forgotten,
Cares what king sets up his rule.
15   If he died long ago
Why do you dread us so?

There in the tomb drops the faint moonlight,
But wind comes up from the shore,
They shake when the winds roar,
Old bones upon the mountain shake.   20

The tower's old cook that must climb and clamber
Catching small birds in the dew of the morn,
When we hale men lie stretched in slumber
Swears that he hears the king's great horn.
But he's a lying hound;   25
Stand we on guard oath-bound!

There in the tomb the dark grows blacker,
But wind comes up from the shore,
They shake when the winds roar,
Old bones upon the mountain shake.   30

January 21, 1939

Cuchulain Comforted
❖❖❖❖

A man that had six mortal wounds, a man
Violent and famous, strode among the dead;
Eyes stared out of the branches and were gone.

Then certain Shrouds that muttered head to head
Came and were gone. He leant upon a tree   5
As though to meditate on wounds and blood.

A Shroud that seemed to have authority
Among those bird-like things came and let fall
A bundle of linen. Shrouds by two and three

Came creeping up because the man was still;   10
And thereupon that linen-carrier said:
'Your life can grow much sweeter if you will

'Obey our ancient rule and make a shroud.
Mainly because of what we only know
15   The rattle of those arms makes us afraid.

'We thread the needles' eyes and all we do
All must together do.' That done, the man
Took up the nearest and began to sew.

'Now must we sing and sing the best we can
20   But first you must be told our character:
Convicted cowards all by kindred slain

'Or driven from home and left to die in fear.'
They sang, but had nor human tunes nor words,
Though all was done in common as before;

They had changed their throats and had the throats
25   of birds.

January 13, 1939

The Statues

❖❖❖

Pythagoras planned it. Why did the people stare?
His numbers though they moved or seemed to
      move
In marble or in bronze, lacked character.
But boys and girls pale from the imagined love
5   Of solitary beds, knew what they were,
That passion could bring character enough;
And pressed at midnight in some public place
Live lips upon a plummet-measured face.

No! Greater than Pythagoras, for the men
10   That with a mallet or a chisel modelled these
Calculations that look but casual flesh, put down
All Asiatic vague immensities,

And not the banks of oars that swam upon
The many-headed foam at Salamis.
Europe put off that foam when Phidias   15
Gave women dreams and dreams their looking-
 glass.

One image crossed the many-headed, sat
Under the tropic shade, grew round and slow,
No Hamlet thin from eating flies, a fat
Dreamer of the Middle Ages. Empty eyeballs knew 20
That knowledge increases unreality, that
Mirror on mirror mirrored is all the show.
When gong and conch declare the hour to bless
Grimalkin crawls to Buddha's emptiness.

When Pearse summoned Cuchulain to his side, 25
What stalked through the Post Office? What
 intellect,
What calculation, number, measurement, replied?
We Irish, born into that ancient sect
But thrown upon this filthy modern tide
And by its formless, spawning, fury wrecked, 30
Climb to our proper dark, that we may trace
The lineaments of a plummet-measured face.

April 9, 1938

News for the Delphic Oracle
❖❖❖❖

I

There all the golden codgers lay,
There the silver dew,
And the great water sighed for love
And the wind sighed too.
Man-picker Niamh leant and sighed 5

By Oisin on the grass;
There sighed amid his choir of love
Tall Pythagoras.
Plotinus came and looked about,
10   The salt flakes on his breast,
And having stretched and yawned awhile
Lay sighing like the rest.

II

Straddling each a dolphin's back
And steadied by a fin
15   Those Innocents re-live their death,
Their wounds open again.
The ecstatic waters laugh because
Their cries are sweet and strange,
Through their ancestral patterns dance,
20   And the brute dolphins plunge
Until in some cliff-sheltered bay
Where wades the choir of love
Proffering its sacred laurel crowns,
They pitch their burdens off.

III

25   Slim adolescence that a nymph has stripped,
Peleus on Thetis stares,
Her limbs are delicate as an eyelid,
Love has blinded him with tears;
But Thetis' belly listens.
30   Down the mountain walls
From where Pan's cavern is
Intolerable music falls.
Foul goat-head, brutal arm appear,
Belly, shoulder, bum,
35   Flash fishlike; nymphs and satyrs
Copulate in the foam.

Long-legged Fly

That civilisation may not sink,
Its great battle lost,
Quiet the dog, tether the pony
To a distant post.
Our master Caesar is in the tent   5
Where the maps are spread,
His eyes fixed upon nothing,
A hand under his head.

Like a long-legged fly upon the stream
His mind moves upon silence.   10

That the topless towers be burnt
And men recall that face,
Move most gently if move you must
In this lonely place.
She thinks, part woman, three parts a child,   15
That nobody looks; her feet
Practise a tinker shuffle
Picked up on a street.

Like a long-legged fly upon the stream
Her mind moves upon silence.   20

That girls at puberty may find
The first Adam in their thought,
Shut the door of the Pope's chapel,
Keep those children out.
There on that scaffolding reclines   25
Michael Angelo.
With no more sound than the mice make
His hand moves to and fro.

Like a long-legged fly upon the stream
His mind moves upon silence.   30

A Bronze Head
❖❖❖

Here at right of the entrance this bronze head,
Human, superhuman, a bird's round eye,
Everything else withered and mummy-dead.
What great tomb-haunter sweeps the distant sky
5 (Something may linger there though all else die)
And finds there nothing to make its terror less
Hysterica passio of its own emptiness?

No dark tomb-haunter once; her form all full
As though with magnanimity of light
10 Yet a most gentle woman; who can tell
Which of her forms has shown her substance right,
Or maybe substance can be composite,
Profound McTaggart thought so, and in a breath
A mouthful hold the extreme of life and death.

15 But even at the starting-post, all sleek and new,
I saw the wildness in her and I thought
A vision of terror that it must live through
Had shattered her soul. Propinquity had brought
Imagination to that pitch where it casts out
20 All that is not itself. I had grown wild
And wandered murmuring everywhere, 'My child,
my child!'

Or else I thought her supernatural;
As though a sterner eye looked through her eye
On this foul world in its decline and fall;
On gangling stocks grown great, great stocks run
25 dry,
Ancestral pearls all pitched into a sty,
Heroic reverie mocked by clown and knave,
And wondered what was left for massacre to save.

John Kinsella's Lament for
Mrs. Mary Moore

I

A bloody and a sudden end,
    Gunshot or a noose,
For death who takes what man would keep,
    Leaves what man would lose.
He might have had my sister,   5
    My cousins by the score,
But nothing satisfied the fool
    But my dear Mary Moore,
None other knows what pleasures man
    At table or in bed.   10
What shall I do for pretty girls
    Now my old bawd is dead?

II

Though stiff to strike a bargain
    Like an old Jew man,
Her bargain struck we laughed and talked   15
    And emptied many a can;
And O! but she had stories
    Though not for the priest's ear,
To keep the soul of man alive,
    Banish age and care,   20
And being old she put a skin
    On everything she said.
What shall I do for pretty girls
    Now my old bawd is dead?

III

The priests have got a book that says   25
    But for Adam's sin

Eden's Garden would be there
    And I there within.
No expectation fails there,
30   No pleasing habit ends,
No man grows old, no girl grows cold,
    But friends walk by friends.
Who quarrels over halfpennies
    That plucks the trees for bread?
35   *What shall I do for pretty girls*
    Now my old bawd is dead?

High Talk

❖❖❖

Processions that lack high stilts have nothing that
    catches the eye.
What if my great-granddad had a pair that were
    twenty foot high,
And mine were but fifteen foot, no modern stalks
    upon higher,
Some rogue of the world stole them to patch up a
    fence or a fire.
Because piebald ponies, led bears, caged lions, make
5   but poor shows,
Because children demand Daddy-long-legs upon
    his timber toes,
Because women in the upper storeys demand a face
    at the pane,
That patching old heels they may shriek, I take to
    chisel and plane.

Malachi Stilt-Jack am I, whatever I learned has
    run wild,
From collar to collar, from stilt to stilt, from father
10   to child.

All metaphor, Malachi, stilts and all. A barnacle
    goose
Far up in the stretches of night; night splits and
    the dawn breaks loose;
I, through the terrible novelty of light, stalk on,
    stalk on;
Those great sea-horses bare their teeth and laugh
    at the dawn.

The Man and the Echo
❖❖❖❖

Man
In a cleft that's christened Alt
Under broken stone I halt
At the bottom of a pit
That broad noon has never lit,
And shout a secret to the stone.   5
All that I have said and done,
Now that I am old and ill,
Turns into a question till
I lie awake night after night
And never get the answers right.   10
Did that play of mine send out
Certain men the English shot?
Did words of mine put too great strain
On that woman's reeling brain?
Could my spoken words have checked   15
That whereby a house lay wrecked?
And all seems evil until I
Sleepless would lie down and die.

Echo
Lie down and die.

Man
                    That were to shirk
20 The spiritual intellect's great work
    And shirk it in vain. There is no release
    In a bodkin or disease,
    Nor can there be a work so great
    As that which cleans man's dirty slate.
25 While man can still his body keep
    Wine or love drug him to sleep,
    Waking he thanks the Lord that he
    Has body and its stupidity,
    But body gone he sleeps no more,
30 And till his intellect grows sure
    That all's arranged in one clear view,
    Pursues the thoughts that I pursue,
    Then stands in judgment on his soul,
    And, all work done, dismisses all
35 Out of intellect and sight
    And sinks at last into the night.

Echo
Into the night.

Man
                    O rocky voice,
    Shall we in that great night rejoice?
    What do we know but that we face
40 One another in this place?
    But hush, for I have lost the theme,
    Its joy or night seem but a dream;
    Up there some hawk or owl has struck
    Dropping out of sky or rock,
45 A stricken rabbit is crying out
    And its cry distracts my thought.

The Circus Animals' Desertion
◇◇◇◇

I

I sought a theme and sought for it in vain,
I sought it daily for six weeks or so.
Maybe at last being but a broken man
I must be satisfied with my heart, although
Winter and summer till old age began   5
My circus animals were all on show,
Those stilted boys, that burnished chariot,
Lion and woman and the Lord knows what.

II

What can I but enumerate old themes?
First that sea-rider Oisin led by the nose   10
Through three enchanted islands, allegorical
   dreams,
Vain gaiety, vain battle, vain repose,
Themes of the embittered heart, or so it seems,
That might adorn old songs or courtly shows;
But what cared I that set him on to ride,   15
I, starved for the bosom of his faery bride?

And then a counter-truth filled out its play,
The Countess Cathleen was the name I gave it,
She, pity-crazed, had given her soul away
But masterful Heaven had intervened to save it.   20
I thought my dear must her own soul destroy
So did fanaticism and hate enslave it,
And this brought forth a dream and soon enough
This dream itself had all my thought and love.

And when the Fool and Blind Man stole the bread   25
Cuchulain fought the ungovernable sea;
Heart mysteries there, and yet when all is said
It was the dream itself enchanted me:

Character isolated by a deed
30   To engross the present and dominate memory.
Players and painted stage took all my love
And not those things that they were emblems of.

III

Those masterful images because complete
Grew in pure mind, but out of what began?
35   A mound of refuse or the sweepings of a street,
Old kettles, old bottles, and a broken can,
Old iron, old bones, old rags, that raving slut
Who keeps the till. Now that my ladder's gone
I must lie down where all the ladders start
40   In the foul rag and bone shop of the heart.

Politics
❖❖❖❖

'*In our time the destiny of man presents its meaning in
political terms.*' – THOMAS MANN

How can I, that girl standing there,
My attention fix
On Roman or on Russian
Or on Spanish politics?
5   Yet here's a travelled man that knows
What he talks about,
And there's a politician
That has both read and thought,
And maybe what they say is true
10   Of war and war's alarms,
But O that I were young again
And held her in my arms.

APPENDIX:
FROM 'SPEAKING TO THE PSALTERY'
◆◇◆◇◆◇

Yeats had strong and interesting ideas about the speaking of verse, especially in dramatic performances. This essay, which first appeared in 1902 and in *Ideas of Good and Evil* (1903), was later supplemented by musical examples, including Yeats's own setting of 'The Song of the Old Mother'. This setting can be compared to Yeats's reading of the poem, which is available on the Caedmon label. The psaltery, which is central to the essay and to the Yeatsian experiment, was a plucked instrument.

An account of Yeats as reader is provided by Edward Marsh: 'After supper he was made to read to us some things out of a new volume of his poems ..., they seemed most beautiful in sound, tho' I never can understand poetry read out. He read them in an extremely monotonous voice, with very strong emphasis on all the accents – it was rather effective, but I think it's possible to read in a more natural way without sacrificing the music of the verse' (Christopher Hassall, *Edward Marsh, Patron of the Arts: A Biography*, 1959). Marsh is describing a reading on 23 April 1899.

Since I was a boy I have always longed to hear poems spoken to a harp, as I imagined Homer to have spoken his, for it is not natural to enjoy an art only when one is by oneself. Whenever one finds a fine verse one wants to read it to somebody, and it would be much less trouble and much pleasanter if we could all listen, friend by friend, lover by beloved. Images used to rise up before me, as I am sure they have arisen before nearly everybody else who cares for poetry, of wild-eyed men speaking harmoniously to murmuring wires while audiences in many-coloured robes listened, hushed and excited. Whenever I spoke of my desire to anybody they said I should write for music, but when I heard anything sung I did not hear the words, or if

I did their natural pronunciation was altered and their natural music was altered, or it was drowned in another music which I did not understand. What was the good of writing a love-song if the singer pronounced love, 'lo-o-o-o-o-ve', or even if he said 'love', but did not give it its exact place and weight in the rhythm? Like every other poet, I spoke verses in a kind of chant when I was making them; and sometimes, when I was alone on a country road, I would speak them in a loud chanting voice, and feel that if I dared I would speak them in that way to other people . . .

Even when one is speaking to a single note sounded faintly on the Psaltery, if one is sufficiently practised to speak on it without thinking about it one can get an endless variety of expression. All art is, indeed, a monotony in external things for the sake of an interior variety, a sacrifice of gross effects to subtle effects, an asceticism of the imagination. But this new art, new in modern life I mean, will have to train its hearers as well as its speakers, for it takes time to surrender gladly the gross efforts one is accustomed to, and one may well find mere monotony at first where one soon learns to find a variety as incalculable as in the outline of faces or in the expression of eyes. Modern acting and recitation have taught us to fix our attention on the gross effects till we have come to think gesture, and the intonation that copies the accidental surface of life, more important than the rhythm; and yet we understand theoretically that it is precisely this rhythm that separates good writing from bad, that is the glimmer, the fragrance, the spirit of all intense literature. I do not say that we should speak our plays to musical notes, for dramatic verse will need its own method, and I have hitherto experimented with short lyric poems alone; but I am certain that, if people would listen for a while to lyrical verse spoken to notes, they would soon find it impossible to listen without indignation to verse as it is spoken in our leading theatres. They would get a subtlety of hearing that would demand new effects from actors and even from public speakers, and they might, it may be, begin even to notice one another's voices till poetry and rhythm had come nearer to common life.

I cannot tell what changes this new art is to go through, or to what greatness or littleness of fortune; but I can imagine little stories in prose with their dialogues in metre going pleasantly to the strings. I am not certain that I shall not see some Order naming itself from the Golden Violet of the Troubadours or the like, and having among its members none but well-taught and well-mannered speakers who will keep the new art from disrepute. They will know how to keep from singing notes and from prosaic lifeless intonations, and they will always understand, however far they push their experiments, that poetry and not music is their object; and they will have by heart, like the Irish *File*, so many poems and notations that they will never have to bend their heads over the book, to the ruin of dramatic expression and of that wild air the bard had always about him in my boyish imagination. They will go here and there speaking their verses and their little stories wherever they can find a score or two of poetical-minded people in a big room, or a couple of poetical-minded friends sitting by the hearth, and poets will write them poems and little stories to the confounding of print and paper. I, at any rate, from this out mean to write all my longer poems for the stage, and all my shorter ones for the Psaltery, if only some strong angel keep me to my good resolutions.

1902

THE SONG OF THE OLD MOTHER

W. B. Y.

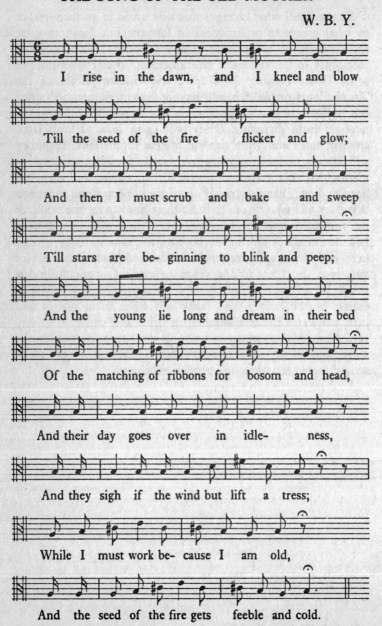

I rise in the dawn, and I kneel and blow

Till the seed of the fire flicker and glow;

And then I must scrub and bake and sweep

Till stars are be- ginning to blink and peep;

And the young lie long and dream in their bed

Of the matching of ribbons for bosom and head,

And their day goes over in idle- ness,

And they sigh if the wind but lift a tress;

While I must work be- cause I am old,

And the seed of the fire gets feeble and cold.

Notes
✦✦✦✦✦✦

Abbreviations Used in the Notes

AFMIM	*A Full Moon in March* (1935)
AU	*Autobiographies* (1955)
AV, 1925	*A Vision* (1925)
AV, 1937	*A Vision* (1937)
BS	*The Bounty of Sweden* (1925)
CK	*The Countess Kathleen and Various Legends and Lyrics* (1892)
CM	*The Cat and the Moon and Certain Poems* (1924)
CP, 1933	*Collected Poems* (1933)
CP, 1949	*Collected Poems* (1949)
CT, 1893	*The Celtic Twilight* (1893)
CT, 1902	*The Celtic Twilight* (1902)
CW	*Collected Works* (1908)
DP	*Dramatis Personae* (1935)
EP	*Eight Poems* (1916)
EPS	*Early Poems and Stories* (1925)
GH, 1910	*The Green Helmet and Other Poems* (1910)
GH, 1912	*The Green Helmet and Other Poems* (1912)
ISW	*In the Seven Woods* (1903)
KGCT	*The King of the Great Clock Tower* (1934)
LDW	*Letters on Poetry from W. B. Yeats to Dorothy Wellesley* (1940; 1964)
LP	*Last Poems and Plays* (1940)
LPTP	*Last Poems and Two Plays* (1939)
M	*Memoirs: Autobiography – First Draft, Journal*, edited by Denis Donoghue (1972)
MRD	*Michael Robartes and the Dancer* (1921)
NP	*New Poems* (1938)
OB	*October Blast* (1927)
OTB	*On the Boiler* (1939)
P	*Poems* (various dates)
PASL	*Per Amica Silentia Lunae* (1918)
PWD	*Poems Written in Discouragement* (1913)
R	*Responsibilities: Poems and a Play* (1914)
SPAF	*Seven Poems and a Fragment* (1922)
SR	*The Secret Rose* (1897)
T	*The Tower* (1928)
TV	*The Trembling of the Veil* (1922)
WFMP	*Words for Music Perhaps and Other Poems* (1932)

WO	*The Wanderings of Oisin and Other Poems* (1889)
WR	*The Wind Among the Reeds* (1899)
WS, 1929	*The Winding Stair* (1929)
WS, 1933	*The Winding Stair and Other Poems* (1933)
WSC, 1917	*The Wild Swans at Coole* (1917)
WSC, 1919	*The Wild Swans at Coole* (1919)

First dates of publication are given only in those cases where poems had appeared in print before they were collected in the volumes to which they were finally assigned. If no date is given, it can be assumed that the poem has no history of previous publication. Books referred to specifically in these notes are indicated by the name of the author alone and can be identified in the Bibliography. If the author is represented by more than one title, the name of the book is also given.

Love Song

First published in *Poems and Ballads of Young Ireland*, 1888; never reprinted by Yeats. Yeats, who knew very little Irish, based his poem on a translation by Edward Walsh in *Irish Popular Songs* (1847) of a stanza from 'Edmund of the Hill' by Edmund O'Ryan: 'My hope, my love, we will proceed / Into the woods, scattering the dews / Where we will behold the salmon, and the ousel in its nest, / The deer and the roebuck calling, / The sweetest bird on the branches warbling, / The cuckoo on the summit of the green hill; / And death shall never approach us / In the bosom of the fragrant wood.' Yeats commented on this version: 'Than which same pastoral aspiration I know nothing more impossibly romantic and Celtic. Nature with these men was a passion.' His own rendering changes Walsh's translation into a lilting verse and, as Colin Meir has remarked, 'the repetition that achieves this lilt also subtly affects the mood, bringing an incantatory dreaminess into what was merely simple statement'.

The Wanderings of Oisin (Book III)

Original title continued: 'and *How a Demon Trapped Him*'. 'The poem is founded upon the Middle Irish dialogues of Saint Patrick and Oisin and a certain Gaelic poem of the last century. The events it describes, like the events in most of the poems in this volume, are supposed to have taken place rather in the indefinite period, made up of many periods, described by the folk-tales, than in any particular century; it therefore, like the later Fenian stories themselves, mixes much that is mediaeval with much that is ancient. The Gaelic poems do not make Oisin go to more than one island' (Yeats's note). Oisin (sometimes spelt *Usheen*, which is a useful guide to pronunciation) was the poet of the Fenian cycle of legend centred on the military order of the Fianna, of which Finn was chief. In *WO* Yeats identified the islands which he visited as the Island of the Living (Book I), the Island of Victories (Book II) and the Island of Forgetfulness (Book III); in 'The Circus Animals' Desertion' he described them as 'allegorical dreams, / Vain gaiety, vain battle, vain repose, / Themes of the embittered heart'. Oisin's fairy tempter was Niamh (spelt *Neave* in 1895 and pronounced *Neeiv*), 'a beautiful woman of the Tribes of Danu, that led Oisin to the Country of the Young, as their country is called' (*WR*). In the third book 'he came back, at last, to bitterness and weariness'. Here he lost that personal immunity from the effects of time which depended on the condition that he never set foot on Irish soil.

As Elizabeth Cullingford has suggested, the poem could be read as a political allegory in which the captive maiden Ireland is rescued from the power of England (the 'Demon' of the subtitle), while the implication of 'Fenians' would also have been unmistakable in the 1880s: 'To select the story of Oisin was no antiquarian fancy, but a deliberate political choice.' After publication the poem was heavily revised, especially in the first two books.

53. *bell-branch* This was a 'legendary branch whose shaking cast all men into a gentle sleep' (*P*, 1895; see 'Dedication to a Book of Stories selected from the Irish Novelists'); *Sennachies* Traditional story-tellers. 70. *moil* Toil, labour. 77. *man of . . . croziers* St Patrick, who is Oisin's questioner, the provoker of his narrative and, in accordance with Gaelic tradition, his antagonist (see the opposition between Ribh and St Patrick in 'Supernatural Songs' and between Crazy Jane and the Bishop in *WFMP*). 80. *demon* Culann made armour for Conchubar (also Conhor or Concobar; pronounced *Conor* or *Conachor*), King of all Ireland, who features in the Red Branch cycle. Other significant legendary characters include Balor, the 'Irish Chimaera, the leader of the hosts of darkness at the great battle of good and evil, life and death, light and darkness, which was fought out on the strands of Moytura, near Sligo' (*P*, 1895), and Grania (pronounced *Grawnya*), 'A beautiful woman, who fled with Dermot to escape from the love of aged Finn' (*P*, 1895). 152. *keened* Wailed, lamented. 156. *grass barnacle* The barnacle goose is a species of wild goose which visits British coasts in winter and which has long been associated with Ireland. 'There stood certaine trees upon the shore of the Irish sea, bearing fruit like unto a gourd, which . . . doe fall into the water, and become birds called Bernacles' (Hakluyt, 1599). 160. Place names do not appear here in the first version. 163. *rath* Hill-fort or place of residence for chief of a tribe, usually circular. 184. Maeve, Queen of Connaught, who features in the Red Branch cycle of stories, 'is rumored to be buried under the cairn on Knocknarea [a mountain in Sligo]' (*P*, 1895; see 'Red Hanrahan's Song about Ireland'). In Book I, Oisin and his companions, 'passing the Firbolgs' burial-mounds, / Came to the cairn-heaped grassy hill / Where passionate Maeve is stony-still' (lines 16–18). 222. *chain of small stones* Rosary beads; 'the rosary of stone beads brought to him in a cargo of silks and laces out of France' ('The Old Men of the Twilight', *SR*).

CROSSWAYS

This never existed as a book in its own right, although Yeats assigned it the date 1889. It was first used as a heading in *P*, 1895. The poems printed under this heading in the present selection are taken from *WO*. In *P*, 1895, Yeats admitted that in these poems he 'tried many pathways', which may help to explain the choice of title. The section bears an epigraph from Blake's *Vala, or The Four Zoas*: 'The stars are threshed, and the souls are threshed from their husks.'

The Indian to His Love

First published as 'An Indian Song' in the *Dublin University Review*, December 1886. 'When I first wrote I went here and there for my subjects as my reading led me, and preferred to all other countries Arcadia and the India of romance, but presently I convinced myself . . . that I should never go for the scenery of a poem to any country but my own' (*CW*).

The Stolen Child

First published in the *Irish Monthly*, December 1886. 'The places mentioned are round about Sligo. Further Rosses is a very noted fairy locality. There is here a little point of rocks where, if anyone falls asleep, there is danger of their waking silly, the fairies having carried off their souls' (*Fairy and Folk Tales of the Irish Peasantry*, 1888). 'Rosses is a little sea-dividing, sandy plain, covered with short grass, like a green table-cloth, and lying in the foam midway between the round cairn-headed Knocknarea and "Ben Bulben, famous for hawks"' ('Drumcliff and Rosses', *CT*, 1893).

Down by the Salley Gardens

First published as 'An Old Song Re-sung' in *WO*. Yeats's note emphasises a debt to oral tradition: 'An extension of three lines sung to me by an old woman at Ballisodare' (*P*, 1895, where 'Salley' is identified as 'Willow'). Various sources have been suggested, including 'Going to Mass last Sunday' and 'You Rambling Boys of Pleasure'. P. J. McCall claimed to have heard in 1875 an 'Old country love song' which he copied down as follows (transcription by Michael Yeats): 'Down by the Sally Gardens my own true love and I did meet; / She passed the Sally Gardens, a tripping with her snow white feet. / She bid me take life easy just as leaves fall from each tree; / But I being young and foolish with my true love would not agree. / In a field by the river my lovely girl and I did stand / And leaning on her shoulder I pressed her burning hand, / She bid me take life easy, just as the stream flows o'er the weirs / But I being young and foolish I parted her that day in tears. / I wish I was in Banagher and my fine girl on my knee / And I with money plenty to keep her in good company. / I'd call for a liquor of the best with flowing bowls on every side / Kind fortune ne'er daunt me, I am young and the world's wide.' In due course Yeats's poem attracted the attention of various composers, including Peter Warlock, and was sung by James Joyce on his concert début; it was also reabsorbed into the mainstream of Irish folksong, from which it seems to have originally emerged.

THE ROSE

Like *Crossways* this heading was introduced by Yeats in 1895, when he dated it 1893. The poems included under *The Rose* in the present selection were from *CK*, *Representative Irish Tales* (1891), *P*, 1895, and *P*, 1912. 'The Rose is a favourite symbol with the Irish poets, and has given a name to several poems both Gaelic and English, and is used in love poems, in addresses to Ireland ... and in religious poems.' (*P*, 1895). The section is dedicated to Lionel Johnson (one of Yeats's fellow poets in the Rhymers' Club) and bears an epigraph from St Augustine: '*Sero te amavi, Pulchritudo tam antiqua et tam nova! Sero te amavi.*'

To the Rose upon the Rood of Time

First published in *CK*. For Yeats's interest in Rosicrucianism and the connection between the rose and the rood (or cross), see note to 'The Secret Rose'.

Fergus and the Druid

First published in the *National Observer*, 21 May 1892. Fergus 'was the poet of the Red Branch cycle, as Usheen was of the Fenian. He was once king of all Ireland, but gave up his throne that he might live at peace hunting in the woods' (*P*, 1895). Because of his great love for Nessa, 'he gave up his throne to Conchobar, her son by another, and lived out his days feasting, and fighting, and hunting. His promise never to refuse a feast from a certain comrade, and the mischief that came by his promise, and the vengeance he took afterwards, are a principal theme of the poets' (*WR*).

35. *quern* Apparatus for grinding corn, usually consisting of two circular stones.

Cuchulain's Fight with the Sea

First published as 'The Death of Cuchulain' in *United Ireland*, 11 June 1892. 'Cuchullin (pronounced Cuhoolin) [correctly, *Coohullin*, hound of Ulster] was the great warrior of the Conorian cycle. My poem is founded on a West of Ireland legend given by Curtin in "Myths and Folklore of Ireland". The bardic tale of the death of Cuchullin is very different' (*CK*). 'We know we shall be long forgetting Cuchulain, whose life is vehement and full of pleasure, as though he always remembered that it was to be soon over' (Yeats in March 1902). Yeats's interest in the myth of Cuchulain was sustained throughout his life and resulted in five plays: *On Baile's Strand*, *The Golden Helmet* (in prose, later *The Green Helmet* in verse), *At the Hawk's Well*, *The Only Jealousy of Emer* and *The Death of Cuchulain*. A principal source was Lady Gregory's book of stories *Cuchulain of Muirthemne* (1902), in which the grotesque elements of the original were softened and the importance of supernatural intervention reduced. Yeats contributed a Preface and pronounced the book 'the best [elsewhere, 'the most important'] that has come out of Ireland in my time' (a phrase which was to be parodied by Buck Mulligan in *Ulysses*). Emer was Cuchulain's wife.

2. *dun* Hill-fortress or fortified eminence.

The Rose of the World

First published as 'Rosa Mundi' in the *National Observer*, 2 January 1892. '*Usna*. The father of Naisi, the lover, and Ardan and Anly, the friends of Deirdre. Deirdre's beautiful lament over their bodies has been finely translated by Sir Samuel Ferguson ['Lament for the sons of Usnach' in *Lays of the Western Gael and Other Poems*, 1864]' (*P*, 1895).

A Faery Song

First published in the *National Observer*, 12 September 1891, with the subtitle 'Sung by "the Good People" over the outlaw Michael Dwyer and his bride, who had escaped into the mountains'. This reference to the rebel leader of 1798 was replaced by an Irish myth which had local associations for Yeats. Grania fled with Diarmuid to escape from the love of the aged Finn. 'She fled from place to place over Ireland, but at last Dermot was killed at Sligo upon the seaward point of Benbulben, and Finn won her love and brought her, leaning upon his neck, into the assembly of the Fenians, who burst into inextinguishable laughter' (*P*, 1895).

Subtitle. *Cromlech* A structure of prehistoric age consisting of a large flat or flattish stone resting on three or more stones set upright' (*OED*); sometimes called by the French name *dolmen* and in Ireland often associated with Diarmuid and Grania.

The Lake Isle of Innisfree

First published in the *National Observer*, 13 December 1890. 'I had still the ambition, formed in Sligo in my teens, of living an imitation of Thoreau on Innisfree, a little island in Lough Gill, and when walking through Fleet Street very homesick I heard a little tinkle of water and saw a fountain in a shop-window which balanced a little ball upon its jet, and began to remember lake water' (*TV*). In the poem the specific setting is generalised into 'the roadway' and 'the pavements grey', while the unpoetic details of the urban epiphany are eliminated. Yeats lived for many years in London, but he carefully omitted almost all traces of the city from his poetry (one exception is the early poem 'Street Dancers').

2. *wattles* See 'The Wanderings of Oisin' (above), line 162.

The Sorrow of Love

First published in *CK*. In the manuscript version the moon in line 10 is 'withered', and the next line reads 'The wearisome loud chaunting of the leaves' (Ellmann, *The Identity of Yeats*).

5–8. See 'a pearl-pale, high-born lady, who rode / On a horse with bridle of findrinny; / And like a sunset were her lips, / A stormy sunset on doomed ships' (*The Wanderings of Oisin*). 7–8. Allusions to the epic subject-matter of the *Odyssey* and the *Iliad* (in which Priam is king of the doomed city of Troy).

When You are Old

First published in *CK*. Yeats's poem takes its inspiration from 'Quand vous serez bien vieille', one of Ronsard's *Sonnets pour Hélène*.

Who Goes with Fergus?

First published in Act II, Scene ii, of *The Countess Kathleen* (*CK*). In the play, Oona 'chants [those verses] with the thin voice of age' to console her foster-daughter Kathleen, who comments after the first verse, 'I hear the horn of Fergus in my heart'. In *P*, 1895, Kathleen asks Oona to sing the song 'he [Aleel] sang in the dim light, / When we first found him in the shadow of leaves, / About King Fergus in his brazen car, / Driving with troops of dancers through the woods'. Oona replies, 'Dear heart, make a soft cradle of old tales, / And songs, and music: wherefore should you sadden / For wrongs you cannot hinder?' For Fergus, see note to 'Fergus and the Druid'.

The Man who Dreamed of Faeryland

First published in the *National Observer*, 7 February 1891. Except for Drumahair, which is in Co. Leitrim, all the place-names are taken from Co. Sligo. Drumahair was reputed to be more than commonly 'gentle' (i.e., conducive to supernatural manifestations).

The Dedication to a Book of Stories selected from the Irish Novelists

First published in *Representative Irish Tales* (1891), in which Yeats collected stories from Maria Edgeworth, John and Michael Banim, William Carleton, Charles Lever, Edward Maginn, Thomas Crofton Croker, Gerald Griffin, Charles Kickham and Rosa Mulholland. In 1924 Yeats remarked that 'Even in its re-written form it is a sheaf of wild oats.' For the bell-branch, see note to *The Wanderings of Oisin*, line 53.

The Lamentation of the Old Pensioner

First published as 'The Old Pensioner' in the *Scots Observer*, 15 November

1890; the final version was first published in *EPS*. 'This small poem is little more than a translation into verse of the very words of an old Wicklow peasant' (*CK*); it is based on 'words spoken by a man on the Two Rock Mountain to a friend of mine [AE]' (*CW*). Yeats provided a prose version in 'A Visionary' in *CT*, 1893 (first published as 'An Irish Visionary' in the *National Observer*, October 1891): 'The peasant was wandering in his mind with prolonged sorrow ... and once he lamented that his old neighbours were gone, and that all had forgotten him: they used to draw a chair to the fire for him in every cabin, and now they said, "Who is that old fellow there?" "The fret" (Irish for doom) "is over me," he repeated, and then went on to talk once more of God and Heaven. More than once also he said, waving his arm towards the mountain, "Only myself knows what happened under the thorn-tree forty years ago"; and as he said it the tears upon his face glistened in the moonlight.' The early version of the poem corresponds to the mood of this second-hand recollection. The vigour and tone of the revised poem may owe something to Synge's description of an Old Pensioner in 'The Vagrants of Wicklow' (as Peter Kuch has suggested).

17. Compare this line to the Old Man in *The Death of Cuchulain*: 'I spit upon the dancers painted by Degas. I spit upon their short bodices, their stiff stays, their toes whereon they spin like peg-tops ... I spit! I spit! I spit!'

The Two Trees

First published in *CK*. The two trees can be interpreted as the Tree of Life and the Tree of Knowledge.

To Ireland in the Coming Times

First published in *CK* as 'Apologia addressed to Ireland in the coming days'.

4. *rann* Verse or strain (an Irish word, as in James Clarence Mangan's 'chant abroad the exulting rann of jubilee'). 18. Thomas Osborne Davis (1814–45), who co-founded the *Nation*, was the leader of the Young Ireland movement, a popular versifier and, in Yeats's view, a maker of 'opinion'. Mangan (1803–49) was a late Romantic who could 'never be popular like Davis': 'In all he wrote there was a sort of intensity, not merely of the intellectual or of the aesthetic nature, but of the whole man'. Sir Samuel Ferguson (1810–86) was a lawyer, antiquary and Ulster Unionist; his Irish mythological poetry caused Yeats to describe him after his death as 'the greatest Irish poet, because his poems and legends embody more completely than in any other man's writings, the Irish character'. Yeats also wrote, 'The nation has found in Davis a battle call, as in Mangan its cry of despair; but he [Ferguson] only, the one Homeric poet of our time, could give us immortal companions still wet with the dew of their primal world' [1886].

NOTES

[The poet, Owen Hanrahan, under a bush of may]

First published in the story 'The Curse of O'Sullivan the Red upon Old Age' in the *National Observer*, 29 September 1894; in 'The Curse of Hanrahan the Red' in *SR*. It was never published by Yeats as a separate poem and was not included in *CP*, 1933, or *CP*, 1949. Hanrahan was a peasant poet invented by Yeats; he features in some of his early stories and also provides one of the personae of *WR* (see notes to that collection and to 'Red Hanrahan's Song about Ireland'). Hanrahan, like O'Sullivan (see note to 'He Reproves the Curlew'), enabled Yeats to come into closer contact with the traditions of poetry in the Irish language (in this case the ritual curse, derived from a sacred energy which is invested in the poet). In *Stories of Red Hanrahan* (1905), where the title was changed to 'Red Hanrahan's Curse', the painful symptoms of old age were first elaborated: 'And he thought of the stiffness of his joints when he first rose of a morning, and the pain of his knees after making a journey, and it seemed to him as if he was come to be a very old man, with cold in the shoulders and speckled shins and his wind breaking and he himself withering away. And with those thoughts there came on him a great anger against old age and all it brought with it.' Again: 'But it is old and broken he looked going home that day with the stoop in his shoulders and the darkness in his face.' (Most of these symptoms had not appeared in the versions of 1894 and 1897: 'But he went towards the Townland of the Bridge [Balladrihid, 1894] with his eyes on the white dust, stooping [stooping greatly, 1894] and seeming an old man indeed.') O'Sullivan/Hanrahan then delivers his curse 'upon old age and upon old men' to the children in his hedge school and tells them: 'You yourselves and the beautiful people of the world are like this blossom, and old age is the wind that comes and blows the blossom away' (1905 and later versions). In the versions of 1894 and 1897 the circumstances of composition are simple: 'He sat down under the bush, and began making his rhyme, crooning it to himself, the May blossoms falling over him the while.' In versions from 1905 onwards these circumstances have changed: 'When he got to his cabin there was no one there, and he went and lay down on the bed for a while as he was used to do when he wanted to make a poem or a praise or a curse.' Quoting stanza VI of 'Among School Children' in 1926, Yeats called it 'a fragment of my last curse upon old age' and explained that 'even the greatest men are owls, scarecrows, by the time their fame has come'.

THE WIND AMONG THE REEDS

All the poems included in the present selection were printed in *WR*. For the wind, see this account of the poems of AE: 'They, with their wild music as of winds blowing in the reeds, seemed to me the very inmost voice of Celtic sadness, and of Celtic longing for infinite things the world has never seen' ('An Irish Visionary' in the *National Observer*, October 1891, later 'A Visionary' in *CT*, 1893). 'When I wrote these poems I had so meditated over the images that came to me in writing "Ballads and Lyrics", "The Rose", and "The Wanderings of Oisin", and other images from Irish folk-lore, that they had become true symbols. I had sometimes when awake, but more often in sleep, moments of vision, a state very unlike dreaming, when these images took upon themselves what seemed an independent life and became a part of a mystic language, which seemed always as if it would bring me some strange revelation' (*CW*). Yeats recognised that this mystic language required some translation for the uninitiated. Like *MRD*, *WR* included detailed notes; Yeats remarked to a friend that these were 'really elaborate essays in the manner of "The Celtic Twilight". They deal with Irish fairy-lore and mythology, and are in most cases made out of quite new material. They have given me a good deal of trouble, and will probably make most of the critics spend half of every review in complaining that I have written very long notes about very short poems. I am in hopes, however, that others will forgive me the poems for the sake of the valuable information in the notes. It is a way of getting the forgiveness of the Philistines which may serve as a useful model' (Wade).

Aedh (pronounced *A* to rhyme with *way*), Hanrahan and Michael Robartes all require explication: 'These are personages in "The Secret Rose"; but, with the exception of some of Hanrahan's and one of Aedh's poems, the poems are not out of that book. I have used them in this book more as principles of the mind than as actual personages. It is probable that only students of the magical tradition will understand me when I say that "Michael Robartes" is fire reflected in water, and that Hanrahan is fire blown by the wind, and that Aedh, whose name is not merely the Irish form of Hugh, but the Irish for fire, is fire burning by itself. To put it in a different way, Hanrahan is the simplicity of an imagination too changeable to gather permanent possessions, or the adoration of the shepherds; and Michael Robartes is the pride of the imagination brooding upon the greatness of its possessions, or the adoration of the Magi; while Aedh is the myrrh and frankincense that the imagination offers continually before all that it loves' (*WR*). In the story 'The Binding of the Hair' Aodh (a variant spelling) is a bard who exercises his poetic powers on the queen: 'the enchantment of his dream-heavy voice was in her ears; the enchantment of his dream-distraught history in her mind: how he would live now in the raths of kings, now alone in the great forest; how, despite the grey hairs mingling before their time with the dark of his beard, he was blown hither and thither by love and anger.' Aodh is beheaded by 'The nations with ignoble bodies and ragged beards', yet he continues to sing in the form of a severed head (the poem is 'He gives his Beloved certain Rhymes'). For Hanrahan, see note to '[The poet, Owen Hanrahan, under a bush of may]'. Robartes, who was based on Yeats's friend Samuel Liddell MacGregor Mathers (see note to 'All Souls' Night'), is described in the story 'Rosa Alchemica': his 'wild red hair, fierce eyes, sensitive, tremulous lips and rough clothes, made him look ... something between a debauchee, a saint, and a peasant'. Unlike Aedh and Hanrahan, he features in Yeats's later poetry, though somewhat changed, and any close conjunction between the fictional character and the figure in the poems must remain problematic.

Yeats once intended *A Vision* to be formed by a series of Robartes papers, while in the Preface to *MRD* he also announced a hope 'that my selection from the great mass of his letters and table talk, which I owe to his friend John Aherne, may be published before, or at any rate but soon after this little book'. Yeats's lengthy explanatory notes for 'An Image from a Past Life' and 'The Second Coming', both of which were published in *MRD*, are attributed to communications from Robartes to Aherne. *AV*, 1937, ultimately included 'Stories of Michael Robartes and his Friends' (first published in 1931) as well as 'The Phases of the Moon', which features a dialogue between Robartes and Aherne. Yeats also wrote but discarded 'Appendix by Michael Robartes', which was originally intended for *AV*, 1925, and 'Michael Robartes Foretells', which was intended for *AV*, 1937 (see Hood).

The Hosting of the Sidhe

First published as 'The Faery Host' in the *National Observer*, 7 October 1893, and as 'The Host' in *CT*, 1893. 'The powerful and wealthy called the gods of ancient Ireland the Tuatha De Danaan, or the Tribes of the goddess Danu, but the poor called them, and still sometimes call them, the Sidhe [pronounced *Shee*], from Aes Sidhe or Sluagh Sidhe, the people of the Faery Hills ... Sidhe is also Gaelic for wind, and certainly the Sidhe have much to do with the wind. They journey in whirling winds, the winds that were called the dance of the daughters of Herodias in the Middle Ages ... If any one becomes too much interested in them, and sees them over much, he loses all interest in ordinary things ... The great of the old times are among the Tribes of Danu, and are kings and queens among them. Caolte [pronounced *Cweeltya*] was a companion of Fiann; and years after his death he appeared to a king in a forest, and was a flaming man, that he might lead him in the darkness. When the king asked him who he was, he said, "I am your candlestick,"' (*WR*). For Niamh and Knocknarea, see note to *The Wanderings of Oisin*.

The Everlasting Voices

First published in the *New Review*, January 1896.
4. Compare 'Who rise, wing above wing, flame above flame, / And, like a storm, cry the Ineffable Name' ('To Some I have Talked with by the Fire', lines 11–12).

Into the Twilight

First published as 'The Celtic Twilight' in the *National Observer*, 29 July 1893; as an epilogue to *CT*, 1893.

The Song of Wandering Aengus

First published as 'A Mad Song' in the *Sketch*, 4 August 1897; included in the story 'Red Hanrahan's Vision' in *SR*.
Title. *Aengus* 'The god of youth, beauty, and poetry. He reigned in

NOTES

Tir-nan-Oge, the country of the young' (*P*, 1895). 'Aengus is the most curious of all the gods. He seems both Hermes and Dionysus. He has some part in all enthusiasm' (Yeats to AE, ? August 1899, *Letters*). Yeats's note to the poem reports in detail on how the Tribes of Danu often take on the shape of fish.

The Song of the Old Mother

First published in the *Bookman*, April 1894. 'The "seed of the fire" is the Irish phrase for the little fragment of burning turf and hot ashes which remains in the hearth from the day before' (Yeats's note after the text in the *Bookman*).

The Lover mourns for the Loss of Love

First published in the *Dome*, May 1898, as the second of Three Songs headed 'Aodh to Dectora'; in *WR*, 'Aedh laments the Loss of Love'.
    2. *beautiful friend* Olivia Shakespear ('Diana Vernon' in Yeats's *AU*), wife of a solicitor and eventually mother-in-law of Ezra Pound; she and Yeats had an affair in 1896 that lasted a year, though their friendship lasted until her death in 1938. 'I wrote her several poems, all curiously elaborate in style ... and thought I was once more in love. I noticed that she was like the wild heroines of my plays.' 6. *your image* Maud Gonne (1865–1953), whose statuesque beauty deeply affected Yeats and left its impress on his life and work. He was also influenced by her passionate commitment to nationalist politics, although he later exaggerated this influence and minimised his own nationalist tendencies. Yeats also believed that Maud Gonne's beauty was misplaced among the abstractions of politics and threatened by her public activities. She is a frequent but unnamed presence behind much of his love poetry.

He mourns for the Change that has come upon him and his Beloved, and longs for the End of the World

First published as 'The Desire of Man and of Woman' in the *Dome*, June 1897; in *WR* retitled 'Mongan laments the Change ...'. A note by Yeats in 1897 relates some of the details to the images of desire in the old Celtic stories. 'The man with the wand of hazel may well have been Angus, Master of Love; and the boar without bristles is the ancient Celtic image of the darkness which will at last destroy the world, as it destroys the sun at nightfall in the west.' For Mongan, see note to 'He thinks of his Past Greatness, when a Part of the Constellations of Heaven'.

He reproves the Curlew

First published as 'Windle-straws. I O'Sullivan Rua to the Curlew' in the *Savoy*, November 1896. In *WR* retitled 'Hanrahan reproves the Curlew'.

O'Sullivan Rua (or the Red), to whom the poem was first attributed, was Eoghan Ruadh Ó Súilleabháin, or Owen Roe O'Sullivan in Anglicised form (1748–84), a Munster peasant poet who was still a potent presence in the oral tradition and who provided one of the models for Red Hanrahan. In 'The Twisting of the Rope' (*National Observer*, 24 December 1892; revised in 1897 as 'The Twisting of the Rope and Hanrahan the Red') Yeats imagines O'Sullivan walking from Munster to Connaught: 'day by day as he wandered slowly and aimlessly he passed deeper and deeper into that great Celtic twilight, that shadowy sunset of the Gaelic world, in which heaven and earth so mingle that each one seems to have taken upon itself some shadow of the other's tragedy' (1892).

He remembers Forgotten Beauty

First published as 'O'Sullivan Rua to Mary Lavell' in the *Savoy*, July 1896. In *WR* retitled 'Michael Robartes remembers Forgotten Beauty'.

To his Heart, bidding it have no Fear

First published in the *Savoy*, November 1896, as 'Windle-Straws. II Out of the Old Days'. In *WR* retitled 'To my Heart, bidding it have no Fear'.
    7. Compare 'the embattled flaming multitude' ('To Some I have Talked with by the Fire', line 10).

The Valley of the Black Pig

First published in the *Savoy*, April 1896, as the second of 'Two Poems concerning Peasant Visionaries'. Yeats's lengthy note includes the following details: 'All over Ireland there are prophecies of the coming rout of the enemies of Ireland, in a certain Valley of the Black Pig, and these prophecies are, no doubt, now, as they were in the Fenian days, a political force . . . A few years before my time, an old man who lived at Lissadell, in Sligo, used to fall down in a fit and rave out descriptions of the Battle; and a man in Sligo has told me that it will be so great a battle that the horses shall go up to their fetlocks in blood, and that their girths, when it is over, will rot from their bellies for lack of a hand to unbuckle them . . . I suggest that the battle between the Tribes of the goddess Danu, the powers of light, and warmth, and fruitfulness, and goodness, and the Fomor, the powers of darkness, and cold, and barrenness, and badness upon the Towery Plain, was the establishment of the habitable world, the rout of the ancestral darkness; that the battle among the Sidhe for the harvest is the annual battle of summer and winter; that the battle among the Sidhe at a man's death is the battle of life and death; and that the Battle of the Black Pig is the battle between the manifest world and the ancestral darkness at the end of all things; and that all these battles are one, the battle of all things with shadowy decay. Once a symbolism has possessed the imagination of large numbers of men, it becomes, as I believe, an embodiment of disembodied powers, and repeats itself in dreams and visions, age after age' (*WR*). In his essay 'War' Yeats recalls a conversation with an old Sligo woman: 'And presently our talk of war shifted . . . to the Battle of the Black Pig, which seems to her a battle between Ireland and England, but to me an Armageddon which shall quench all things in the Ancestral Darkness again' (*CT*, 1902).

The Secret Rose

First published in the *Savoy*, September 1896, as 'O'Sullivan Rua to the Secret Rose'. The story of the love of Cuchulain for the goddess Fand is 'one of the most beautiful of our old tales'. 'When Cuchulain saw her going, his love for her fell upon him again, and he went mad, and wandered among the mountains without food or drink, until he was at last cured by a Druid drink of forgetfulness.' Emer was his mortal wife.

Yeats's interest in the symbol of the rose was given particular point and focus by his association with the Hermetic Order of the Golden Dawn and with the mystic rituals and images of Rosicrucianism (see note to 'The Mountain Tomb'); these sometimes included a 'mystic marriage' between rose and cross. Yeats also published a volume of stories under the title of *The Secret Rose* (1897). The back cover design was 'intended to make the book resemble a *grimoire*' (Ellmann, *The Identity of Yeats*); it is also suggestively similar to the textbook of the magical order described in 'Rosa Alchemica' (*SR*), which shows a cross, a four-petalled rose, the serpentine Tree of Life and the kissing heads of a man and woman. While the back cover of *SR* bears a precise resemblance to the cover of the book described in 'Rosa Alchemica', the front cover resembles the front cover of the book as described in cancelled page proofs of the story (O'Donnell). Another sacred book is described in 'The Tables of the Law'. For some later implications of this approach to the book, see Hugh Kenner, 'The Sacred Book of the Arts': 'Against the poet as force of nature he placed . . . the poet as deliberate personality, and correspondingly against the usual "Collected Poems" (arranged in the order of composition) he placed the oeuvre, the deliberated artistic Testament, a division of that new Sacred Book of the Arts of which, Mr Pound has recalled, he used to talk. It was as a process of fragmentation, into little people and little poems, that he viewed the history of European poetry, from the *Canterbury Tales* to the Collected Poems of, say, Lord Byron.'

16. *him . . . liss* Caolte drove the gods out of their liss, or fort. 19. *dreaming king* Fergus (see notes to 'Fergus and the Druid'). 22. *him who sold tillage* This man features in a folktale in which he discovers a woman's lock of hair which shines in the darkness (*WR*).

The Travail of Passion

First published in the *Savoy*, January 1896; with 'The Shadowy Horses' (later 'He bids his Beloved be at Peace') as one of 'Two Love Poems'.

Title. *Travail* Trouble, hardship, suffering. See *SR*: 'He was of those ascetics of passion who keep their hearts pure for love or for hatred as other men for God, for Mary and for the Saints, and who, when the hour of their visitation arrives, come to the Divine Essence by the bitter tumult, the Garden of Gethsemane, and the desolate Rood ordained for immortal passions in mortal hearts.' 5. *hissop* Hyssop is a plant, the twigs of which are used for sprinkling in Jewish rites (*OED*). In 'Rosa Alchemica' Michael Robartes brings incense: 'I got it from an old man in Syria, who said it was made from flowers, of one kind with the flowers that laid their heavy purple petals upon the hands and upon the hair and upon the feet of Christ, in the Garden of Gethsemane, and folded Him in their heavy breath, until He cried against the cross and his destiny' (*SR*); *Kedron* (Kidron) A stream which flows between Jerusalem and the Mount of Olives.

The Lover pleads with his Friend for Old Friends

First published as 'Song' in the *Saturday Review*, July 1897; in *WR* retitled 'The Poet pleads with his Friend for Old Friends'. See: '"Time's bitter flood!" Oh, that's all very well, / But where's the old friend hasn't fallen off, / Or slacked his hand-grip when you first gripped fame?' (Ezra Pound, 'In Exitum Cuiusdam', *Ripostes*, 1912).

The Lover speaks to the Hearers of his Songs in Coming Days

First published in the story 'The Vision of O'Sullivan [Hanrahan in *SR*] the Red' in the *New Review*, April 1896; retitled 'Hanrahan speaks to the Lovers of his Songs in Coming Days'; in 1906 'A Lover . . .'. 'His fingers began to play with the wires of the little square harp and his lips to murmur as the mood shaped itself into a song; and presently he sang to the now forgotten tune so full of fathomless regret, despite its uncouth name, "The Herdsmen of the Children of Byrne" ["The Herdsmen of Roughley O'Byrne", 1896]' (*SR*); the poem follows.

8. *pentitential throng* The souls in Purgatory.

He wishes his Beloved were Dead

First published as 'Aodh to Dectora' in the *Sketch*, 9 February 1898; in *WR* retitled 'Aedh wishes his Beloved were Dead'.

He wishes for the Cloths of Heaven

First published as 'Aedh wishes for the Cloths of Heaven' in *WR*.

He thinks of his Past Greatness when a Part of the Constellations of Heaven

First published as 'Song of Mongan' in the *Dome*, October 1898; in *WR* retitled 'Mongan thinks . . .'. 'Mongan, in the old Celtic poetry, is a famous wizard and king who remembers his passed lives. "The Country of the Young" is a name in the Celtic poetry for the country of the gods and of the happy dead. The hazel tree was the Irish tree of Life or of Knowledge, and in Ireland it was doubtless, as elsewhere, the tree of the heavens. The Crooked Plough and the Pilot Star are translations of the Gaelic names of the Plough and Pole Star' (Yeats's note after the text in the *Dome*).

3ff. See the pattern of metamorphosis in 'Fergus and the Druid', lines 31–7 and in 'Mohini Chatterjee'. In 'Kanva on Himself' (printed in *WO* but thereafter excluded from the canon) Yeats provided a still earlier version of the theme: 'Now wherefore hast thou tears innumerous? / Hast thou not known all sorrow and delight / . . . Hast thou not sat of yore upon the knees / Of myriads of beloveds, and on thine / Have not a myriad swayed below strange trees / In other lives?' (lines 1–2, 9–12). See the account of 'Dreaming Back' in *A Vision*. For another modern version of reincarnation, see T. S. Eliot's 'The Death of Saint Narcissus'.

[I walked among the Seven Woods of Coole]

First published as 'Introduction to a Dramatic Poem' in the *Speaker*, 1 December 1900; untitled dedication to *The Shadowy Waters* (1900), from which the present text is derived (the 1906 version differs in spelling, punctuation and one minor substantive detail). After 1900 it was not printed as a separate poem. The Seven Woods were a feature of the estate at Coole Park in Co. Galway, owned by Isabella Augusta Gregory (1852–1932), whom Yeats first met in 1896 and who was the hearer and heartener of his work. Yeats assisted Lady Gregory in her collection of Irish folklore for *Visions and Beliefs in the West of Ireland* (1920) and collaborated with her in the writing of prose and plays, and in the creation and management of a national theatre for Ireland. Forgael and Dectora are the central characters in a play which went through several stages, with first publication in 1900, a revised version in 1906 which Yeats descibed as 'entirely new', and an acting version in 1907. Yeats claimed that it was 'woven to a very great extent out of certain visionary experiences'. He wrote of it in a letter of 1904: 'I would not now do anything so remote, so impersonal . . . The whole picture as it were moves together – sky and sea and cloud are as it were actors. It is almost religious, it is more a ritual than a human story. It is deliberately without human characters.' The dedicatory verses ignore those markedly Anglo-Irish elements which feature so strongly in later celebrations of Coole. Compare the resonances of the Gaelic name in the coda to *R*, where Yeats looks forward to finding 'when June is come / At Kyle-na-no under that ancient roof / A sterner conscience and a friendlier home' ('[*While I, from that reed-throated whisperer*]', lines 6–8). Yeats was obviously influenced by his recent experiences of collecting local folklore with Lady Gregory, and the Gaelic element comes out strongly in the place-names.

15. *Biddy Early* A 'famous Clare witch' who had been dead 'some twenty years'. She is the central focus in Yeats's 'Ireland Bewitched', which was based on Lady Gregory's collection of folk materials and which appeared in September 1899. 'She is believed to have journeyed all over the country with the fairies.'

IN THE SEVEN WOODS

Poems under this heading in the present selection were collected by Yeats from *ISW* and from *P*, 1906. 'I made some of these poems walking about among the Seven Woods, before the big wind of nineteen hundred and three blew down so many trees, & troubled the wild creatures, & changed the look of things' (*ISW*). The volume was subtitled 'Being Poems chiefly of the Irish Heroic Age'.

In the Seven Woods

First published in *ISW*. For the Seven Woods, see note to '[I walked among the Seven Woods of Coole]'. The sylvan idyll of Coole is set against the disturbance of Tara, the legendary seat of the High Kings of Ireland, by English excavators in search of the Ark of the Covenant (which provoked Yeats to complain to *The Times*).

6. *new commonness* This is in keeping with his attitude to the visit of Queen Victoria to Ireland in 1900: 'What can these Royal Processions mean to those who walk in the procession of heroic and enduring hearts that has followed Kathleen Ny Hoolihan through the ages? Have they not given her their wills and their hearts and their dreams? What have they left for any less noble Royalty?' ('Noble and Ignoble Loyalties', *United Irishman*, 21 April 1900). 7–9. A reference to the coronation celebrations of Edward VII.

The Folly of Being Comforted

First published in the *Speaker*, 11 January 1902.

Adam's Curse

First published in the *Monthly Review*, December 1902. According to Maud Gonne in *A Servant of the Queen* (1938), the poem is based on a conversation between Yeats, herself and her sister Kathleen, who 'remarked that it was hard work being beautiful'. For Adam's curse, see Genesis 3:17–19, where God tells Adam, 'In the sweat of thy face shalt thou eat bread, till thou return unto the ground.' The woman's speech and especially 'we must labour to be beautiful' is a reminder that the curse also extended to Eve, who was told, 'In sorrow thou shalt bring forth children.' Yeats wrote of 'the heroic discipline of the looking-glass' (*Discoveries*, 1906). See '[A woman's beauty is like a white]' and note.

Red Hanrahan's Song about Ireland

First published in the *National Observer*, 4 August 1894, in the story 'Kathleen-ny-Hoolihan', where the central figure is O'Sullivan, not Hanrahan; in 'Kathleen the Daughter of Hoolihan and Hanrahan the Red' in *SR*; in 'Hanrahan and Cathleen the Daughter of Hoolihan' in *Stories of Red Hanrahan* (1905). The stories provide a precise context and an audience for the poem. '"It is not of that I am thinking," he said, "but of Ireland and the weight of grief that is on her." And he leaned his head against his hand, and began to sing these words, and the sound of his voice was like the wind in a lonely place' (*Stories of Red Hanrahan*, 1905, and later versions). '"No," he said, laying his hand upon her head, "I am thinking of Ireland and her sorrows." Then he began to sing these words to a wild and fitful air of his own making which rose and fell like the cry of the wind' (*SR*). 'While he was singing, his voice began to break, and tears came rolling down his cheeks, and Margaret Rooney put down her face into her hands and began to cry along with him. Then a blind beggar by the fire shook his rags with a sob, and after that there was no one of them all but cried tears down' (1905). 'While he sang he became greatly moved, and a tear rolled down his cheek, and Margaret Rooney put her face upon her hands and wept too. Then a blind beggar by the fire shook his rags with a sob, and after that every one wept and tossed about as does Shroon-a-Melea when the tide runs strong and the wind blows high' (1894). Yeats's patriotic play *Cathleen ni Houlihan* (1902) was also based on this traditional personification of Ireland. The title role was strikingly played by Maud Gonne (for the possible political consequences, see 'The Man and the Echo', line 11). For Maeve and Knocknarea, see note on *The Wanderings of Oisin*, line 184. Except for Drumahair (see 'The Man who Dreamed of Faeryland'), the place-names all refer to Co. Sligo. The rood is the cross; this both recalls the imagery of some of Yeats's early poems and accords with his remark that this song 'embodied the tragic patriotism of Catholic Ireland', which was to be distinguished from that of Protestant Anglo-Ireland (Torchiana). The 'black wind that blows from the left hand' is an evil omen. For a more elaborate system of winds, see the passage from 'The Adoration of the Magi' (1897), where a dying woman is asked to reveal the names of the immortals and tells, among other things, of 'the immortals of Ireland and of their love for the cauldron, and the whetstone, and the sword, and the spear, and the hills of the Shee, and the horns of the moon, and the Grey Wind, and the Yellow Wind, and the Black Wind, and the Red Wind' (see also note on 'An Irish Airman Foresees his Death').

The Old Men Admiring Themselves in the Water

First published in the *Pall Mall Magazine*, January 1903.

O Do Not Love Too Long

First published in the *Acorn*, October 1905.

[The friends that have it I do wrong]

First published as 'Preliminary Poem' in Vol. 2 of *CW*; not in *CP*, 1933, or *CP*, 1949, in fact, never reprinted by Yeats.

From THE GREEN HELMET AND OTHER POEMS

Although Yeats dates this section 1910, there were two editions of *The Green Helmet* (1910 and 1912). Most of the poems selected here appeared in the 1910 volume; those which first appeared in 1912 are specifically indicated in the notes. The 1910 volume concludes with *The Green Helmet: An Heroic Farce*, which matches the tone of some of the poems. This is a revision in verse form of the prose play *The Golden Helmet* (1908), which centres on Cuchulain and which presents a satirical picture of Irish discord. See, for example, 'Here neighbour wars on neighbour and why there is no man knows, / And if a man is lucky all wish his luck away, / And take his good name from him between a day and a day' (lines 16–18). Yeats's application of the Homeric myth can be compared to Joyce's use of 'Troy measure' in *Ulysses*; it may perhaps owe something to Ronsard. In 'Dust Hath Closed Helen's Eye' (*CT*, 1902) Yeats suggests that the figure of Helen of Troy engaged the imaginations of country people: 'though they can be hard, they grow gentle as the old men of Troy grew gentle when Helen passed by on the walls'.

A Woman Homer Sung

First published in *GH*, 1910, under the general title 'Raymond Lully and his wife Pernella' together with 'His Dream', 'Words', 'No Second Troy', 'Reconciliation', 'King and No King', 'Peace' and 'Against Unworthy Praise'. An erratum slip reads: 'By a slip of the pen when I was writing out the heading for the first group of poems, I put Raymond Lully's name in the room of the later Alchemist, Nicolas Flamel.' For Yeats's interest in Ramon Lully (*c.* 1232?–1315), Catalan philosopher and missionary to the Moors, and in Nicolas Flamel (*c.* 1330–1417), Parisian scribe and alchemist, see the description of the library of Michael Robartes in 'Rosa Alchemica' (*SR*); this library included the works 'of Lully, who transformed himself into the likeness of a red cock; of Flamel, who with his wife Parnella [suggestive misprint for *Pernella*] achieved the elixir many hundreds of years ago, and is fabled to live still in Arabia among the Dervishes'. George Mills Harper (*Yeats's Golden Dawn*) has discovered that 'Pernelle the wife and fellow worker of Nicolas Flamel' was referred to in a lecture to Neophytes in the Hermetic Order of the Golden Dawn first given by William Wynn Westcott in 1888. By his own account Yeats envisaged the close conjunction between Flamel and his wife as a model for his relationship with Maud Gonne: 'We ... were initiated in the Hermetic

Students, and I began to form plans of our lives devoted to mystic truth, and spoke to her of Nicolas Flamel and his wife, Pernella. In a propaganda, secret and seeking out only the most profound and subtle minds, that great beauty would be to others, as it was always to me, symbolic and mysterious' (*M*). While Yeats was writing the sequence of poems which he associated with Flamel, he and Maud Gonne experienced a series of mystic visions which were recorded but not published (Harper). Yeats's interest in Ramon Lully is also illuminated by a passage in 'Rosa Alchemica'. The narrator, who recognises that 'even in my most perfect moment I would be two selves, the one watching with heavy eyes the other's moment of content', buys a set of alchemical apparatus which may have belonged to Lully: 'I understood the alchemical doctrine, that all beings, divided from the great deep where spirits wander, one and yet a multitude, are weary; and sympathised . . . with the consuming thirst for destruction which made the alchemist veil under his symbols of lions and dragons, of eagles and ravens, of dew and of nitre, a search for an essence which would dissolve all mortal things' (*SR*).

The 'Woman Homer Sung' was Helen of Troy. This poem and the next four are all centred on Maud Gonne, the daughter of a British army officer (Assistant Adjutant-General in Dublin, with leanings towards Home Rule); she had long been the object of Yeats's unrequited affections and the inspiration of many of his early love poems. In 1903 she married Major John MacBride (who had fought against the British in the Boer War and who was to be executed after the Easter rising of 1916) but separated from him in 1906. (See 'The People' and 'The Leaders of the Crowd' and note to 'The Lover mourns for the Loss of Love', line 6.) In 1902 Maud Gonne acted the title role in *Cathleen ni Houlihan* with such electrical consequences that Yeats later wondered, 'Did that play of mine send out / Certain men the English shot?' ('The Man and the Echo', lines 11–12).

The Fascination of What's Difficult

First published in *GH*, 1910, with ten other poems under the general title of 'Momentary Thoughts'. The poem continues the Greek mythological strain by introducing Pegasus, the winged horse, and Olympus, the mountain home of the gods. It also refers to Yeats's work in the management of the Abbey Theatre. Yeats's plan for the poem involved using the word *difficult* three times at the line-ending. The draft of lines 10–11 at one stage took this form: 'On the day's letters / Theatre business / On correspondence, management of men' (*M*).

8. *road metal* Broken stone used for macadamising roads.

The Coming of Wisdom with Time

First published as 'Youth and Age' in *McClure's Magazine*, December 1910.

On hearing that the Students of our New University have joined the Agitation against Immoral Literature

First published in *GH*, 1912, as 'On hearing . . . joined the Ancient Order of Hibernians and the Agitation . . .'. The Royal University (later the National University of Ireland) was founded in 1908. The Ancient Order of Hibernians was a sectarian organisation which 'drew its main strength from Ulster, where it represented the Catholic reaction to the Orange Order'. By about 1909 it had 60,000 members in Ireland (Lyons, *Ireland since the Famine*). See Yeats's note of 1927 to *P*, 1895, where he recalls that 'The Politician or the newspaper persuaded some forty Catholic students to sign a protest' against *The Countess Kathleen*.

The Mask

First published in *GH*, 1910, as 'A Lyric from an Unpublished Play' (*The Player Queen*, 1922) under the heading 'Momentary Thoughts'. For Yeats's doctrine of the mask, see *TV*: 'Among subjective men (in all those, that is, who must spin a web out of their own bowels) the victory is an intellectual daily re-creation of all that exterior fate snatches away, while what I have called "The Mask" is an emotional antithesis to all that comes out of their internal nature. We begin to live when we have conceived life as tragedy.'

Upon a House shaken by the Land Agitation

First published in *McClure's Magazine*, December 1910, as 'To a Certain Country House in Time of Change'; in *GH*, 1910, under the heading 'Momentary Thoughts'. The house is Coole Park, home of the Gregory family (see note to *ISW*). 'The gifts that govern men' encompass, among other family achievements, the career of the late Sir William Gregory (died 1892) in colonial administration, while 'the written speech' refers to Lady Gregory's development of 'Kiltartan' dialect based on the speech of local people which was still close to its Gàelic roots. The poem was inspired by legislation of 1909 (including the Land Purchase Act), which imposed new taxes on landowners such as Lady Gregory, and by the Land Commissioner's decision of 30 July that the rents of her tenants ('Mean roof-trees') should be reduced by approximately 20 per cent. For Yeats's concern with the fate of the great house and its traditions, see *Purgatory*, lines 74–6: 'to kill a house / Where great men grew up, married, died, / I here declare a capital offence'. See also 'The New Faces', 'Coole Park, 1929' and 'Coole Park and Ballylee, 1931'.

2. See a letter of 1912 in which Yeats thanks the scholar H. J. C. Grierson for a copy of his edition of Donne; Yeats noticed 'that the more precise and learned the thought the greater the beauty, the passion; the intricacy and subtleties of his imagination are the length and depths of the furrow made by his passion'. 4. *lidless eye* Of the eagle. 7. See *OTB*: 'It may be, or it must be, that the best bred from the best shall claim again their ancient omens.' See

also *M*: 'One feels always that where all must make their living they will not live for life's sake but the work's, and all be the poorer.'

At the Abbey Theatre

First published in *GH*, 1912. The poem is addressed to Douglas Hyde (1860–1949), whose pseudonym was *An Craoibhín Aoibhinn* (The Pleasant Little Branch). Hyde was a poet who captured in his translations from the Irish, such as *Love Songs of Connacht* (1893), something of the syntactical and linguistic flavour of the originals. Yeats celebrated what 'seemed all spontaneous, all joyous, every speech born out of itself' and thought Hyde 'had the folk mind as no modern man has had it, its qualities and its defects'; he also regretted a failure to apply those talents and to make the most of those materials which might have turned him into 'another and happier Synge' (*DP*). Hyde founded the Gaelic League and became the first President of the new Irish state. Yeats's poem is a version of a sonnet by Ronsard.

11. *Proteus* An old man of the sea whose elusiveness was based on his ability to change shape.

At Galway Races

First published as 'Galway Races' in the *English Review*, February 1909; in *GH*, 1910, under the heading 'Momentary Thoughts'.

All Things can Tempt Me

First published as 'Distraction' in the *English Review*, February 1909; in *GH*, 1910, under the heading 'Momentary Thoughts'.

Brown Penny

First published in *GH*, 1910, as 'The Young Man's Song' under the heading 'Momentary Thoughts'.

RESPONSIBILITIES

The poems from this volume included in the present selection first appeared in book form in *The Green Helmet* (1912), *A Selection from the Poetry of W. B. Yeats* (1913), *Poems Written in Discouragement* (1913) and *Nine Poems* (1914). (*Poems Written in Discouragement* comprised 'To a Wealthy Man who promised a Second Subscription to the Dublin Municipal Gallery if it were proved the People wanted Pictures', 'September 1913', 'To a Friend whose Work has come to Nothing', 'Paudeen' and 'To a Shade'.) There are two epigraphs: 'In dreams begins responsibility' (Old Play) and 'How am I fallen from myself, for a long time now / I have not seen the Prince of Chang in my dreams' (Khoung-Fou-Tseu).

[Pardon, old fathers, if you still remain]

Dated 1912–14 in *R*, December 1913 in Ellmann's *The Identity of Yeats*. Inspired by George Moore's attack in extracts from *Vale* which appeared in the *English Review* in January and February 1914. Moore maliciously reported that when Yeats 'spoke the words, the middle classes, one would have thought that he was speaking against a personal foe' and wondered why 'our Willie Yeats should feel himself called upon to denounce his own class; millers and shipowners on one side, and on the other a portrait-painter of distinction'. The poem invokes ancestors among Yeatses, Pollexfens, Butlers and Armstrongs. Yeats made two mistakes. In 1914 he acknowledged one misapprehension: '"Free of ten and four" is an error I cannot now correct, without more rewriting than I have a mind for. Some merchant in Villon, I forget the reference, was "free of the ten and four". Irish merchants exempted from certain duties by the Irish Parliament were, unless memory deceives me again, ... "Free of the eight and six" [six and ten per cent tax].' The first version of lines 9–12 was also based on an incorrect assumption – that some of his ancestors had supported James II against William of Orange at the Battle of the Boyne in 1690. This error was not corrected till 1929. The 'barren passion' was Yeats's unrequited love for Maud Gonne.

8. *huckster's* Retailer of small goods, in a petty shop or booth, or at a stall; pedlar, hawker (*OED*).

September 1913

First published in the *Irish Times* on 8 September 1913 as 'Romance in Ireland (On reading much of the correspondence against the Art Gallery)'. In a note dated 1914 Yeats refers to the controversies over Parnell, Synge's *Playboy of the Western World* and the refusal of the Dublin Corporation to provide a building for the collection of pictures assembled by Lady Gregory's nephew, Sir Hugh Lane. 'These controversies, political, literary, and artistic, have showed that neither religion nor politics can of itself create minds with enough receptivity to become wise, or just and generous enough to make a nation ... Against all this [the influences of religion and politics] we have but a few educated men and the remnants of an old traditional culture among the poor. Both were stronger forty years ago, before the rise of our new middle class which made its first public display during the nine years of the Parnellite split, showing how base ... at moments of excitement are minds without culture.' The poem appeared at a moment of great political tension in Dublin, following a sequence of labour disturbances, public meetings, police intervention and rioting. Yeats did not mention this specifically in the poem, though he did contribute a letter to James Connolly's *Irish Worker* in November; nor did he mention the charismatic labour leader James Larkin, whom Constance Markievicz described as 'some great primeval force, rather than a man'. Yet he was probably affected by the lockout of strikers in Dublin, in which the employers were led by William Martin Murphy, the Catholic proprietor of the *Irish Independent* who incorrectly assumed that he had been attacked for tight-fisted philistinism in 'To a Wealthy Man . . .'.

8. *O'Leary* John O'Leary (1830–1907), a Fenian who had been released from penal servitude, exercised a major influence on the young Yeats through his striking appearance and the generous and literary patriotism of his old age. In his Introduction to *The Words upon the Window Pane* (dated 1931, published 1934), Yeats recalled how O'Leary read the poems of Thomas Davis: 'though he never thought them good poetry they shaped his future life, gave him the moral simplicity that made him so attractive to young men in his old age, but we can no longer permit life to be shaped by a personified ideal, we must serve with all our faculties some actual thing. The old service was moral, at times lyrical; we discussed perpetually the character of public men and never asked were they able or well-informed, but what would they sacrifice? How many times did I hear on the lips of J. F. Taylor these words: "Holy, delicate white hands"? His patriotism was a religion, never a philosophy.' Yeats also declared that O'Leary belonged to 'the romantic conception of nationality on which Lionel Johnson and myself founded, so far as it was founded on anything but literature, our art and our Irish criticism.' 17. *wild geese* Those who left Ireland in 1691 to serve in the armies of Catholic Europe after the defeat of James II (described in *KGCT* as 'those Catholic gentlemen who, in the words of Swift, carried into foreign service "a valour" above "that of all nations"'). 20–21. Mentioned here are three revolutionaries of Protestant origin who gave their lives for the nationalist cause, Lord Edward Fitzgerald (1763–98), Robert Emmet (1778–1803) and Theobald Wolfe Tone (1763–98).

To a Friend whose Work has come to Nothing

First published in *PWD*. By Yeats's own account, addressed to Lady Gregory; her dishonourable but unnamed antagonist is William Martin Murphy.

Paudeen

First published in *PWD*. Paudeen is the diminutive of Patrick and may be taken here to represent less than a flattering racial archetype (see 'Let Paudeens play at pitch and toss' in 'To a Wealthy Man . . .'), marking Yeats's distaste for an emergent Catholic middle class and for the imperatives of commerce.

To a Shade

First published in *PWD*. Addressed to Charles Stewart Parnell (1846–91), the leader of the Irish Parliamentary Party who was buried in Glasnevin Cemetery in Dublin and whose tragically early death was the subject of the poem 'Mourn – And Then Onward!' Here Parnell is aligned with Hugh Lane and set against 'an old foul mouth', which may suggest the eternal enmity between the noble and the malicious but which can also be seen as a reference to William Martin Murphy and the power of the press. Murphy (see note to 'September 1913') had played a leading part in the movement to depose Parnell in 1890 after the public scandal of his affair with Katharine O'Shea and the subsequent proceedings. See 'Parnell's Funeral'.

Beggar to Beggar Cried

First published in *Poetry*, May 1914. *R* also focuses on beggars in 'The Three Beggars' and 'The Hour before Dawn'.

4. *make my soul* To prepare for death (see 'The Tower', line 181, and Yeats's remark that 'it is right for an old man to make his soul', which is one of the themes of 'Sailing to Byzantium').

Running to Paradise

First published in *Poetry*, May 1914.

I The Witch
II The Peacock

First published separately in *Poetry*, May 1914; as a pair in *R*. Ezra Pound, who stayed with Yeats at Stone Cottage, Coleman's Hatch, Sussex, in the winter of 1913 was responsible for the publication of these poems in *Poetry*. In *The Cantos* he associated the opening lines of 'The Peacock' with the experience of hearing Yeats composing his poetry 'as it were the wind in the chimney' (*Cantos*, 83). See Whistler's plan for 'a great peacock ten feet high'.

II. 5. *Three Rock* This may be Three Rock Mountain near Dublin.

The Mountain Tomb

First published in *Poetry*, December 1912. In 'The Body of the Father Christian Rosencrux' (first printed as the opening paragraph in the essay 'Contemporary Irish Poets', third part of the series 'Irish National Literature' in the *Bookman*, September 1895; later in *Ideas of Good and Evil*, 1903), Yeats explained the tradition that the members of the Rosicrucian order 'wrapped his imperishable body in noble raiment and laid it under the house of their Order, in a tomb containing the symbols of all things in heaven and earth, and in the waters under the earth, and set about him inextinguishable magical lamps'. The myth of Christian Rosencreuz had an influence on the initiatory ritual of the Order of the Golden Dawn. In his unfinished autobiographical novel *The Speckled Bird* Yeats parodies this ritual when his hero discovers a body 'lying on his back and quite naked' in 'a long box slightly tipped on one end with a lid of orange glass'. He applied this Rosicrucian myth to the history of the imagination which had been laid 'in a great tomb of criticism' for two hundred years. For Yeats's interest in Rosicrucianism, see note to 'The Secret Rose'.

I To a Child Dancing in the Wind
II Two Years Later

The former first published in *Poetry*, December 1912; the latter in *Poetry*, May 1914. Both poems are addressed to Iseult Gonne, Maud's daughter by the French political journalist Lucien Millevoye.

A Memory of Youth

First published as 'Love and the Bird' in *Poetry*, December 1912. The unnamed woman is Maud Gonne.

Fallen Majesty

First published in *Poetry*, December 1912.
  8. Ezra Pound deleted *as it were*, but Yeats at first restored it before deleting it himself in 1913 (Ellmann, *The Identity of Yeats*).

The Magi

First published in *Poetry*, May 1914; paired with 'The Dolls' in *R*. Yeats remembered in a note to 'The Dolls': 'After I had made the poem, I looked up one day into the blue of the sky, and suddenly imagined, as if lost in the blue of the sky, stiff figures in procession. I remembered that they were the habitual image suggested by blue sky, and looking for a second fable called them "The Magi", complementary forms of those enraged dolls' (*R*). The Magi were the wise men from the East who came to Bethlehem, bearing gifts at the birth of Christ (in the poem they are unsatisfied by his death on Calvary). Yeats's early interest in this myth is revealed in his story 'The Adoration of the Magi' (1897), while in *WR* Michael Robartes is defined as 'the adoration of the Magi'. Yeats had a particular interest in the magus, exemplified by Father Christian Rosencreuz (see notes to 'The Secret Rose' and 'The Mountain Tomb') and by Michael Robartes, notably in 'Rosa Alchemica' (*SR*). Madame Blavatsky and MacGregor Mathers 'believed in the existence of magi and claimed to have been personally instructed by "masters" or magi' (O'Donnell). 'This belief that mortals could be turned into magi was the central organising principle for the Golden Dawn's ritual initiations' (Yeats had joined in 1890).

A Coat

First published in *Poetry*, May 1914.

[A woman's beauty is like a white]

First published in *Poetry*, January 1919, in *The Only Jealousy of Emer*. Sung at the opening of the play by the Musicians. It was not included by Yeats in any edition of his poetry. Yeats quotes from this song in *TV* when he analyses Maud Gonne's hatred for her own beauty, which demanded 'the denial or the dissolution of the self'. He claims that 'her whole body seemed a master-work of long labouring thought, as though a Scopas [Greek sculptor] had measured and calculated, consorted with Egyptian sages, and mathematicians out of Babylon'.

8. *sedentary* Requiring continuance in a sitting posture; see 'A style is found by sedentary toil' ('Ego Dominus Tuus', line 65) and 'sedentary trade' ('The Tower', line 180). 7–14. See 'Adam's Curse' and note. In *M* Yeats quotes Castiglione, who says, 'speaking the high Urbino thought, that all such beauty "is the spoil and monument of the victory of the soul"'. *Archimedes* Greek mathematician and inventor (*c*. 287–212 BC).

THE WILD SWANS AT COOLE

The first version of this volume was published in 1917 when it included *At the Hawk's Well*. The 1919 volume printed, in addition to the poems from the 1917 edition, material from *Nine Poems* (1918) and other poems which had not appeared previously in book form. The 1919 volume concludes with a sequence of eight poems which are derived from, or associated with, the automatic writing of Yeats's wife and which articulate his developing philosophical system. These poems are: 'Ego Dominus Tuus', 'A Prayer on Going into my House', 'The Phases of the Moon', 'The Cat and the Moon', 'The Saint and the Hunchback', 'Two Songs of a Fool', 'Another Song of a Fool' and 'The Double Vision of Michael Robartes'. Of these only one had appeared in *WSC* (1917) – this was 'Ego Dominus Tuus', identified as 'the germinal poem of the cycle' though it was 'more tentative than those that followed' (Sidnell).

The Wild Swans at Coole

First published in the *Little Review*, June 1917, when it was dated October 1916; in *WSC* (1917). In the *Little Review* version, lines 25–30 were placed between lines 12–13. For Coole, see notes to '[I walked among the seven woods of Coole]' and 'In the Seven Woods'. Yeats's depression was partly caused by Maud Gonne's recent refusal of his latest proposal of marriage. For swans and subjectivity, see note to 'The Tower'.

In Memory of Major Robert Gregory

First published in the *English Review*, August 1918; in *WSC*, 1919. Lady Gregory's son (born 1881) was killed in action as a member of the Royal Flying Corps on the Italian Front on 23 January 1918; his death is the focus of three other poems, 'Shepherd and Goatherd', 'An Irish Airman Foresees his

Death' and 'Reprisals' (not published till 1948). Robert Gregory was a sportsman, a painter who had worked at the atelier of Jacques Blanche, and a theatrical designer. The tower in the poem is the Norman tower Thoor Ballylee, which Yeats had bought in 1917; it was close to Coole Park and featured in one of Robert Gregory's pictures. Yeats associates Gregory with Lionel Johnson (1867–1902), one of the sources for Owen Aherne, dedicatee of 'The Rose', a fellow member of the Rhymers' Club whose works included *Ireland, with Other Poems* (1897), and a fellow worker in the interests of Irish literature whom Yeats anthologised as an Irish poet and with whom he collaborated on *Poetry and Ireland*, 1908 (see also note to 'September 1913'); with the playwright John Millington Synge (1871–1909), whom he celebrated in 'J. M. Synge and the Ireland of his Time'; and with his maternal uncle George Pollexfen (1839–1910). All three men feature in *AU*. Yeats's elegy makes an interesting comparison with his *Observer* obituary of 17 February 1918 ('A Note of Appreciation').

19. See 'Mystic and Cavalier': 'Go from me: I am one of those, who fall'. Johnson was notable for his falls, which were physical as well as moral, and involved hansom cabs, stairs and a final collapse in the Green Dragon in Fleet Street. 24. A reference to the concept of *Straminis Deflagratio* (burning of straw), which Yeats and Lionel Johnson discovered in their reading of Joachim de Fiore. As Warwick Gould has shown, this 'attempt to light the "fires of the Last Day"' is associated with Yeats's image of the arts as the destroyers of nations and finally of life itself; they sow 'everywhere unlimited desires, like torches thrown into a burning city'. See note to 'In Memory of Eva Gore-Booth and Con Markiewicz', lines 26ff. 39. *trine* denoting the 'aspect' of two heavenly bodies which are a third part of the Zodiac, i.e., 120° distant from each other (*OED*). 47. *Sidney* Sir Philip Sidney (1554–86), English poet and aristocrat, who died an exemplary death on a foreign field. 65–6. '. . . in a few years I came to care for his paintings of the Clare coast, with its cloud-shadows upon blue-grey stony hills, and for one painting of a not very different scenery by his friend, Innes, more than for any contemporary landscape painting' ('A Note of Appreciation'). 67–8. 'One always understood by something in his selection of line and of colour that he had read his Homer and his Virgil and his Dante; that they, while giving something of themselves, had freed him from easy tragedy and trivial comedy' ('A Note of Appreciation'). 70–72. 'Though he often seemed led away from his work by some other gift, his attitude to life and art never lost intensity – he was never the amateur. I have noticed that men whose lives are to be an ever-growing absorption in subjective beauty . . . seek through some lesser gift, or through mere excitement, to strengthen that self which unites them to ordinary men' ('A Note of Appreciation'). 74. *a house* Coole Park.

An Irish Airman Foresees his Death

For Robert Gregory, in whose voice this poem is delivered, and for Yeats's 'A Note of Appreciation', see notes to 'In Memory of Major Robert Gregory'.

Robert Gregory's 'lonely impulse of delight' suggests a Wordsworthian sensibility. For confirmation of this, see 'A Note of Appreciation': 'Is it merely that these men share certain moods with great lyric poetry, with, let us say, the "Leach Gatherer" [*sic*; correctly, 'Resolution and Independence'] of Wordsworth; or that their moods, unlike those of men with more objective curiosity, are a part of the traditional expression of the soul?' Gregory's attitude to death may also owe something to Yeats's reading of Nietzsche and to his interpretation of Cuchulain. Yeats was reported as claiming that his poem was written to express Protestant Irish patriotism, which 'was a hesitating thing, but had its own nobility, its own heroism' and which always involved a choice (see note on 'Red Hanrahan's Song about Ireland'). Compare 'September 1913' and the Introduction to *Fighting the Waves*: 'Here in Ireland we have come to think of self-sacrifice when worthy of public honour, as the act of some man at the moment when he is least himself, most completely the crowd. The heroic act, as it descends through tradition, is an act done because a man is himself, because, being himself, he can ask nothing of other men but room amid remembered tragedies; a sacrifice of himself to himself, almost, so little may he bargain, of the moment to the moment . . . So lonely is that ancient act, so great the pathos of its joy.'

5–6. *Kiltartan* A barony near Coole Park. The name came to be associated with the version of Irish-influenced English which Lady Gregory popularised in her plays and stories.

Men Improve with the Years

First published in the *Little Review*, June 1917, and dated 19 July 1916; in *WSC* (1917).

2. *triton* Sea-deity of semi-human form.

The Collar-Bone of a Hare

First published in the *Little Review*, June 1917, and dated 5 July 1915; in *WSC* (1917).

Solomon to Sheba

First published in the *Little Review*, October 1918; in *Nine Poems*. 'It seems to me that love, if it is fine, is essentially a discipline, but it needs so much wisdom that the love of Solomon and Sheba must have lasted for all the silence of the Scriptures. In wise love each divines the high secret self of the other and, refusing to believe in the mere daily self, creates a mirror where the lover or the beloved sees an image to copy in daily life. Love also creates the mask' (*M*). See 'The Mask'.

8. *pound* Place of confinement, originally used in the context of animals or goods which were detained by authority.

NOTES

The Living Beauty

First published in the *Little Review*, October 1918; in *Nine Poems*. According to Jeffares, the poem refers to Maud Gonne's daughter Iseult, whom Yeats unsuccessfully attempted to marry in 1917.

A Song

First published in the *Little Review*, October 1918; in *Nine Poems*. In lines 3–4 Yeats may be recalling the fencing lessons which he received from Ezra Pound when they shared Stone Cottage in the winter of 1913. Yeats used his experience of fencing to provide an image for his encounter with the spirit world both in *PASL* and in his letters to Leo Africanus (see Adams and Harper, 'The Manuscript of Leo Africanus'). 'It was only by watching my own plays that I came to understand that this reverie, this twilight between sleep and waking, this bout of fencing, alike on the stage and in the mind, between man and phantom, this perilous path as on the edge of a sword, is the condition of tragic pleasure, and to understand why it is so rare and so brief' (Preface to *Plays for an Irish Theatre*, 1911).

The Scholars

First published in the *Catholic Anthology* in 1915; in *WSC* (1917). The *Catholic Anthology* was edited by Ezra Pound and included T. S. Eliot's 'The Love Song of J. Alfred Prufrock' and 'Portrait of a Lady'. Yeats's poem, with which it begins, seems to show the influence of Pound in its general attitude to scholarship and perhaps in its invocation of the Roman love poet Catullus, who exemplifies the romantic extravagance of youth. Compare St Patrick's attack on the Irish scholars in the story originally (1895) called 'St Patrick and the Pedants' (later 'The Old Men of the Twilight') as 'men who have no part in love, who have no part in song, who have no part in wisdom, but dwell with the shadows of memory' (1897).

Lines Written in Dejection

First published in *WSC*, 1917.
7. *centaurs* Fabulous creatures, with the head, trunk, and arms of a man, joined to the body and legs of a horse.

On Woman

First published in *Poetry*, February 1916; in *EP*; in *WSC* (1917).

The Fisherman

First published in *Poetry*, February 1916; in *EP*; in *WSC* (1917).
4. *grey Connemara clothes* Connemara is a region in Co. Galway. See

'The Phases of the Moon', line 4. 14. *dead man* Deliberately unidentified but a specific figure is suggested, probably Synge. Other references seem to merge the particular into the general with calculated elusiveness.

Memory

First published in *Poetry*, February 1916; in *EP*; in *WSC* (1917).

Her Praise

First published in *Poetry*, February 1916, as 'The Thorn Tree'; in *EP*; in *WSC* (1917). The subject is Maud Gonne, who had virtually retired from political life.

11. *the long war* Translates the First World War into the language of the peasantry (see 'the great war beyond the sea' in 'Shepherd and Goatherd').

The People

First published in *Poetry*, February 1916, as 'The Phoenix'; in *EP*; in *WSC* (1917). For Yeats's association of Maud Gonne with the phoenix, see 'His Phoenix'. Yeats had praised the patronage of Duke Ercole of Ferrara in 'To a Wealthy Man'; here he finds another antithesis to the philistinism of shabby Dublin in the images of Castiglione's *The Book of the Courtier* (1528), which evoke the cultured and aristocratic court life of Urbino.

A Thought from Propertius

First published in *WSC* (1917). Another tribute to Maud Gonne.

6. *Pallas Athene* The virgin goddess who presided over Athens (see 'Beautiful Lofty Things'). 7. *centaur* See note to 'Lines Written in Dejection'.

A Deep-sworn Vow

First published in the *Little Review*, June 1917, where it is dated 17 October 1915; in *WSC* (1917). Jeffares interprets Maud Gonne's vow as 'not to marry'.

Presences

First published in the *Little Review*, June 1917; in *WSC* (1917). The queen is Maud Gonne, the child is her daughter Iseult, the harlot less obviously identifiable. For Yeats's identification of the regal qualities of Maud Gonne, see 'The Old Age of Queen Maeve' (first published in April 1903): 'For there is no high story about queens / In any ancient book but tells of you; / And when I've heard how they grew old and died, / Or fell into unhappiness, I've said, / "She will grow old and die, and she has wept!"' (lines 134-8).

NOTES

On being asked for a War Poem

First published in 1916 in *The Book of the Homeless* (edited by Edith Wharton, with many distinguished contributors) as 'A Reason for Keeping Silent'; in *WSC* (1917). Originally titled 'To a friend who has asked me to sign his manifesto to the neutral nations' (Jeffares). Apart from the poems on Robert Gregory, Yeats carefully avoided the subject of the war, although it clearly contributed to the sense of threat and impending chaos in 'The Second Coming'.

Upon a Dying Lady

First published as 'Seven Poems' in the *Little Review*, August 1917; in *WSC* (1917). Yeats began the poem in 1912: Mabel Beardsley died of cancer in 1916. Her 'dead brother' (V. 11) was Aubrey, the artist and art editor of *The Yellow Book* who had died in 1898. 'In Beardsley I found that noble courage that seems to me at times, whether in man or woman, the greatest of human faculties. I saw it in all he said and did, in the clear logic of speech and in [the] clean swift line of his art' (*M*).

I.8. *Petronius Arbiter* Roman author of *The Satyricon*; in *The Player Queen* associated with 'witty, scandalous tales'. III.7. *domino* Loose cloak . . . chiefly worn to masquerades, with a small mask covering the upper part of the face (*OED*); *panniered* distended at the hips by a frame; *Longhi* Pietro Longhi (1702–62), Venetian painter of genre scenes which provide a vivid picture of Venetian life and fashion. VI.4–9. For Diarmuid and Grania, see note to 'A Faery Song'. Giorgione (*c.* 1476/8–1510) was one of the greatest Venetian painters. Achilles is the hero of the *Iliad*, Timor the Mongol conqueror Tamburlaine, Babar the founder of the Moghul Empire, and Bahram probably 'that great Hunter' in Edward Fitzgerald's *Rubáiyát of Omar Khayyám*. VII.1. *great enemy* Death.

Ego Dominus Tuus

First published in *Poetry*, October 1917; in *WSC* (1917), dated December 1915. The title is derived from Dante's *Vita Nuova* and means 'I am thy master.' The poem also refers to Dante's exile, to his love for Beatrice, and to his friends Lapo and Guido Cavalcanti. This dialogue between *Hic* and *Ille* ('this man' and 'that man') is set in the vicinity of Yeats's tower at Ballylee. For Michael Robartes, see headnote to *WR*. Yeats noted: 'I now consider that I used the actual names of two friends [Robartes and Aherne, who began as fictional characters], and that one of these friends, Michael Robartes, has but lately returned from Mesopotamia, where he has partly found and partly thought out much philosophy. I consider that Aherne and Robartes, men to whose namesakes I had attributed a turbulent life or death, have quarrelled with me. They take their place in a phantasmagoria in which I endeavour to explain my philosophy of life and death. To some extent I wrote these poems as a text for exposition.' He playfully noted also: 'I have the fancy that I read the name John Aherne among those of men prosecuted for making a disturbance at the first production of "The Play Boy", which may account for his animosity to myself.' For an example of Yeats's reflexiveness and the complexities of his use of Michael Robartes, see the following passage from 'A People's Theatre' (1919), which seems to attribute to Robartes two other poems in *WSC* in which Robartes is implicated, whether as speaker in the poem's dialogue or in the title: 'Are we approaching a supreme moment of self-consciousness, the two halves of the soul separate and face to face? A certain friend of mine has written upon this subject a couple of intricate poems called "The Phases of the Moon" and "The Double Vision" respectively, which are my continual study.' 'Ego Dominus Tuus', which should be read with *PASL* and *A Vision*, expounds Yeats's theory that 'all happiness depends on the energy to assume some other self'. See, for example: 'The Daemon comes not as like to like but seeking its own opposite, for man and Daemon feed the hunger in one another's hearts' ('Anima Hominis' in *PASL*). Yeats's investment in this antithetical patterning encouraged him to exaggerate the poverty of John Keats.

The Phases of the Moon

Included in *AV*, 1925, under the heading 'What the Caliph Partly Learned / I The Wheel and the Phases'. When he had finished *AV*, 1925, Yeats seemed to tire of 'texts for exposition': 'I can now, if I have the energy, find the simplicity I have sought in vain. I need no longer write poems like "The Phases of the Moon" nor "Ego Dominus Tuus", nor spend barren years, as I have done some three or four times, striving with abstractions' ('To Vestigia', *AV*, 1925). For Robartes, see headnote to *WR* and note to 'Ego Dominus Tuus'; his 'death' (see lines 27–8) is mentioned in the story 'Rosa Alchemica' (*SR*). For a description of Aherne, see this passage from 'The Tables of the Law' (first published in the *Savoy*, November 1896; in book form, 1897): 'the impression [is still vivid with me] of a man holding a flame in his naked hand. He was to me, at that moment, the supreme type of our race, which when it has risen above, or is sunken below, the formalisms of half-education and the rationalisms of conventional affirmation and denial, turns away, unless my hopes for the world and for the church have made me blind, from practicable desires and intuitions towards desires so unbounded that no human vessel can contain them, intuitions so immaterial that their sudden and far-off fire leaves heavy darkness about hand and foot. He had the nature, which is half monk, half soldier of fortune, and must needs turn action into dreaming, and dreaming into action; and for such there is no order, no finality, no contentment in this world.' He features later in the poem 'Owen Aherne and his Dancers'. Perhaps by mistake, in later years Yeats 'split the one Aherne into a pair of brothers; and so a character [John Aherne] got himself born' (Sidnell, who may have overlooked the fact that 'John' is an English form of 'Owen'). See also note to 'Ego Dominus Tuus'.

3–4. 'The essential aspect of Robartes's book lies not in its content (whatever that may be) but in that . . . it is the phenomenal evidence of the reality of an image, and moreover an image created by Yeats. Images and ideas precede their material embodiments' (Sidnell). **15.** *tower* From Milton's 'Il Penseroso'. **16.** *Shelley's visionary prince* Shelley's Prince Athanase (in the poem of that name) whose 'solitary light' has not moved as many readers as it might have done because 'it has not entered into men's prayers nor lighted any through the sacred dark of religious contemplation'. **17.** *lonely light* This refers to Samuel Palmer's illustration of line 186 of Milton's 'Il Penseroso'. **27–8.** 'Robartes makes no complaint about your description of his death and says nobody would have thought the Aherne and Robartes of such fantastic stories real men but for Owen's outcry' (John Aherne in *A Vision*). The reference is to a passage in 'Rosa Alchemica'; *Pater* Walter Pater (1839–94) was an influence on Yeats's richly mannered early prose style and on his cultivation of the intensity of experience. From an early stage, though, Yeats marked his own resistance to the Paterian. **45–6.** References to the *Iliad*, in which Hector was killed by Achilles; *Nietzsche* (Friedrich Nietzsche, 1844–1900), author of *The Birth of Tragedy*, reinterpreter of the Greek tradition and expounder of the theory of the Superman, was highly congenial to Yeats, who first read him in 1902 and who was influenced by his view of the heroic and of 'gaiety'. **67.** Moses received the Ten Commandments on Mount Sinai. **118.** Hunchback and Saint and Fool belong to Phases 26–8 in *A Vision*.

The Double Vision of Michael Robartes

For title, see Blake's 'double the vision my Eyes do see, / And a double vision is always with me' (letter to Thomas Butts, 22 November 1802). For Michael Robartes, see headnote to *WR* and to 'The Phases of the Moon', lines 3–4.
 1. *Cashel* The Rock of Cashel in Co. Tipperary is famous for its ruins which include a chapel built by Cormac MacCarthy. **28.** In *A Vision*, Phase 15 is that of complete subjectivity and complete beauty. **42.** *minute particulars* Yeats, who shared Blake's hatred of the 'abstract', may have derived from him this phrase which embodies the alternative to dangerous generalisation. **56.** *Homer's Paragon* Helen of Troy.

Reprisals

First published in *Rann: An Ulster Quarterly of Poetry*, Autumn 1948; written for publication in the *Nation* in 1921 but withheld out of respect for the feelings of Robert Gregory's widow. It was not included in *CP*, 1933, or *CP*, 1949. For the circumstances of the death of Robert Gregory, who is addressed in the poem, see note to 'In Memory of Major Robert Gregory'. This poem is written from a later perspective and refers to atrocities committed by the Black and Tans (see 'Nineteen Hundred and Nineteen', lines 26–8), which had been chronicled and criticised by Lady Gregory in a series of articles in the *Nation*. Yeats's indignation with a British government which countenanced such brutality led him to reinterpret Gregory's role in the war: in 'An Irish

Airman Foresees his Death' his involvement is presented as self-delighting, whereas here Yeats writes of 'the cause you served'.

5–6. 'Major Gregory told Mr. Bernard Shaw, who visited him in France, that the months since he joined the Army [*sic*] had been the happiest of his life. I think they brought him peace of mind, an escape from that shrinking, which I sometimes saw upon his face, before the growing absorption of his dream, the loneliness of his dream, as from his constant struggle to resist those other gifts that brought him ease and friendship. Leading his squadron in France or in Italy, mind and hand were at one, will and desire' ('A Note of Appreciation'). 23–4. See 'To a Shade', lines 18–20.

MICHAEL ROBARTES AND THE DANCER

The Cuala edition is dated 1920 but was not published till February 1921. For Michael Robartes, see headnote to *WR*.

An Image from a Past Life

First published in the *Nation*, 6 November 1920. Yeats's lengthy note is based on letters supposedly written by Michael Robartes to Aherne. On the subject of 'substitution' in dreams, Robartes distinguishes different sources. 'Those that come in sleep are (1) from the state immediately preceding our birth; (2) from the *Spiritus Mundi* – that is to say, from a general storehouse of images which have ceased to be a property of any personality or spirit.' Robartes also writes: 'No lover, no husband has ever met in dreams the true image of wife or mistress. She who has perhaps filled his whole life with joy or disquiet cannot enter there. Her image can fill every moment of his waking life but only its counterfeit comes to him in sleep; and he who classifies these counterfeits will find that just in so far as they become concrete, sensuous, they are distinct individuals; never types but individuals. They are the forms of those whom he has loved in some past earthly life, chosen from *Spiritus Mundi* by the subconscious will, and through them, for they are not always hollow shades, the dead at whiles outface a living rival.' Yeats commented: 'When I wrote "An Image from a Past Life", I had merely begun my study of the various papers upon the subject, but I do not think I misstated Robartes' thought in permitting the woman and not the man to see the Over Shadower or Ideal Form, whichever it was. No mind's contents are necessarily shut off from another, and in moments of excitement images pass from one mind to another with extraordinary ease, perhaps most easily from that portion of the mind which for the time being is outside consciousness.'

Under Saturn

First published in the *Dial*, November 1920. The title suggests a gloomy, cold or sluggish frame of mind, under the influence of Saturn. The poem invokes a number of Yeats ancestors and pays a tribute to Mrs Yeats (whom he had married in 1917) for her contributions to the marriage, including perhaps her gift of automatic writing (line 4) which ultimately led to *A Vision*. For competition between living and dead, see 'The Two Kings' and *The Only Jealousy of Emer*.

Easter 1916

First published in the *New Statesman*, 23 October 1920, but printed privately in 1916. Yeats explores his responses to the Proclamation of the Republic of Ireland in Dublin on 24 April 1916, to the subsequent fighting and to the execution of the fifteen leaders of the insurrection (with whom Yeats also numbered Roger Casement). Yeats, who had been in England at the time, was initially despondent: 'At the moment I feel that all the work of years has been overturned, all the bringing together of classes, all the freeing of Irish literature and criticism from politics.'

The Easter rising also inspired the play *The Dreaming of the Bones* (set in 1916, finished in August 1917 and published in January 1919, but not performed at the Abbey till 1931), which, by Yeats's own account, is based on the 'point of view' that England had once treated Ireland as Germany had recently treated Belgium. One of its central characters is a young man who had fought in the Post Office, and its presiding presences are Diarmuid and Dervorgilla, the lovers who still carry a burden of guilt for invoking the aid of Henry II and so bringing the English to Ireland. The play introduces images of the ideal city, which link it with the poems of *R*, and images of destruction which look towards the poems of *T* and Yeats's later elegies for Coole Park (see note to 'Coole Park and Ballylee, 1931', lines 27 ff.). For a useful collection of poems on the Easter rising, see Roger McHugh, *Dublin 1916* (1976), which includes work by Francis Ledwidge, James Stephens, Lady Gregory and AE.

14. *motley* Parti-coloured dress worn by a professional fool or jester. 15. In the 1916 edition of *R*, Yeats conceded: '"Romantic Ireland's dead and gone" [see 'September 1913'] sounds old-fashioned now. It seemed true in 1913, but I did not foresee 1916. The late Dublin Rebellion, whatever one can say of its wisdom, will long be remembered for its heroism. "They weighed so lightly what they gave," and gave too in some cases without hope of success.' 17–23. *That woman* Constance Markievicz (*née* Gore-Booth, 1868–1927), whom Yeats had known in Sligo and who had been second-in-command in St Stephen's Green, in 1916, but whose death sentence was commuted. 'She had often passed me on horseback, going or coming from some hunt, and was acknowledged beauty of the county' (*M*). See notes to 'In Memory of Eva Gore-Booth and Con Markiewicz'. 24–5. *This man* Patrick Pearse (b. 1879), who was a poet, playwright and educationalist (Yeats took a close interest in his school, St Enda's, which tried to provide a genuinely Irish education); *winged horse* Pegasus (see 'The Fascination of What's Difficult'). 26–30. Thomas McDonagh (b. 1878), poet, playwright (whose *When the Dawn is Come* was produced by Yeats), teacher at St Enda's, university lecturer. 31–40. Major John MacBride

(b. 1865), formerly the husband of Maud Gonne. 32. Compare: '*I knew a woman none could please, | Because she dreamed when but a child | Of men and women made like these* [the figures of mythology]; *| And after, when her blood ran wild, | Had ravelled her own story out, | And said, "In two or in three years | I needs must marry some poor lout," | And having said it, burst in tears*' ('The Grey Rock', lines 41–8). 68. *England may keep faith* The British government had promised to activate the suspended Home Rule Bill when the war was over. Yeats remarked in a letter: 'if the English Conservative party had made a declaration that they did not intend to rescind the Home Rule Bill there would have been no Rebellion'. 75–6. Yeats now names the names he had previously withheld but Constance Markievicz is replaced by the labour leader James Connolly (b. 1870).

Sixteen Dead Men

First published in the *Dial*, November 1920. For Lord Edward Fitzgerald and Wolfe Tone, see notes to 'September 1913'.

On a Political Prisoner

First published in the *Dial*, November 1920. Constance Markievicz was imprisoned in Holloway Gaol.

14. The mountain Bel Bulben is a prominent feature of the landscape near Sligo.

The Leaders of the Crowd

6. *Helicon* Mountain sacred to the Muses.

The Second Coming

First published in the *Dial*, November 1920. Yeats included a lengthy note. 'Robartes copied out and gave to Aherne several mathematical diagrams from the *Speculum*, squares and spheres, cones made up of revolving gyres intersecting each other at various angles, figures sometimes of great complexity. His explanation of these, obtained invariably from the followers of Kusta-ben-Luki, is founded upon a single fundamental thought. The mind, whether expressed in history or in the individual life, has a precise movement, which can be quickened or slackened but cannot be fundamentally altered, and this movement can be expressed by a mathematical form ... It is possible in this way, seeing that death is itself marked upon the mathematical figure, which passes beyond it, to follow the soul into the highest heaven and the deepest hell ... The figure while the soul is in the body, or suffering from the consequences of that life, is frequently drawn as a double cone, the narrow end of each cone being in the centre of the broad end of the other ... This figure is also true of history, for the end of an age, which always receives the revelation of the character of the next age, is represented by the coming of one gyre to its point of greatest expansion and of the other to that of its greatest contraction. At the present moment the life gyre is sweeping outward, unlike that before the birth of Christ which was narrowing, and has almost reached its greatest expansion. The revelation which approaches will however take its character from the contrary movement of the interior gyre. All our scientific, democratic, fact-accumulating, heterogeneous civilisation belongs to the outward gyre and prepares not the continuance of itself but the revelation as in a lightning flash, though in a flash that will not strike only in one place, and will for a time be constantly repeated, of the civilisation that must slowly take its place. This is too simple a statement, for much detail is possible.' The drafts (printed in Stallworthy, 'The Second Coming') show that Yeats began with a view of history in which 'armed tyranny' was replaced by 'mob led anarchy'. There are specific references to history in the drafts: 'The Germany of Marx has led to Russian Com' [*sic*] includes the Russian Revolution of 1917 and the downfall of the Romanovs; and the French Revolution is also invoked through references to Marie Antoinette and a regret that 'there's no Burke to cry aloud no Pit[t]'. As Donald Torchiana has suggested, the rough beast of Yeats's poem may be associated with the revolutionary monster envisaged by Burke in *Letters on a Regicide Peace*: 'There is no centaur of fiction, no poetic satyr of the woods, nothing short of the hieroglyphic monsters of Egypt, dog in head and man in body, that can give an idea of it.' Further details suggest that Yeats was thinking of the turbulence of contemporary Ireland. Yet the final version of the poem is entirely void of all historical specificity. Yeats also abandoned the rhyme scheme which can be faintly perceived in an early draft.

5. *blood-dimmed tide* An earlier version was 'bloodstained'. 6. There are suggestions here both of the Massacre of the Innocents by Herod and of the purificatory rite of baptism; earlier versions include 'innocence most foully put to death'; and 'ceremonious innocence has died' (see 'A Prayer for my Daughter'). 10. The Second Coming is predicted by Christ in Matthew 24. 12. *Spiritus Mundi* See note to 'An Image from a Past Life'. 13–17. In *A Vision* these lines are quoted to illustrate the following passage: 'The approaching *antithetical* influx and that particular *antithetical* dispensation for which the intellectual preparation has begun will reach its complete systematisation at that moment when ... the Great Year comes to its intellectual climax. Something of what I have said it must be, the myth declares, for it must reverse our era and resume past eras in itself; what else it must be, no man can say, for always at the critical moment, the *Thirteenth Cone*, the sphere, the unique intervenes.' In an Introduction to *The Resurrection* in *Wheels and Butterflies* (1934) Yeats wrote: 'Had I begun "On Baile's Strand" or not when I began to imagine, as always at my left side just out of the range of the sight, a brazen winged beast that I associated with laughing, ecstatic destruction?' (A note adds: 'Afterwards described in my poem "The Second Coming"'.) 18–22. The Christian phase of history which began 2,000 years ago with a 'rocking cradle' is now reaching its point of furthest extension and will be followed by

an antithetical phase initiated by another birth which brutally and parodically usurps the traditional associations of Bethlehem. The 'rough beast' is based on the beast of the Apocalypse in the Book of Revelation.

A Prayer for my Daughter

First published in *Poetry*, November 1919. Yeats's daughter Anne was born on 26 February 1919. The setting is Thoor Ballylee, near the Gregory estate. In draft stanzas which were excluded from later versions Yeats imagined his daughter at the age of twenty-five walking through Coole Park and visiting the 'stony edges of the lake', where every year he had counted the swans; he also told her that his spirit would be visible in his favourite haunts if she had 'perfect sight'. These self-references were later removed (Stallworthy, *Between the Lines*).

5–6. In the draft the wind has resonances which are more obviously political. It is figured as 'A popular tempest' and 'some demagogue's song / To level all things'. Compare: 'Not by that storm am I perplexed / But by the storm that seems to shake mankind' (Stallworthy, *Between the Lines*). 25–9. Helen was married to Menelaus before she left him for Paris; Aphrodite, goddess of love (literally, born from the foam), was attracted to lame Hephaestus. 59–64. Maud Gonne. 67–8. *self-delighting* ... For the rhetorical device, compare Samuel Ferguson's hope in 'Lament for Thomas Davis' that the young men would 'make Erin a nation yet; / Self-respecting, self-relying, self-advancing, / In union or in severance, free and strong'; and see also Yeats's comment on the Elizabethan dramatists in the Introduction to his *Poems of Spenser* (1906): 'Their subject was always the soul, the whimsical, self-awakening, self-exciting, self-appeasing soul.' 79. For ceremony, see 'The Second Coming', line 6, and reference to 'ancient ceremony' in 'While I, from that reed-throated whisperer' in *R*.

THE TOWER

Yeats's volume was largely based on three smaller collections published by the Cuala Press: *Seven Poems and A Fragment* (1922), *The Cat and the Moon and Certain Poems* (1924) and *October Blast* (1927); 'Fragments' was assigned to *The Tower* only in *CP*, 1933. The cover design by T. Sturge Moore (whose lyric 'The Dying Swan' Yeats unconsciously echoed in Section III of 'The Tower') was the result of careful consultation with Yeats; it shows in the top half Thoor Ballylee and its cottages and in the bottom half the inverted image of the tower as reflected in water (but without the cottages). Yeats told Sturge Moore: 'I need not make any suggestions, except that "The Tower" should not be too unlike the real object. I like to think of that building as a permanent symbol of my work plainly visible to the passer-by. As you know all my art theories depend upon just this – rooting of mythology in the earth.' The tower is also the setting of 'Michael Robartes Foretells' intended for *AV*, 1925, but discarded by Yeats (see headnote to *WR*).

Sailing to Byzantium

First published in *OB* but written in autumn 1926; printed as introductory poem to *Stories of Red Hanrahan and The Secret Rose* (1927). Yeats shared with some of the *symbolistes* a fascination with the eastern capital of Christianity. For him it exhibited a unity of culture which could not be matched in more fragmented modern times: 'I think that in early Byzantium, maybe never before or since in recorded history, religious, aesthetic and practical life were one, that architect and artificers – though not, it may be, poets, for language had been the instrument of controversy and must have grown abstract – spoke to the multitude and the few alike. The painter, the mosaic worker, the worker in gold and silver, the illuminator of sacred books, were almost impersonal, almost perhaps without the consciousness of individual design, absorbed in their subject-matter and that the vision of a whole people' (*AV*, 1937, with very minor differences from *AV*, 1925). Yeats admired the highly stylised forms of Byzantine art which he had seen on visits to Ravenna and Palermo (but never to Byzantium itself). In the earlier stages of drafting the voyage was presented in vivid detail, evoking the process of travelling (Stallworthy, *Between the Lines*), but the final version of the poem concentrates the process in the participle 'Sailing' (which is merely 'Towards' in one of the drafts). In a BBC broadcast of 1931 Yeats later emphasised the symbolic and the spiritual when he said that he was 'trying to write about the state of my soul, for it is right for an old man to make his soul' and explicitly declared, 'I symbolise the search for the spiritual life by a journey to that city.' 'Sailing to Byzantium' opens the volume and is balanced against 'All Souls' Night', which brings it to an end.

1. *Country* Often identified as Ireland. The drafts make this identification very specific and even refer to 'Teig' (a pejorative term for an Irish Catholic), yet the published version is less obviously localised and suggests less a particular location than a Land of Youth whose details may be drawn from the Irish landscape. While preparing for a broadcast, Yeats criticised the opening of the poem as 'the worst bit of syntax I ever wrote' and changed the first line to 'Old men should visit a country where the young'. 17–18. The image is derived from Yeats's visit to Ravenna, which reinforced his interest in Byzantine art. See 'Rosa Alchemica' (*SR*): 'a marvellous passage, along whose sides were so many divinities wrought in a mosaic, not less beautiful than the mosaic in the Baptistery at Ravenna, but of a less severe beauty'. See also 'The Tables of the Law' (1908 and 1914 versions only): 'the Byzantine style, which so few care for to-day, but which moves me because these tall, emaciated angels and saints seem to have less relation to the world about us than to an abstract pattern of flowing lines, that suggest an imagination absorbed in the contemplation of Eternity'. 19. *perne in a gyre* 'When I was a child at Sligo I could see above my grandfather's trees a little column of smoke from "the pern mill" and was told that "pern" was another name for the spool, as I was accustomed to call it, on which thread was wound' (note to 'he unpacks the loaded pern' in 'Shepherd and Goatherd', *WSC*). For another use, see 'When I remember that Shelley calls our minds "mirrors of the fire for which all thirst", I cannot but ask the question all have asked, "What or who has

cracked the mirror?" I begin to study the only self that I can know, myself, and to wind the thread upon the perne again' (*PASL*). It is clear from the *Dialect Dictionary* that 'pern' was once widely used in Scotland, Ireland and several English counties. Yeats's innovation is to use it in a specialised sense and in conjunction with 'gyre' (see note to 'The Second Coming') to signify the passage between the spiritual and the physical realms. He also described a gull 'gyring down and perning' in 'Demon and Beast'. **29.** 'I have read somewhere that in the Emperor's palace at Byzantium was a tree made of gold and silver, and artificial birds that sang' (Yeats's note in *T*). **30–32.** Yeats had also imagined himself in a Byzantine context in the narrative poem *The Old Age of Queen Maeve*: '*A certain poet in outlandish clothes* | *Gathered a crowd in some Byzantine lane,* | *Talked of his country and its people, sang* | *To some stringed instrument none there had seen,* | *A wall behind his back, over his head* | *A latticed window*' (lines 1–6).

The Tower

First published in the *New Republic*, 29 June 1927; dated 1925 in *OB*. For the tower, see 'Ego Dominus Tuus' and note to 'In Memory of Major Robert Gregory'. In 'Dust hath closed Helen's Eye' in *CT*, 1902, Yeats described 'the old square castle, Ballylee, inhabited by a farmer and his wife, and a cottage ... and a little mill with an old miller, and old ash-trees throwing green shadows upon a little river and great stepping-stones'.

12. *Plato and Plotinus* The Greek philosopher and the most celebrated Neo-Platonist, respectively. Plotinus developed his ideas in the *Enneads*, and here stands for a commitment to the intellectual and the abstract rather than the physical. In a note dated 1928 Yeats commented: 'When I wrote the lines about Plato and Plotinus I forgot that it is something in our own eyes that makes us see them as all transcendence. Has not Plotinus written: "Let every soul recall, then, at the outset the truth that soul is the author of all living things . . .?"' (*CP*, 1933). In his Introduction to *The Resurrection* Yeats also noted: 'All our thought seems to lead by antithesis to some new affirmation of the supernatural. In a few years perhaps we may have much empirical evidence, the only evidence that moves the mass of men to-day that man has lived many times . . . This belief held by Plato and Plotinus, and supported by weighty argument, resembles the mathematical doctrines of Einstein before the experimental proof of the curvature of light.' **25ff.** 'The persons mentioned are associated by legend, story and tradition with the neighbourhood of Thoor Ballylee or Ballylee Castle, where the poem was written. Mrs. French lived at Peterswell in the eighteenth century and was related to Sir Jonah Barrington, who described the incident of the ears and the trouble that came of it [in *Personal Sketches of his own Time*]. The peasant beauty and the blind poet are Mary Hynes and [Anthony] Raftery [*c.* 1784–1835], and the incident of the man drowned in Cloone Bog is recorded in my "Celtic Twilight". Hanrahan's pursuit of the phantom hare and hounds is from my "Stories of Red Hanrahan". The ghosts have been seen at their game of dice in what is now my bedroom, and the old bankrupt man lived about a hundred years ago' (*CP*, 1933). 'It may be that in a few years Fable ... will have changed Mary Hynes and Raftery to perfect symbols of the sorrow of beauty and of the magnificence and penury of dreams' (*CT*, 1902). **57.** *Hanrahan* 'Red Hanrahan is an imaginary name – I saw it over a shop, or rather part of it over a shop in a Galway village – but there were many poets like him in the eighteenth century in Ireland'; see also headnote to *WR*. **62.** *broken knees* See note to '[The poet, Owen Hanrahan, under a bush of may]'. **65.** *bawn* Fortified enclosure or cattlefold. **85.** *Great Memory* The storehouse or matrix of images to which we all have access. **91–3.** Raftery and Red Hanrahan. **132.** *Burke and Grattan* Edmund Burke (1729–97), politician, orator and author of *Reflections on the Revolution in France*, and Henry Grattan (1746–1820), leading parliamentarian. Yeats invoked both of these names in his celebrated pronouncement on divorce in the Irish Senate in June 1925, aligning himself with the Protestant minority to which Burke and Grattan had both belonged: 'We against whom you have done this thing are no petty people. We are one of the great stocks of Europe. We are the people of Burke; we are the people of Grattan; we are the people of Swift, the people of Emmet, the people of Parnell. We have created the most of the modern literature of this country. We have created the best of its political intelligence.' See also 'The Seven Sages'. **139–44.** 'I have unconsciously echoed one of the loveliest lyrics of our time – Mr Sturge Moore's "Dying Swan"' (*CP*, 1933). **156.** *Translunar* Beyond or above the moon (and its unstable influence); a secondary meaning is ethereal, insubstantial, visionary. **178.** *metal* The 'stuff' of which a man is made, with reference to character. **180.** *sedentary trade* Writing (see 'Aherne ... was stout and sedentary-looking', *AV*, 1937). **186.** *Testy* Prone to be irritated by small checks and annoyances; impatient of being thwarted; irascible, short-tempered (*OED*).

Meditations in Time of Civil War

First published in the *Dial*, January 1923; in *CM*. The Civil War of 1922–3 was fought between the forces of the newly established Irish Free State and the Republicans. 'These poems were written at Thoor Ballylee in 1922, during the civil war. Before they were finished the Republicans blew up our "ancient bridge" one midnight. They forbade us to leave the house, but were otherwise polite, even saying at last "Good-night, thank you," as though we had given them the bridge' (*CP*, 1933). In fact, 'Ancestral Houses' was written in England in 1921 and includes in its composite imagery impressions of Garsington, the home of Lady Ottoline Morrell. Yeats may also have been influenced by the time he spent in the house which had once belonged to John Hampden. Book I of *A Vision* ends with the subscription, 'Finished at Thoor Ballylee, 1922, / in a time of Civil War.'

I Ancestral Houses

9ff. 'I thought of this house, slowly perfecting itself and the life within it in ever-increasing intensity of labour, and then of its probably sinking

away through courteous incompetence, or rather sheer weakness of will'
(16 September 1909; *M*). 27. *Juno* Consort of Jupiter and queen of the gods.

II My House
14. See note to 'The Phases of the Moon', line 14. 16. *daemonic* Of, or relating
to, or of the nature of, supernatural power or genius (*OED*); see VII.39.

III My Table
2. Yeats was presented a ceremonial sword by Junzo Sato, Japanese Consul
at Portland, Oregon. 8. Geoffrey Chaucer was born *c*. 1340.

IV My Descendants
17. *Primum Mobile* Prime source of motion, prime mover; supposed outer-
most sphere added in the Middle Ages to the Ptolemaic system and believed
to carry with it the inner spheres.

V The Road at my Door
1. An Irregular is a Republican, in opposition to the 'brown Lieutenant',
who is a member of the Government forces. 2. *Falstaffian* Refers not only to
the man's build but to his attitude to war.

VI The Stare's Nest by my Window
'In the West of Ireland we call a starling a stare, and during the civil war one
built in a hole in the masonry by my bedroom window' (*CP*, 1933). In the
first printed version the bird was called a 'Jay' in the title.

*VII I see Phantoms of Hatred and of the Heart's Fullness and of the Coming
Emptiness*
'A cry for vengeance because of the murder of the Grand Master of the
Templars seems to me fit symbol for those who labour for hatred, and so for
sterility in various kinds. It is said to have been incorporated in the ritual of cer-
tain Masonic societies of the eighteenth century, and to have fed class-hatred.

   'I suppose that I must have put hawks into the fourth stanza because I have
a ring with a hawk and a butterfly upon it, to symbolise the straight road of
logic, and so of mechanism, and the crooked road of intuition: "For wisdom is
a butterfly and not a gloomy bird of prey"' (*CP*, 1933).

Nineteen Hundred and Nineteen

First published in the *Dial*, September 1921, as 'Thoughts upon the Present
State of the World'; in *SPAF*. Lady Gregory had described to Yeats atrocities
committed at Gort in Co. Galway during the struggle between the Black and
Tans and the Auxiliaries and the Irish Republican Army (see note to 'Re-
prisals').
   7. *Phidias'* Greek sculptor who was responsible for the sculptures of the
Parthenon in Athens and who was celebrated for his work in gold and ivory.

8. Thucydides records that the Athenians used grasshopper brooches made of gold. 17–24. 'There will never be another war, that was our opium dream' (cited by Torchiana from unpublished draft of speech). 25–8. A specific reference to the murder of the pregnant Ellen Quinn, who was carrying a baby in her arms (described by Lady Gregory in 'Murder by the Throat' which appeared in the *Nation*). 48–50. Loie Fuller (1862–1928) was an American dancer whose performance at the Folies Bergère featured a virtuoso whirling of draperies and who was much celebrated by poets and artists (including Toulouse-Lautrec and Mallarmé). '*Au bain terrible des étoffes se pâme, radieuse, froide, la figurante qui illustre maint thème giratoire où tend une trame loin épanouie, pétale et papillon géants, déferlement, tout d'ordre net et élémentaire ... L'enchanteresse fait l'ambiance, la tire de soi et l'y rentre, par un silence palpité de crêpes de chine*' (Mallarmé; see Kermode). 54. *Platonic Year* The Great Year is that period of time which is required for the constellations to return to their original starting points; variously calculated and discussed at length in *A Vision*. 59–60. In a note on *Calvary* in *Four Plays for Dancers* (1921) Yeats said: 'I use birds as symbols of subjective life' and cited a letter from Robartes to Aherne as partial explanation. Robartes recalls his initiation into the beliefs of the Judwalis in the Middle East and articulates the philosophy which he has developed as a result: 'Certain birds, especially as I see things, such lonely birds as the heron, hawk, eagle, and swan, are the natural symbols of subjectivity, especially when floating upon the wind alone or alighting upon some pool or river, while the beasts that run upon the ground, especially those that run in packs, are the natural symbols of objective man.' 97. *levelling wind* See 'the haystack- and roof-levelling wind' of 'A Prayer for my Daughter' which originally was 'A popular tempest'. 118. See Yeats's note to 'The Hosting of the Sidhe'. 128. 'The country people see at times certain apparitions whom they name now "fallen angels", now "ancient inhabitants of the country", and describe as riding at whiles "with flowers upon the heads of the horses". I have assumed in the sixth poem [Section VI] that these horsemen, now that the times worsen, give way to worse. My last symbol, Robert Artisson incubus of the witch Dame Alice Kyteler, was an evil spirit much run after in Kilkenny at the start of the fourteenth century. Are not those who travel in the whirling dust also in the Platonic Year? W.B.Y. May, 1921' (September/November 1921).

The Wheel

First published in *SPAF*. The title suggests that the sequences both of nature and of human life are part of that larger cyclical pattern which is the subject of 'The Great Wheel' (Book I of *AV*, 1937; discussed also in *AV*, 1925). Graham Hough has explained: 'The same rhythm runs through all human activity. The same cycle is traversed in the succession of incarnations, in an individual life, in a single judgement or act of thought. It is the rhythm of every completed act of mind or life. It is also therefore the rhythm of collective life, the rhythm of history.'

The New Faces

First published in *SPAF*. Written in 1912 and addressed to Lady Gregory.

    2. *catalpa-tree* This was a feature of the gardens at Coole. See 'Upon a House Shaken by the Land Agitation', 'Coole Park, 1929' and 'Coole Park and Ballylee, 1931'.

Two Songs from a Play

First published in the Adelphi, June 1927, then in *OB*, except for stanza 2 of the second song, which was printed as part of the complete version in *Stories of Michael Robartes and his Friends* (1931). 'These songs are sung by the Chorus in a play [*The Resurrection*, 1931] that has for its theme Christ's first appearance to the Apostles after the Crucifixion. It is meant to be played in a drawing-room or studio' (*OB*). The songs accompany the unfolding and folding of a black cloth (in the drawing-room version, or the curtain in the stage version) at the beginning of the play and the reverse process at the end. Yeats invokes a fertility myth according to which the virgin goddess Athene took the heart of the dead Dionysus (or Bacchus) to Zeus, who swallowed it and, in due course, fathered the dead god once more.

    7. *Magnus Annus* (The great year) is another term for one of the great cycles of time (see note to 'Nineteen Hundred and Nineteen', line 54). 9–12. These lines invoke Shelley's chorus in *Hellas* (1822): 'The world's great age begins anew', which, in its turn, is a version of Virgil's prophecy of the return of the golden age in *Eclogues*, IV.6; *Argo's* The ship in which the Argonauts went in search of the Golden Fleece. 15. *fierce virgin* The Virgin Mary. 24. *Doric* One of the orders of Greek architecture.

Fragments

I first published in the *Dublin Magazine*, October–December 1931, as part of Yeats's 'Commentary' on *The Words upon the Window Pane*; II first published in *CP*, 1933. In his Introduction to the play (which centres on Swift) Yeats recorded 'a sort of nightmare vision' in which he could see 'the "primary qualities" torn from the side of Locke, Johnson's ponderous body bent above the letter to Lord Chesterfield, some obscure person somewhere inventing the spinning-jenny'. Like Blake, Yeats regarded John Locke (1632–84) as one of the founders of a mechanistic system of philosophy which was the enemy of the spirit, poetry and the imagination. This was largely responsible for the unfortunate development of modern society, including the Industrial Revolution and its influence (referred to in the image of the birth of the spinning-jenny, which is also a parody of the creation of Eve in Genesis). See Yeats's claim that Berkeley 'defined . . . the philosophy of Newton and Locke, in three sentences, [and] wrote after each that Irishmen thought otherwise' (Introduction to J. M. Hone and M. M. Rossi, *Bishop Berkeley*, 1931).

Leda and the Swan

First published in the *Dial*, June 1924; in *CM*; in *AV*, 1925. 'I wrote Leda and the Swan because the editor of a political review [AE] asked me for a poem. I thought, "After the individualist, demagogic movement, founded by Hobbes and popularised by the Encyclopaedists and the French Revolution, we have a soil so exhausted that it cannot grow that crop again for centuries." Then I thought, "Nothing is now possible but some movement from above preceded by some violent annunciation." My fancy began to play with Leda and the Swan for metaphor, and I began this poem; but as I wrote, bird and lady took such possession of the scene that all politics went out of it, and my friend tells me that his "conservative readers would misunderstand the poem".' In *AV*, 1925, he wrote: 'all things are from antithesis, and when in my ignorance I try to imagine what older civilisation she refuted ['civilisation that annunciation rejected', 1937], I can but see bird and woman blotting out some corner of the Babylonian mathematical starlight'.

The swan is Zeus, inventively lecherous father of the gods; his union with Leda produced Helen, whose fatal beauty led to the Trojan War and indirectly, after the war, to the murder of King Agamemnon by his wife, Clytemnestra (who was also Leda's daughter). In Yeats's theory of history this brutal impregnation was the initiation of a new age, and Leda analogous to the Virgin Mary, whose impregnation inaugurated the Christian phase of history. The word 'annunciation' in Yeats's note and as a title in the draft (see *M*), shows that he was reading the Greek myth in terms of its Christian parallel. Yeats devoted more attention to the swan in the drafts than he did in the published texts (see *M* and Ellmann, *The Identity of Yeats*). One version began: 'The swooping godhead is half hovering still, / Yet climbs upon her trembling body pressed / By the webbed toes; and that all powerful bill / Has suddenly bowed her face upon his breast.' The second line was revised to read: 'But mounts until her trembling thighs are pressed' (*M*). Possible artistic influences are discussed by Melchiori, and by Henn and Loizeaux. For a different perspective on Zeus and Leda, see the last stanza of 'Lullaby' (XVI in *WFMP*): 'Such a sleep and sound as fell / Upon Eurotas' grassy bank / When the holy bird, that there / Accomplished his predestined will, / From the limbs of Leda sank / But not from her protecting care.'

On a Picture of a Black Centaur by Edmund Dulac

First published in *SPAF*. Edmund Dulac (1882–1953) was the dedicatee of *The Winding Stair*. He translated Yeats's works into musical and pictorial form, illustrating some of his books and setting poems to music. He also designed the masks for *At the Hawk's Well*.

11. *Ephesian topers* The Seven Sleepers of Ephesus who slumbered for centuries in a cave during the persecution of the Christians under the Roman Empire; they awoke at the Resurrection. In a letter to Henry James in August 1915, Yeats declared his intention to keep their 'neighbourhood, hoping to

catch their comfortable snores till bloody frivolity [the First World War] is over'. 13. *Saturnian* Saturn presided over a golden age.

Among School Children

First published in the *Dial*, August 1927; in *OB*. See note to '[The poet, Owen Hanrahan, under a bush of may]'.

4. Text emended from the *London Mercury*, August 1927. 9–16. For Leda, see note to 'Leda and the Swan'; the lines refer to Maud Gonne. Plato's 'parable' in *The Symposium* supposes that each human being is half of what was originally a spherical whole and that love is the desire for the restoration of that primal unity. 26. *Quattrocento* Of the fifteenth century (Yeats originally printed 'quinto-cento', or sixteenth century). 'What quinto-cento finger fashioned it' (*Dial*, August 1927); 'Da Vinci' finger so had fashioned it' (*London Mercury*, August 1927). 33–40. 'A mother that saw her son / Doubled over a speckled shin, / Cross-grained with ninety years, / Would cry, "How little worth / Were all my hopes and fears / And the hard pain of his birth!"' (*At the Hawk's Well*, lines 11–16). 34. *Honey of generation* 'I have taken "the honey of generation" from Porphyry's essay on "The Cave of the Nymphs", but find no warrant in Porphyry for considering it the "drug" that destroys the "recollection" of pre-natal freedom' (*OB*). 41–8. Three Greek philosophers: Plato insisted on the superior reality of the world of ideas to that of the shadowy physical universe; Aristotle, who was tutor to Alexander the Great, was more empirical ('Solider') and established the foundations of scientific classification; Pythagoras investigated the mathematical basis of music. 42. *paradigm* Pattern, example; used by Thomas Taylor the Platonist to signify an archetype (Parkinson, *W. B. Yeats: The Later Poetry*). 43. *taws* Leather strap or thong, divided at the end into narrow strips (defined by Yeats as a 'form of birch').

The Hero, the Girl, and the Fool

First published as 'Cuchulain the Girl and the Fool' in *SPAF*; lines 18–29 only in *AV*, 1925; as 'The Hero, the Girl and the Fool' in *T*; and lines 18–29 as 'The Fool by the Roadside' in *CP*, 1933.

1. See 'The Indian to his God', line 5. 22. *spool* Yeats made elaborate use of this image in 'Shepherd and Goatherd', one of his elegies for Robert Gregory, in which Gregory 'unpacks the loaded pern / Of all 'twas pain or joy to learn'. The poem continues to imagine him living his life backwards through 'victories of the mind' until he reaches the cradle. 'Having no active intelligence he owns nothing of the exterior world but his mind and body. He is but a straw blown by the wind, with no mind but the wind and no act but a nameless drifting and turning' (*AV*, 1925). 26. *coagulate* Clothed, congealed, converted into a soft solid mass.

All Souls' Night

First published in the *New Republic*, 9 March 1921; in *SPAF*; in *EPS*; as conclusion to *AV*, 1925, and as 'An Epilogue' to *AV*, 1937. On 2 November, the day after the Irish Samhain (pronounced approximately *Sahwin*), it is Catholic practice to pray for the souls of the faithful departed who are still in Purgatory. Yeats's poem, which was the product of one of his 'moments of exaltation', concludes both versions of *A Vision*; in 1925 it is matched by the opening 'Dedication: To Vestigia' (Moina, the wife of MacGregor Mathers and the sister of Henri Bergson; see note to 'XVII After Long Silence' in *WFMP*). Yeats noted: 'It is a constant thought of mine that what we write is often a commendation of, or expostulation with the friends of our youth, and that even if we survive all our friends we continue to prolong or to amend conversations that took place before our five-and-twentieth year.' Remembering those friends with whom he shared occult interests and who are the focus of this act of commendation and expostulation, he suggests a concern which bound them together: 'We all, so far as I can remember, differed from ordinary students of philosophy or religion through our belief that truth cannot be discovered but may be revealed.'

1. *the great Christ Church Bell* This bell, also known as Great Tom, would have been audible in the house where Yeats was staying in Oxford and where the poem was written. See also: 'At Oxford I went constantly to All Souls' Chapel, though never at service time, and parts of "A Vision" were thought out there' ('A Packet for Ezra Pound' in *AV*, 1937). 4. *muscatel* Strong sweet wine made from the muscat or similar grape. 21. *Horton* William Thomas Horton (1864–1919), a mystical painter, 'whose work had little of his personal charm and strangeness'. Yeats wrote a Preface to his *A Book of Images* (1898), in which he described Horton as a 'disciple of perhaps the most medieval movement in modern mysticism' and observed that his images were 'part of the history of a soul; for Mr. Horton tells me he has made them spectral, to make himself feel all things but a waking dream'. 'He was my close friend and had he lived I would have asked him to accept the dedication of a book I could not expect him to approve, for in his later life he cared for little but what seemed to him a very simple piety' ('To Vestigia'). Yeats exercised particular caution with his name: in *AV*, 1925, he was introduced as X, while in other versions of the poem before *T* he was H. Strangely, perhaps, he does not feature in either *M* or *AU*. When Yeats reprinted his Introduction to *A Book of Images* as 'Symbolism in Painting' in *Ideas of Good and Evil* (1903), he removed Horton's name from the list of modern Symbolists and also entirely omitted the final section, which was specifically devoted to a review and appraisal of Horton's work. Both his 'platonic love' and the apparition of his dead beloved are described in *A Vision*. For the house lit up, see also 'O but I saw a solemn sight' in *KGCT*, 'V Crazy Jane on God' in *WFMP*, 'The Curse of Cromwell' and *Purgatory*. 26. *Anodyne* A medicine or drug which alleviates pain; anything that soothes wounded or excited feelings or that lessens the sense of misfortune (*OED*). 41. *Florence Emery* Florence Farr Emery (1869–1917), 'accomplished speaker of verse, less accomplished actress' who in later years taught in a Buddhist convent in Ceylon; the dedicatee of 'In the Seven Woods' in *P*, 1906. Yeats admired her 'incomparable sense of rhythm and . . .

beautiful voice' and acclaimed her as the 'only reciter of lyric poetry who is always a delight'. His essay 'Speaking to the Psaltery' (see Appendix) includes three of her settings of Yeats's poems. **61–80.** *Mathers* Samuel Liddell MacGregor Mathers (1854–1918), author of *The Kabbalah Unveiled*, with whom Yeats shared occult interests in his earlier years in London and who stimulated his experiments and research into the source of images in the Anima Mundi. Having studied Mathers's symbolic system, Yeats discovered that 'for a considerable minority ... the visible world would completely vanish, and that world summoned by the symbol take its place'. This scholar of magic and the occult was the main source for the character of Michael Robartes in Yeats's early stories. Yeats recorded that 'in body and in voice at least he was perfect; so might Faust have looked in his changeless aged youth' (*TV*). He was also a student of the theory of war and his prediction in the 1890s of 'immense wars' may have 'made' Yeats write 'The Valley of the Black Pig'. Like Yeats, Horton and Florence Farr Emery, Mathers was a member of the Hermetic Order of the Golden Dawn. **86.** *mummy truths* The mysterious truths of death.

THE WINDING STAIR AND OTHER POEMS

The first collection under this title appeared in New York in 1929. The 1933 edition was based on this and on *WFMP*. Two poems were published for the first time: 'VI Crazy Jane Talks with the Bishop' and 'The Choice' (which had previously appeared as a stanza of 'Coole Park and Ballylee, 1931'). Yeats noted: 'In this book and elsewhere I have used towers, and one tower in particular, as symbols and have compared their winding stairs to the philosophical gyres, but it is hardly necessary to interpret what comes from the main track of thought and expression. Shelley uses towers constantly as symbols, and there are gyres in Swedenborg, and in Thomas Aquinas and certain classical authors.' The winding stair is also, at the most basic level, a translation into symbolic form of the stone staircase of the tower at Ballylee.

In Memory of Eva Gore-Booth and Con Markiewicz

First published in *WS*, 1929. Lissadell, ten miles from Sligo, is the home of the Gore-Booth family. It is a Neo-Classical country house which was built in the 1830s; on the south side, its bay windows have a view over Rosses Point towards Knocknarea. Yeats registered its social significance in the world of his childhood in *M*. Eva Gore-Booth (1870–1926) had a much lower public profile than her sister, but she shared her active concern for the poor, wrote poetry and worked persistently for women's rights. The abbreviated 'Con' in the title may suggest greater intimacy with Constance, but Yeats recorded in *M* that he was 'at once in closer sympathy' with Eva, 'whose delicate, gazelle-like beauty reflected a mind far more subtle and distinguished'. Constance (1868–1927) (see 'Easter 1916' and 'On a Political Prisoner') was released from penal servitude in 1917 and would have been the first woman MP had she taken her seat at Westminster; later she was twice appointed a Government Minister in the Dáil. On first meeting her, Yeats had been surprised by 'some small' physical resemblance and 'a very exact resemblance in voice' to Maud Gonne, whose example was later to influence her own approach to politics.

4. *gazelle* A small delicately formed antelope ... especially noted for the grace of its movements and the softness of its eyes (*OED*). 26. See note to 'In Memory of Major Robert Gregory', line 26. The burning of time is a recurrent idea in Yeats: see, for example, 'The Man who Dreamed of Faeryland', line 47, and 'He Tells of the Perfect Beauty', line 7. 30. *gazebo* A turret or lantern on the roof of a house, usually for the purpose of commanding an extensive prospect; a belvedere or look-out (*OED*). Also, a show or gaping-stock; any object which attracts attention (*Dialect Dictionary*, which cites Irish examples including 'He became a holy show, and gazabo to the entire world,' 1869). In the draft Yeats originally wrote 'I' rather than 'We' (Stallworthy, *Between the Lines*). 'Gazelle' may have suggested 'gazebo' by a process of association which occurs elsewhere in Yeats.

Death

First published in *WS*, 1929. 'I think that I was roused to write *Death* and *Blood and the Moon* by the assassination of Kevin O'Higgins, the finest intellect in Irish public life, and, I think I may add, to some extent, my friend.' Kevin O'Higgins (1892–1927), whom Churchill described as 'a figure from the Antique, cast in bronze', was Vice-President and Minister of Justice when he was assassinated on 10 July 1927. In a letter to Olivia Shakespear, Yeats described the mysterious but vivid intimations of this event which he had experienced on the night before it took place. See also 'The Municipal Gallery Revisited'.

A Dialogue of Self and Soul

First published in *WS*, 1929. 'The Tower is Thoor Ballylee, or Ballylee Castle, where I have written most of my poems of recent years. My poems attribute to it most of the meanings attributed in the past to the Tower – whether watch tower or pharos, and to its winding stair those attributed to gyre or whorl. What those meanings are let the poems say' (*WS*, 1929, referring also to 'Blood and the Moon'). This poem, which was written in the spring of 1928 during a long illness, enacts an internal dialogue which has many parallels throughout the work of Yeats, but which may owe a particular debt to the example of metaphysical poetry (see Marvell's 'A Dialogue between the Soul and Body').

10. *Sato's ancient blade* See Section III of 'The Tower' for the ceremonial sword made by Bishu Osafumé Motoshigé.

Blood and the Moon

First published in the *Exile*, Spring 1928; in *WS*, 1929. 'Part of the symbolism of "Blood and the Moon" was suggested by the fact that Thoor Ballylee has a waste room at the top and that butterflies come in through the loopholes and die against the window-panes.' See note to 'A Dialogue of Self and Soul'.

13. *Alexandria's tower . . . Babylon's* The pharos or lighthouse referred to in Yeats's note to 'A Dialogue of Self and Soul'; the Tower of Babel. 15. More precisely: 'those skiey towers / Where Thought's crowned powers / Sit watching our dance, ye happy hours!' (*Prometheus Unbound*, IV, 102–4). For Shelley's towers, see Yeats's essay 'The Philosophy of Shelley's Poetry' (dated 1900 in *Ideas of Good and Evil*, 1903), where he gives a number of examples and comments that 'The tower, important in Maeterlinck, as in Shelley, is, like the sea, and rivers, and caves with fountains, a very ancient symbol, and would perhaps, as years went by, have grown more important in his poetry.' 18. *Goldsmith and the Dean, Berkeley and Burke* Oliver Goldsmith (1728–74), Jonathan Swift (1667–1745), George Berkeley (1685–1753) and Edmund Burke (1729–97): exemplars in Yeats's reading of history of the traditions of eighteenth-century Protestant Ireland which he increasingly cultivated at this period in resistance to the degeneracy both of England and of contemporary Irish life (see 'The Seven Sages'). 19. *sibylline* Oracular, occult, mysterious (named after prophetesses of antiquity). 28 *Saeva Indignatio* Yeats translated this phrase from Swift's epitaph as 'Savage indignation'; the epitaph adopts it from the Roman satirist Juvenal, who attributes to *saeva indignatio* the motive power of his satire.

Oil and Blood

First published in *WS*, 1929. See 'Vacillation', lines 80–82, on the undecayed body of Saint Teresa; see also 'The Mountain Tomb'.

The Seven Sages

First published in *WFMP*. See section III of 'Blood and the Moon' for Yeats's development of a myth of eighteenth-century Ireland which was centred on Burke, Goldsmith, Berkeley (the Bishop of Cloyne, who believed in the medical efficacy of tar-water) and Swift (whose friendship with Esther Johnson is immortalised in his *Journal to Stella*).

2. For Grattan, see 'The Tower', line 132, and note. 15–16. The major points of focus in Burke's political career. 17–20. In *The Deserted Village*, which is based on his memories of Ireland rather than being the picture of English country life for which it is often taken; *trefoil* The shamrock, emblem of Irish nationality. 26. For Yeats's interest in beggars, see note to 'Beggar to Beggar Cried' and 'Dream of the noble and the beggar-man' ('The Municipal Gallery Revisited', line 47), which illustrates Yeats's propensity for discovering kindred qualities in the aristocrat and the beggar (or the peasant) to the exclusion of the bourgeoisie.

The Crazed Moon

First published in *WFMP*; written in April 1923.

Coole Park, 1929

First published as 'Coole Park' in *Coole* by Lady Gregory (1931) and dated 7 September 1929; in *WFMP*. A prose draft reads: 'Describe house in first stanza. Here Synge came, Hugh Lane, Shaw Taylor, many names. I too in my timid youth. Coming and going like migratory birds. Then address the swallows fluttering in their dream like circles. Speak of the rarity of the circumstances that bring together such concords of men. Each man more than himself through whom an unknown life speaks. A circle ever returning into itself' (Parkinson, *W. B. Yeats: The Later Poetry*). In 'Michael Robartes Foretells' (see headnote to *WR*) one of the characters has come to stay in Yeats's tower because of its nearness to Coole; he desires to 'look into the empty rooms, walk the woods and the grass-grown gardens, where a great Irish social order climaxed and passed away' (edited by Hood).

9. For Douglas Hyde, see 'At the Abbey Theatre'. 13. *meditative man* 'Synge found the check that suited his temperament in an elaboration of the dialects of Kerry and Aran. The cadence is long and meditative, as befits the thought of men who are much alone' ('J. M. Synge and the Ireland of his Time', 1910). 13–14. *John Synge . . . Shawe-Taylor and Hugh Lane* For Synge, see 'In Memory of Major Robert Gregory', lines 25–32 and note. John Shawe-Taylor (1866–1911) was, like Sir Hugh Lane, a nephew of Lady Gregory. He is the subject of an essay by Yeats which finds fault with his portrait and which includes the following assessment of his character and 'moral genius': 'Men like him live near this power [some power deeper than our daily thought] because of something simple and impersonal within them which is, as I believe, imaged in the fire of their minds, as in the shape of their bodies and their faces' (*Observer*, 2 July 1911; *The Cutting of an Agate*, 1912). Yeats described his impetuosity and placed him among those men who 'copying hawk or leopard, have an energy of swift decision, a power of sudden action, as if their whole body were their brain'. In politics this manifested itself in his calling for a Land Conference between landlords and tenants, for which, according to Yeats, he found the necessary 'independence from class and family' at Coole (*TV*). For Hugh Lane (1875–1915), patron of the arts, see note to 'September 1913'. 24. *withershins* (1) In a direction opposite to the usual; the wrong way; (2) in a direction contrary to the apparent course of the sun, considered as unlucky or causing disaster (*OED*).

Coole Park and Ballylee, 1931

First published in *WFMP* as 'Coole Park and Ballylee, 1932'.

4. *'dark'* An Irish usage meaning blind; *Raftery* see 'The Tower', lines 34ff. Raftery's poem about Mary Hynes includes the line 'There is a strong cellar in Ballylee.' Yeats's informant in 'Dust hath closed Helen's Eye' told him that

'the strong cellar was the great hole where the river sank underground' (*The Celtic Twilight*). 8. In 'Earth, Fire and Water' (*CT*, 1902) Yeats attributed to Porphyry both the belief that water is the principle of generation for the human soul and that 'even the generation of images in the mind is from water'. 12. *buskin* The high boot of the tragic actor which is a symbol for the tragic mode. 27ff. The house was described by Yeats in *DP*; he also produced pastels of the façade and the library. See the evocation of the great house in *Purgatory*, and see these images of threat in *The Dreaming of the Bones*: 'The enemy has toppled roof and gable, / And torn the panelling from ancient rooms; / What generations of old men had known / Like their own hands, and children wondered at, / Has boiled a trooper's porridge.' 40. After this line the poem as printed in *WFMP* included eight lines which later became 'The Choice' (see variant). 43–4. Lady Gregory quoted this phrase from Raftery in *Poets and Dreamers*. See 'The Municipal Gallery Revisited', lines 40–47. 46. For Pegasus, see 'The Fascination of What's Difficult'.

At Algeciras – A Meditation upon Death

First published in *A Packet for Ezra Pound* (1929) as one of two 'Meditations upon Death' (with 'Mohini Chatterjee'). In November 1927 Yeats stayed at Algeciras in southern Spain near the Straits of Gibraltar.

11. Newton's words were: 'To myself I seem to have been only like a boy, playing on the seashore, and diverting myself, in now and then finding another pebble or prettier shell than ordinary, while the great ocean of truth lay all undiscovered before me'. For Rosses in Co. Sligo, see 'The Stolen Child'.

Byzantium

First published in *WFMP*. Yeats's prose draft reads: 'Subject for a poem. Death of a friend ... Describe Byzantium as it is in the system towards the end of the first Christian millennium. A walking mummy. Flames at the street corners where the soul is purified. Birds of hammered gold singing in the golden trees, in the harbour [dolphins] offering their backs to the wailing dead that they may carry them to Paradise' (*Pages from a Diary Written in 1930*). Byzantium is also evoked in detail in *A Vision* (see note to 'Sailing to Byzantium'). The poem was provoked by Sturge Moore's objection to the final stanza of 'Sailing to Byzantium' on the grounds that the golden bird is as much nature as the human body which it supposedly transcends.

5–8. 'Amidst the abstract splendour of its basilicas stood saints with thought-tortured faces and bodies that were but a framework to sustain the patterns and colours of their clothes. The mosaics of the Apse displayed a Christ with a face of pitiless intellect, or a pinched, flat-breasted virgin holding a child like a wooden doll. Nobody can stray into that little Byzantium chapel at Palermo ... without for an instant renouncing the body and all its works' ('The Censorship and St. Thomas Aquinas', *Irish Statesman*, 22 September 1928). 11. *Hades' bobbin* A bobbin is an article round which thread or yarn is wound, in order to be wound off again with facility, and as required, in weaving, sewing, etc. (*OED*). Hades' bobbin is defined by Ellmann as the soul, which 'winds up the mummy-cloth of experience' in life and unwinds the cloth (which is 'the winding path' of nature) when it returns after death to the underworld, which is the realm of Hades. **17–24.** See lines 27–32 of 'Sailing to Byzantium'. **33.** The dolphins transport the souls of the dead to the afterlife. Yeats had introduced them into the draft of 'Sailing to Byzantium', where he had written, 'Or send the dolphins back and gather me / Into the artifice of eternity' (Stallworthy, *Between the Lines*). **34ff.** See the dance of 'flame-like figures' in 'Rosa Alchemica' (*SR*): 'I saw that the floor was of a green stone, and that a pale Christ on a pale cross was wrought in the midst. I asked Robartes the meaning of this, and was told that they desired "To trouble His unity with their multitudinous feet."'

The Mother of God

First published in *WFMP*. 'In "The Mother of God" the words "A fallen flare through the hollow of an ear" are, I am told, obscure. I had in my memory Byzantine mosaic pictures of the Annunciation which show a line drawn from a star to the ear of the Virgin. She received the Word through the ear, a star fell, and a star was born' (*CP*, 1933).

Vacillation

First published in *WFMP* with the sections titled as follows: 'I What is Joy'; 'II The Burning Tree' (subsequently II and III); 'III Happiness' (subsequently IV); 'IV Conscience' (subsequently V); 'V Conquerors' (subsequently VI); 'VI A Dialogue' (subsequently VII); 'VII Von Hügel' (subsequently VIII). Yeats originally called the sequence 'Wisdom'. The poem is based on two experiences separated by a considerable number of years. The first is described in *PASL* (see note to lines 35ff. below); the second is described in a letter of 23 November 1931 to Olivia Shakespear: 'I suddenly seemed to understand [a lofty philosophical conception] at last and then I smelt roses. I had realised the nature of the timeless spirit. Then I began to walk and with my excitement came – how shall I say? – that old glow so beautiful with its autumnal tint. The longing to touch it was almost unendurable. The next night I was walking in the same path and now the two excitements came together. The autumnal image, remote, incredibly spiritual, erect, delicate featured, and mixed with it the violent physical image, the black Mass of Eden.' The poem was, he thought, 'a poor shadow of the intensity of the experience'.

    11–14. This tree appears in *The Mabinogion*. **16–18.** *Attis'* A vegetation god whose image was hung on a tree during an annual festival when his followers performed a ritual self-castration. **27.** *Lethean* That which brings forgetfulness. **35.** *fiftieth year* Yeats was fifty in 1915. In *PASL* he remembered an experience which he had had during the First World War: 'At certain moments, always unforeseen, I become happy, most commonly when at hazard I have opened some book of verse ... Perhaps I am sitting in some crowded restaurant, the book open beside me, or closed, my excitement having over-brimmed the page. I look at the strangers near as if I had known them all my life, and it seems strange that I cannot speak to them: everything fills me with affection, I have no longer any fears or any needs: I do not even remember that this happy mood must come to an end.' 51–6. See 'The Man and the Echo'. 59. *lord of Chou* Perhaps Chou-kung, Duke of Chou in the twelfth century. 74. *Isaiah's coal* One of the seraphim lays a live coal on the mouth of Isaiah and says, 'Lo, this hath touched thy lips, and thine iniquity is taken away and thy sin purged' (Isaiah 6:6–7). The draft has 'Ezekiel' (Ellmann, *The Identity of Yeats*). 77. One of the drafts has 'grandad Homer'; Homer is also coupled with Shakespeare (Ellmann, *The Identity of Yeats*). 78. Baron Friedrich von Hügel (1852–1925) was the author of *The Mystical Element of Religion*, in which he contrasts Homeric and Christian projections of the life after death. 80–82. See 'Oil and Blood'. 88. Judges 14:5–18: 'Out of the strong came forth sweetness.'

The Results of Thought

First published in *WFMP*.
   2. *One dear brilliant woman* Identified by Jeffares as Lady Gregory.

Remorse for Intemperate Speech

First published in *WFMP*.
   4. *Fit* See 'fit audience find, though few' (*Paradise Lost*, 7.31).

Words for Music Perhaps

This sequence was first published in *WFMP* (though in different order) with the exception of 'I Crazy Jane talks with the Bishop', which first appeared in *WS*, 1933. Yeats wanted the poems to be 'all emotion and all impersonal ... all praise of joyous life'. Crazy Jane is partly based on Cracked Mary, 'the local satirist' who lived near Lady Gregory. Many years earlier, in a note to *The Pot of Broth* (1902), Yeats had attributed both words and air of a tramp's song to 'an old woman known as Cracked Mary, who wanders about the plain of Aidhne'. Ellmann (*The Identity of Yeats*) has printed the previously unpublished 'Cracked Mary's Vision', which favourably contrasts 'Long-bodied Tuatha de Danaan' with George V.

I Crazy Jane and the Bishop
First published in the *New Republic*, 12 November 1930, when the title was 'Cracked Mary and the Bishop'; in *WS*, 1933.

7. *solid* Sober-minded, of reliable judgement, in practical matters; steady, sedate, staid (*OED*). 9. *Jack the Journeyman* first appears in the song in *The Pot of Broth* mentioned above.

V Crazy Jane on God
13–17. See note on 'All Souls' Night', line 21.

VI Crazy Jane talks with the Bishop
First published in *WS*, 1933.

VII Crazy Jane Grown Old looks at the Dancers
First published in the *New Republic*, 12 November 1930.
    18. *thraneen* Little stalk of grass, something of no value (Irish word).

X Her Anxiety
First published in the *New Republic*, 22 October 1930.

XVII After Long Silence
Commentators have long thought that this is addressed to Olivia Shakespear, but David L. Clark has plausibly suggested that it is written to Moina Mathers (see notes to 'All Souls' Night').
    2. In 'To Vestigia' (*AV*, 1925), which is certainly addressed to Mrs Mathers, Yeats wrote: 'All other students who were once friends or friends' friends were dead or estranged'.

XXV The Delphic Oracle upon Plotinus
This is based on a passage in Stephen MacKenna's translation of Porphyry's *Life of Plotinus*; it is in effect a translation into the Yeatsian mode. The Delphic oracle envisages Plotinus entering the afterlife. Plotinus (AD 205–70) was the founder of Neo-Platonism; his mystical philosophy was of particular interest to Yeats; see also 'The Tower', lines 12 and 146, and especially 'News for the Delphic Oracle', which is a revisionary version of 'The Delphic Oracle upon Plotinus'.
    3. *Rhadamanthus* In early Greek tradition a stern judicial presence in the underworld. 8. *Minos* King of Crete, also a judge in the underworld. 9. *Pythagoras* A mystic as well as a mathematician (see 'Among School Children', lines 45–7).

A Woman Young and Old

The sequence was first published in *WS*, 1929. The complete sequence is composed of eleven poems in the following order: 'I Father and Child', 'II Before the World was made', 'III A First Confession', 'IV Her Triumph', 'V Consolation', 'VI Chosen', 'VII Parting', 'VIII Her Vision in the Wood', 'IX A Last Confession', 'X Meeting', 'XI From the "Antigone"'. *The Tower* has a sequence entitled *A Man Young and Old*.

VIII Her Vision in the Wood

12–16. A reference to the myth of Adonis, who was killed by a boar. An interest in fertility ritual can be traced in a number of Yeats's poems. **19.** *Quattrocento* Of the fifteenth century. **20.** *Mantegna* Andrea Mantegna (1431–1506); see 'Among School Children', line 26.

From A FULL MOON IN MARCH

With the exception of four 'Supernatural Songs' and 'Two Songs Rewritten for the Tune's Sake', all the poems in this volume had previously appeared in *KGCT*. The volume also included two plays: *A Full Moon in March* and *The King of the Great Clock Tower* (in verse).

Parnell's Funeral

First published in full in the *Spectator*, 19 October 1934, with the two sections titled 'A Parnellite at Parnell's Funeral' and 'Forty Years Later'; in *KGCT*. 'In "At Parnell's Funeral" I rhymed passages from a lecture I had given in America.' Yeats wrote of the impact of Parnell's fall: 'The modern literature of Ireland, and indeed all that stir of thought which prepared for the Anglo-Irish war, began when Parnell fell from power in 1891. A disillusioned and embittered Ireland turned from parliamentary politics; an event was conceived; and the race began as I think, to be troubled by that event's [the rising of 1916] long gestation' (*BS*). In the Introduction to *The Words upon the Window Pane* (1931) Yeats also wrote: 'The fall of Parnell has freed imagination from practical politics, from agrarian grievance and political enmity, and turned it to imaginative nationalism, to Gaelic, to the ancient stories, and at last to lyrical poetry and to drama.' In his 'Commentary' on the poem Yeats treated the subject at length: 'Dublin had once been a well-mannered, smooth-spoken city ... Then came agrarian passion; Unionists and Nationalists ceased to meet, but each lived behind his party wall an amiable life. This new dispute broke through all walls; there were [*sic*] old men and women I avoid because they have kept that day's bitter tongue. Upon the other hand, we began to value truth. According to my memory and the memory of others, free discussion appeared among us for the first time, bringing the passion for reality, the satiric genius that informs "Ulysses", "The Playboy of the Western World", "The Informer", "The Puritan" and other books and plays; the accumulated hatred of years was suddenly transferred from England to Ireland' (*KGCT*). See 'To a Shade'.

1. *Great Comedian* Daniel O'Connell (1775–1847), the 'Liberator', Catholic politician, champion of Catholic Emancipation and eloquent agitator for Repeal of the Union, the most charismatic and popular figure in Irish politics in the nineteenth century. O'Connell was a brilliant exponent of the 'monster' public meeting, and Yeats distrusted his association with the crowd which he connected with O'Connell's Catholicism: 'O'Connell, the one great Catholic figure, was formless. The power of self-conquest, of elevation has been Protestant, and more or less a thing of class. All the tragedians were Protestant

– O'Connell was a comedian. He had the gifts of the market place, of the clown at the fair' (*M*). His particular brand of politics had left an unfortunate legacy for his successors: 'O'Connell was a great man but there is too much of his spirit in the practical politics of Ireland,' wrote Yeats in a speech on Robert Emmet delivered in New York on 28 February 1904. The failure of Emmet was much more fruitful: 'I sometimes think that O'Connell was the contrary principle to Emmet. He taught the people to lay aside the pike and the musket, the song and the story, and to do their work now by wheedling and now by bullying. He won certain necessary laws for Ireland. He gave her a few laws, but he did not give her patriots. He was the successful politician, but it was the unsuccessful Emmet who has given her patriots'. 7. Yeats's note recalls 'the star that fell in broad daylight as Parnell's body was lowered into the grave – was it a collective hallucination or an actual event?' He connected this epiphany with the symbolism of his own vision of a naked woman shooting an arrow at a star, which he explicated in a note to *TV*. He traced the woman back to early Cretan religion and identified her in part as Artemis: 'She was, it seems, the Mother-Goddess, whose representative priestess shot the arrow at the child, whose sacrificial death symbolised the death and resurrection of the tree-spirit, or Apollo.' On the phenomenon which occurred at Parnell's funeral, he commented: 'I ask if the fall of a star may not, upon occasion, symbolise an accepted sacrifice' (*KGCT*). 14. Yeats's note to *TV* records that the Cretan Jupiter made an image of his son in gypsum which he placed in the boy's heart. The image was kept in a temple, and the heart became the occasion of 'festivals and noisy processions'. 15. *Sicilian coin* Yeats had a particular admiration for Sicilian coinage: 'the most famous and beautiful coins are the coins of the Greek Colonies, especially of those in Sicily'. The Sicilian example exercised an influence on his contribution towards the design of the new Irish coinage. See 'What we did, or tried to do', *Coinage of Saorstát Éireann* (1928). 16. 'I had seen Ireland in my own time turn from the bragging rhetoric and gregarious humour of O'Connell's generation and school, and offer herself to the solitary and proud Parnell as to her anti-self, buskin followed hard on sock [tragedy followed comedy], and I had begun to hope, or to half hope, that we might be the first in Europe to seek unity as deliberately as it had been sought by theologian, poet, sculptor, architect, from the eleventh to the thirteenth century' (*TV*). 'As we discussed and argued, the national character changed. O'Connell, the great comedian, left the scene and the tragedian Parnell took his place. When we talked of his pride; of his apparent impassivity when his hands were full of blood because he had torn them with his nails, the preceding epoch with its democratic bonhomie seemed to grin through a horse collar. He was the symbol that made apparent, or made possible ... that epoch's contrary' (*KGCT*, spelling corrected). 17–18. For Emmet, Fitzgerald and Tone, see 'September 1913', lines 20–21; see also note to line 1 above. The word 'murdered' is loosely applied, since Emmet was executed, Fitzgerald was wounded fatally while being arrested and Tone took his own life. Yet all three died in their resistance to the rule of 'strangers' (the English), while Parnell was the victim of the Irish people themselves. 18. See

'Easter 1916', line 14, and 'The Circus Animals' Desertion', lines 31–2. **21.**
See *King Lear*, Act II, Scene iv, line 57: 'Hysterica passio! down, thou
climbing sorrow'. A favourite Yeatsian phrase to suggest that 'sheer madness'
which he identified in Irish public life ('*Hysterica passio* dragged this quarry
Parnell down') and in himself ('I had to subdue a kind of Jacobin rage. I
escaped from it all as a writer through my sense of style', *M*). **32.** Yeats's sense
of decline in the character of politicians after Parnell was expressed in 'Poetry
and Tradition' (dated August 1907, first printed in *Discoveries*, 1908): 'I could
not foresee that a new class, which had begun to rise into power under the
shadow of Parnell, would change the nature of the Irish movement, which,
needing no longer great sacrifices, nor bringing any great risk to individuals,
could do without exceptional men and those activities of the mind that are
founded on the exceptional moment.' **33.** Eamonn de Valera (1882–1975), who
later was for many years the leading political presence in the Irish Free State
and became President, took part in the rising of 1916, became President of
Sinn Féin (1917–26) and President of the political party Fianna Fáil from
1926. Since 1932 he had been President of the Executive Council of the Irish
Free State. Yeats would have known from his reading of *The Golden Bough* by
Sir James Frazer that in certain more 'primitive' societies the hearts of men
had been eaten in order to acquire their qualities, while the hearts of dead
kings were sometimes eaten by their successors. **34.** *loose-lipped* Refers to the
easy rhetoric of O'Connell and those who followed him, but may also carry
something of the ethnic caricature of the Irish and of Irish Catholics in
particular which was very notable in the nineteenth century. **36.** *Cosgrave*
William T. Cosgrave (1880–1966) had been the first President of the Dáil
from 1922 to 1932 and subsequently continued to be a member. **39.** *O'Higgins*
See 'Death'. **40.** Eoin O'Duffy (1892–1944), who had been for many years
head of the Garda Síochána, was a leader of the Blueshirts and later fought
with the Nationalists in the Spanish Civil War. Yeats was interested in his
Fascist activities, but he soon became disillusioned. **42–3.** For Swift, see
'Blood and the Moon' and 'The Seven Sages'.

A Prayer for Old Age

First published in the *Spectator*, 2 November 1934, as 'Old Age'; in *KGCT*.

Supernatural Songs

First published in *Poetry*, December 1934; in *KGCT*; as a sequence of eight
poems which was completed in *AFMIM*. There are twelve poems in the
complete sequence, with the following not included in the present selection:
'II Ribh denounces Patrick', 'III Ribh in Ecstasy', 'IV There', 'VI He and
She', 'VII What Magic Drum?' 'IX The Four Ages of Man', 'X Conjunctions'
and 'XI A Needle's Eye'.

I Ribh at the Tomb of Baile and Aillinn

Yeats explained that 'that old hermit Ribh' [pronounced *Reeve*] was 'an imaginary critic of St. Patrick' [founder of Irish Christianity and patron saint of Ireland]. 'Saint Patrick must have found in Ireland ... men whose Christianity had come from Egypt, and retained characteristics of those older faiths that have become so important to our invention ... I would consider Ribh, were it not for his ideas about the Trinity, an orthodox man' (*KGCT*). Baile and Aillinn [pronounced *Bollya* and *Allyin*] were the subject of Yeats's 'half lyrical half narrative poem' which bears their name and which was published in July 1902. 'Baile and Aillinn were lovers, but Aengus, the Master of Love, wishing them to be happy in his own land among the dead, told to each a story of the other's death, so that their hearts were broken and they died' (Yeats's note to the poem, 1902).

4. *tonsured* With head partly or completely shaven as sign of priestly or monastic dedication (*OED*). See 'the circular grey patch of hair in the middle of his bald head looked like the cairn upon Knocknarea, for in Connaught they had not yet abandoned the ancient tonsure' ('The Crucifixion of the Outcast', 1925 version). 8. *apple and yew* 'And poets found, old writers say, / A yew-tree where his body lay, / But a wild apple hid the grass / With its sweet blossom where hers was; / And being in good heart, because / A better time had come again / After the deaths of many men, / And that long fighting at the ford, / They wrote on tablets of thin board, / Made of the apple and the yew, / All the love stories that they knew' (*Baile and Aillinn*, lines 187–97). 15–16. See Yeats's reference in a letter to 'that saying of Swedenborg that the sexual intercourse of angels is a conflagration of the whole being' (21 February, 1933, *Letters*). 'I do not doubt that they [the dead] make love in that union which Swedenborg has said is of the whole body and seems from far off an incandescence' (*PASL*). 24. *aquiline* Eagle-like and therefore able to endure the light without blinking.

V Ribh considers Christian Love insufficient
First published in *Poetry*, December 1934.

VIII Whence had they come?
First published in *AFMIM*.

4. *Dramatis Personae* The characters of the play. This was the title of one of Yeats's volumes of autobiography (1935). For Yeats's tendency to think dramatically, see: 'I am satisfied, the Platonic Year in my head, to find but drama' (Introduction to *The Resurrection* in *Wheels and Butterflies*, 1934). 7. *Flagellant* One who scourges himself by way of religious discipline or penance, especially one of a sect of fanatics that arose in the thirteenth century (*OED*). 12. *Charlemagne* Charlemagne (742–814) was crowned as Holy Roman Emperor in 800; for parallels to the 'sacred drama' enacted by his mother Berthe au Grand Pied as she gave birth, compare 'Leda and the Swan' and 'The Mother of God'. The term 'sacred drama' is used by Sir James Frazer in connection with the rituals which marked the birth and resurrection of Osiris and with

rituals at the sanctuary of Semiramis. 'A nation should be like an audience in some great theatre – "In the theatre," said Victor Hugo, "the mob becomes a people" – watching the sacred drama of its own history' (*KGCT*). In *KGCT* Yeats also suggested that if any government or political party wishes to achieve unity of culture, 'it will promise not this or that measure but a discipline, a way of life; that sacred drama must to all native eyes and ears become the greatest of the parables'.

XII Meru

This poem is closely associated with Yeats's Introduction to *The Holy Mountain* (1934) by Shri Purohit Swāmi. The Swāmi's book describes the initiation of his master on Kailās, or Mount Meru, in Tibet, which Sven Hedin called 'the most famous of all mountains'. In his Introduction Yeats evoked in some detail both the mountain and its place in Eastern religion. Cave, ice and snow are vividly described, as are the conditions in which the Swāmi sought for Turiyā [pure personality] 'in hollows of the ice, his overcoat about his head, his feet drawn up to his ribs'.

NEW POEMS

This collection was published by the Cuala Press in 1938. For its relation to *Last Poems* and its inclusion under that heading in *CP*, 1949, and afterwards, see 'A Note on the Text', pp. xli–xliii above. Only 'The Municipal Gallery Revisited' and 'A Crazed Girl' had previously appeared in book form. A number of poems (including 'The Curse of Cromwell') had been published as broadsides; this reflects Yeats's interest at this time in ballads, which feature prominently in *NP*. The volume printed thirteen poems completely new to the reading public; the most notable of these was, perhaps, 'The Gyres'.

The Gyres

For gyres, see notes on 'The Second Coming' and 'Sailing to Byzantium', line 19.

1. *Old Rocky Face* Variously identified as the Delphic Oracle 'who spoke through a cleft in the rock' and 'a proper muse for a prophetic poem' (Ellmann, *The Identity of Yeats*), the prophetic Jew, Ashasuerus, who inhabited a cavern in Shelley's *Hellas* (Henn, Jeffares) and (fancifully) as Blake's Urizen (Moore, *The Unicorn*). In drafts, 'Old cavern man, old rocky face,' and 'wrinkled rocky face' (Stallworthy, *Vision and Revision*). 4. *lineaments* A word which carries much resonance with Yeats and suggests archetypal patterns and firm outlines; see 'The Statues' and Blake's use of the word (for example, in 'The lineaments of gratified desire', line 2 of 'What is it men in women do require?'). 6. *Empedocles* Greek philosopher and poet (*c.* 493–*c.* 433 BC) who denied the unity and immobility of real being. 'Generation and decay are nothing save the compounding . . . and dissolution of eternally unchanging "elements". Empedocles imagines a world-cycle in which Love, the unifier of

unlikes, and Strife, which divides and so joins like to like, alternately predominate' (*Oxford Classical Dictionary*). In *AV*, 1937, Yeats quotes Empedocles on Concord and Discord at the opening of Book I: 'Never will boundless time be emptied of that pair; and they prevail in turn as that circle [the Great Wheel] comes round, and pass away before one another and increase in their appointed turn.' In this context he notes that Love and War came from the eggs of Leda. 7. *light in Troy* The burning of the city which eventually followed the death of Hector, its champion.

Lapis Lazuli

First published in the *London Mercury*, March 1938. Lapis Lazuli is a complex silicate containing sulphur, of light blue colour, used as a pigment (*OED*). See this passage from 'Rosa Alchemica' in *SR* (first published in the *Savoy*, April 1896): 'There is Lear, his head still wet with the thunder-storm, and he laughs . . . and there is Beatrice . . . and there is the mother of the God of humility.'

3. Yeats's insistence on 'gaiety' in the face of death and destruction is probably indebted to the writings of Nietzsche (including *The Gay Science*). For a much earlier use, see 'We who are old, old and gay' ('A Faery Song'), line 1). 6. *Zeppelin* This reference to the dirigible airship recalls the period of the First World War, when Yeats had experienced German air-raids on London. 7. *King Billy* A name full of political resonance, especially in Northern Ireland. It is common Irish parlance for William of Orange (William III), the victor of the Battle of the Boyne. Yeats's ancestors had taken part in the fighting (see notes to '[*Pardon, old fathers, if you still remain*]'); *bomb-balls* These seem to be derived from an Irish ballad. 15. An example of characterisation which falls short of the genuinely tragic. 'Always at the noble moment, the great moment, when the actor must speak thinking lyrically or musically, these are the very moments when he desired to characterise'. 'No tragedy is legitimate unless it leads some great character to his final joy. Polonius may go out wretchedly, but I can hear the dance music in "Absent thee from felicity awhile", or in Hamlet's speech over the dead Ophelia, and what of Cleopatra's last farewells, Lear's rage under the lightning, Oedipus sinking down at the story's end into an earth "riven" by love?' (*OTB*). 19. *Black out* (1) The darkening of a stage during a performance; a darkened stage (2) a temporary loss of memory (3) the action of extinguishing, covering, or obscuring lights as a precaution against air-raids, etc; the resulting darkness (*OED*, which first records 3 in 1935). 22. *drop-scenes* Painted curtain(s) let down between the acts of a play to shut off the stage from the view of the audience; also used for the final scene of a drama or play in real life (*OED*). 29. *Callimachus* Greek sculptor of the fifth century BC who is said to have invented the Corinthian capital and whose works included a 'bronze lamp, shaped like a palm' for the Erechtheum at Athens.

An Acre of Grass

First published in the *Atlantic Monthly*, April 1938. The house is Riversdale in Rathfarnham, Co. Dublin, which Yeats had leased in 1932.

What Then?

First published in the *Erasmian*, April 1937.
   12. *small old house* Riversdale (see 'An Acre of Grass').

Beautiful Lofty Things

1. For John O'Leary, see notes to 'September 1913'. 2–4. John Butler Yeats (1839–1922), portrait painter, contributed to a debate at the Abbey Theatre on 4 February 1907 on the subject of Synge's *The Playboy of the Western World*; this had provoked riots among the audience during its early performances. 'No man of all literary Dublin dared show his face but my own father, who spoke to, or rather in the presence of, that howling mob with sweetness and simplicity' (*Estrangement*, 1936). Yeats himself played a prominent role in the debate. 5–6. Standish James O'Grady (1846–1928), member of the 'old Irish land-owning aristocracy' and writer of political works such as *Toryism and Tory Democracy* (1886), historian of Ireland's epic past, notably in *The History of Ireland: Heroic Period* (1878–81), and author of historical novels such as *Finn and His Companions* (1892) and *The Coming of Cuchulain* (1894). On at least two occasions Yeats quoted the claim of this Irish prose Homer that a day would come 'when Slieve-na-mon [which features in Yeats's own 'The Grey Rock'] will be more famous than Olympus' (see last line of the poem). See also O'Grady's claim: 'The heroic age of Ireland is not a tradition, but a prophecy; unfulfilled, but which is to be fulfilled' (*All Ireland*, 1898). In *DP* Yeats remembered that O'Grady 'could delight us with an extravagance which we were too critical to share' and recalled his drunken but prophetic speech on the destiny of Ireland. 7–10. This incident in the life of Lady Gregory occurred during the Irish Civil War. 10–11. Howth (pronounced to rhyme with *growth*), where the Yeats family lived from late 1881 till 1884, is a village with a small fishing harbour situated on a promontory north of Dublin. Howth Head, which overlooks Dublin Bay, is the setting of the first amorous encounter between Leopold and Molly Bloom in Joyce's *Ulysses*. Yeats and Maud Gonne spent a day on the cliff paths of Howth after he had unsuccessfully proposed to her (the day is remembered in 'The White Birds'). This is the only occasion on which Yeats names Maud Gonne in his poetry; *Pallas Athene* See note to 'A Thought from Propertius'. 13. The Olympians are the Greek gods who inhabited Mount Olympus (see note to lines 5–6 above).

A Crazed Girl

First published in *The Lemon Tree* by Margot Ruddock, 1937, as 'At Barcelona'. The girl is Margot Collis (her pseudonym was Margot Ruddock), whose breakdown is described by Yeats in a letter of 22 May 1936. Yeats's poem appeared in her book of poetry, *The Lemon Tree*, to which he contributed an Introduction. She is also the subject of 'Sweet Dancer' and of 'Margot' (printed in McHugh).

The Curse of Cromwell

First published in *A Broadside*, August 1937. Oliver Cromwell's Irish expedition, which included the Drogheda and Wexford massacres, was followed by the confiscation of land on an extensive scale; these episodes were deeply seared into the consciousness of the Irish, particularly the Catholics. The speaker in Yeats's poem is a 'wandering peasant poet'. In the MS of 'A General Introduction for my Work' Yeats quoted the first verse in the context of his own divided loyalties towards England and the English tradition and of his relation to the wider historical context: 'The "Irishry" have preserved their ancient "deposit" through wars which, during the sixteenth and seventeenth centuries, became wars of extermination. No people, Lecky said at the opening of his "Ireland in the Eighteenth Century", have undergone greater persecution. Nor did that persecution altogether cease up to our own day. No people hate as we do in whom that past is always alive. There are moments when hatred poisons my life and I accuse myself of effeminacy because I have not given it adequate expression.' The peasant poet comes out of the same poetic tradition as the historical Raftery and Yeats's Red Hanrahan, and his lament for the great houses and for the ancient customs of poetic patronage owes something to the example of Gaelic poetry. It also provides an interesting alternative perspective to Yeats's own laments for Coole Park. See *KGCT*: 'At the base of the social structure, but hardly within it, the peasantry dreamed on in their medieval sleep; the Gaelic poets sang of the banished Catholic aristocracy; "My fathers served their fathers before Christ was crucified" sang one of the most famous. Ireland had found new masters.'

17–19. According to Plutarch, the boy maintained the code of Spartan heroism by uncomplainingly concealing a stolen fox under his tunic. 25–8. See note to line 4 of 'All Souls' Night'. 30. See the end of *Gulliver's Travels*.

The Great Day

First published in the *London Mercury*, March 1938.

Parnell

First published in the *London Mercury*, March 1938. For Parnell, see notes to 'To a Shade' and 'Parnell's Funeral'. According to Yeats, the poem 'contains an actual saying of Parnell's' (*LDW*); see also Introduction, p. xxv.

The Spur

First published in the *London Mercury*, March 1938.

The Municipal Gallery Revisited

First published in *A Speech and Two Poems* (1937). Yeats's speech of 17 August 1937 provides both a prose gloss and a context for the poem. In the Municipal Gallery of Modern Art in Dublin, Yeats saw 'Ireland not as she is displayed in guide book or history, but, Ireland seen because of the magnificent vitality of her painters, in the glory of her passions ... In those rooms of the Municipal Gallery I saw Ireland in spiritual freedom, and the Corots, the Rodins, the Rousseaus were the visiting gods.' For identification of the pictures, see Jeffares, *A New Commentary*.

3. *Casement* Roger Casement (1864–1916), who had worked for twenty years in the British Consular Service, was executed for high treason; he had been arrested after landing in Ireland from a German submarine on his way to assist in the rising of 1916. Yeats, who had interceded for him at the highest level, made him the subject of 'Roger Casement' and 'The Ghost of Roger Casement'. 4. *Griffith* Arthur Griffith (1871–1922), politician, influential political journalist and editor of the *United Irishman* and *Sinn Féin*, and leader of the Irish delegation that negotiated the Anglo-Irish Treaty, approved by the Dáil on 7 January 1922. He had frequently crossed swords with Yeats and had nicknamed him 'Pensioner Yeats' after his acceptance of a Civil List Pension. 5. *O'Higgins*' For Kevin O'Higgins, see notes on 'Death'. 10. *Tricolour* The Flag of the Irish Free State in which equal vertical stripes of green, white and orange follow the pattern of blue, white and red established by the French Republic during the Revolution. 21–2. For Robert Gregory and Hugh Lane, see notes to 'In Memory of Major Robert Gregory' and 'September 1913'. 23. *Hazel Lavery* This refers to two portaits of Hazel, the American wife of the Irish artist Sir John Lavery (1856–1941), who painted a number of the pictures specifically alluded to by Yeats in this poem. 25–7. In *A Vision* Yeats links Synge and Rembrandt in the Twenty-third phase: 'both delight in all that is wilful, in all that flouts intellectual coherence, and conceive of the world as if it were an overflowing cauldron.' 39–40. 'He now is gone, the whiles the foxe is crept / Into the hole, the which the Badger swept' (from 'The Ruines of Time' in which Spenser lamented the death of his patron, the Earl of Leicester). Yeats here identified that kind of coincidence between the diction of poetry and the 'common tongue' which featured in Lady Gregory's ideal, 'To think like a wise man, but to express oneself like the common people.' Spenser's lines also coincide with local realities, since Yeats's account in *The Celtic Twilight* made it clear that the woods of Coole were home to badgers and foxes. This stanza is one line short, though there is a draft version in which it runs to the expected total. 41–7. 'Folk-art is, indeed, the oldest of the aristocracies of thought, and because it refuses what is passing and trivial, the merely clever and pretty, as certainly as the vulgar and insincere, and because it has gathered into itself the simplest and most unforgettable thought of the generations, it is the soil where all great art is rooted' ('By the Roadside', *CT*, 1902); 'Aristocracies have made beautiful manners, because their place in the world puts them above the fear of life, and

the countrymen have made beautiful stories and beliefs, because they have nothing to lose and so do not fear, and the artists have made all the rest, because Providence has filled them with recklessness' ('Poetry and Tradition', dated 1907, first published in *Discoveries*, 1908). Synge and Lady Gregory specifically created a dramatic style out of the speech of the peasantry. Yeats also made use of dialect in some of his plays and stories, with help from Lady Gregory, while the 'common tongue' added concreteness and an unromantic edge to his poetry in its later stages. 'We three have conceived an Ireland that will remain imaginary more powerfully than we have conceived ourselves' (*M*). *Antaeus-like* Antaeus was a giant whose strength depended on direct contact with the Earth, who was his mother.

Are You Content?

First published in the *Atlantic Monthly*, April 1938. The title seems to allude to a vision experienced by Shelley towards the end of his life. According to one version, he met 'a figure of himself' on the terrace at Lerici, which asked, 'How long do you mean to be content?' In another version a cloaked figure visited him in the night and asked '*Siete soddisfatto?*' The question seems appropriate, since the later Yeats is much concerned with final reckonings and with last things. Compare '[*Pardon, old fathers, if you still remain*]', 'A Dialogue of Self and Soul' and 'The Man and the Echo'.

6. *old loins* See 'blood / That has not passed through any huckster's loin' ('[*Pardon, old fathers* . . .]', lines 7–8). 9–16. Ancestors from both sides of Yeats's family (see his accounts in *AU* and *M*). 22–3 Yeats is invoking one of his 'favourite quotations', a passage from Browning's youthful confessional poem *Pauline* (1833), in which the poet recalls his early impressions of Greek literature: 'an old hunter / Talking with gods, or a high-crested chief / Sailing with troops of friends to Tenedos' (lines 323–5). Shelley is a significant presence in this poem.

From ON THE BOILER

This prose essay is an irascible, mocking prophetic discourse on eugenics, education and politics which owes not a little to Yeats's interpretation of Swift. For the significance of the title, see note to 'Why Should not Old Men be Mad?'

Why Should not Old Men be Mad?

In its original context in *OTB* the poem immediately follows an account of a mad ship's carpenter who denounced his neighbours from a rusty old boiler: 'I saw him at a Rosses Point regatta alone in a boat; sculling it in whenever he saw a crowd, then, bow to seaward, denouncing the general wickedness, then sculling it out amid a shower of stones.' This explains the title of *OTB* itself and suggests some ironical qualification of Yeats's own prophetic voice.

4. *drunken journalist* This reference cannot be identified precisely. 5. *A girl* Maud Gonne's daughter, Iseult, who married the writer Francis Stuart. 7–8. *Helen* This would seem to be Maud Gonne but may also carry traces of Constance Markievicz. Compare the oblique method of naming historical figures in 'Easter 1916' and the more generalised figures of 'The Fisherman'.

Crazy Jane on the Mountain

For Crazy Jane and the Bishop, see the poem of that name.

7–10. Probably alludes to the killing of the Russian royal family in July 1918 and to the unsuccessful effort of George V to save their lives by bringing them to England. For Yeats's distaste for the king, see note to 'I Crazy Jane and the Bishop'. Kathleen Raine has read these lines as a reference to Conchubar and the sons of Usna, 'whom he treacherously murdered because of Deirdre, who had preferred Naoise to himself' (Introduction to *The Celtic Twilight*, 1981). *And he stuck* The co-ordinative syntax is characteristically Irish. 15. *Great bladdered Emer* In *OTB* Yeats noted that 'In a fragment from some early version of *The Courting of Emer*, Emer [wife of Cuchulain] is chosen for the strength and volume of her bladder. This strength and volume were certainly considered signs of vigour.' 22. See: 'there was no one of them all but cried tears down' in note to 'Red Hanrahan's Song about Ireland'.

LAST POEMS

See 'A Note on the Text', pp. xli–xliii above.

Under Ben Bulben

First published in the *Irish Times*, February 1939. According to tradition, Ben Bulben was associated with the Fianna; the door of Faeryland was located on its southern side (*The Celtic Twilight*).

2. *Mareotic Lake* One of the focal points of Egyptian monasticism (see 'Through barren Thebaid, / Or by the Mareotic sea' in 'Demon and Beast'). The enigmatic witch in Shelley's *The Witch of Atlas* (written 1820) passes along the Nile 'by Moeris and the Mareotid lakes, and sees all human life shadowed upon its waters', as Yeats noted in 'The Philosophy of Shelley's Poetry', in which he compared Shelley to Porphyry and observed that 'Water is his great symbol of existence, and he continually meditates over its mysterious source' (1903). 5–11. See 'The Hosting of the Sidhe' and Yeats's note. Compare also, 'I meet those long pale faces, / Hear their great horses, then / Recall what centuries have passed / Since they were living men' (*The Death of Cuchulain*, lines 204–7). 13–24. Reincarnation is discussed in *OTB*. 25–6. A quotation from 'that marvellous' *Jail Journal* (1854) of John Mitchel; Yeats wrote, he 'thundered from his convict hulk a thunder that was half Carlyle's against England and the gods of his master' ('Irish National Literature', I, 1895). Mitchel (1815–75), founder of the *United Irishman*, was transported to

Tasmania, though he eventually escaped. He believed that 'wars and revolutions (the truest moral force) are needed to purify and vivify a comatose world'. **36.** At this stage the draft includes a passage which does not appear in the final version: 'So what's the odds if war must come / From Moscow, from Berlin, or Rome. / Let children should an aeroplane / Some neighbouring city pavement stain, / Or Should the deafening cannon sound / Clasp their hands & dance in a round. / The passing moment makes it sweet / When male & female organ meet' (Stallworthy, *Vision and Revision*). **42–52.** See 'The Statues' and notes. For the sexual qualities of Michelangelo's art, see 'Long-Legged Fly', lines 21–6, where there is a specific reference to the creation of Adam. See also the passage in *A Vision* which claims that in the eighth gyre (1550– 1650), beginning with Raphael, Michelangelo and Titian, 'the forms, as in Titian, awaken sexual desire – we had not desired to touch the forms of Botticelli or even of Da Vinci – or they threaten us like those of Michel Angelo, and the painter himself handles his brush with a conscious facility or exultation.' Compare also: 'Michael Angelo's Sistine roof, / His "Morning" and his "Night" disclose / How sinew that has been pulled tight, / Or it may be loosened in repose, / Can rule by supernatural right / Yet be but sinew' ('Michael Robartes and the Dancer', lines 32–7). **53.** *Quattrocento* Fifteenth century; see 'Among School Children', line 26, and 'Her Vision in the Wood', line 19. **64–6.** Edward Calvert (1779–1883), Richard Wilson (1714–82), William Blake (1757–1827), Claude Lorrain (1600–1682) and Samuel Palmer (1805–81). All in different ways created visionary landscapes and offered intimations of Eden or Paradise. In his essay on Blake's illustrations to Dante (1897) Yeats quoted Palmer on Thornton's illustrations to Virgil: 'There is in all such a misty and dreamy glimmer as penetrates and kindles the inmost soul and gives complete and unreserved delight, unlike the gaudy daylight of this world. They are like all this wonderful artist's work, the drawing aside of the fleshly curtain, and the glimpse which all the most holy, studious saints and sages have enjoyed, of the rest which remains to the people of God [referring to Hebrews 4:9].' **79–9.** The collapse of the Irish aristocratic tradition (see 'The Curse of Cromwell'). **83.** *Irishry* Native Irish as distinct from English settlers in Ireland; used by Burke to differentiate them from 'Englishry'. Yeats may have employed with proud defiance a term which was often used abusively, as in Holland's 'They that refuse to be under lawes, . . . are termed the Irishry, and commonly the Wilde Irish' (1610). See 'A General Introduction for my Work': 'If Irish literature goes on as my generation planned it, it may do something to keep the "Irishry" living'; and 'The "Irishry" have preserved their ancient "deposit" through wars which, during the sixteenth and seventeenth centuries, became wars of extermination.' **86–7.** John Yeats (1774–1848) was rector of Drumcliff, which is 'a wide green valley, lying at the foot of Ben Bulben' (*The Celtic Twilight*).

The Black Tower

This is Yeats's last poem. According to Henn, the poem celebrates the warrior

Eoghan Bel, who was buried standing near the summit of Knocknarea, his javelin defiantly in his hand, after the Battle of Sligo in 537.

Cuchulain Comforted

For the Cuchulain theme, see notes to 'Cuchulain's Fight with the Sea' and especially *The Death of Cuchulain*, which was first published in *LPTP*. Towards the end of the play, Cuchulain tells the Blind Man who is about to cut off his head: 'There floats out there / The shape that I shall take when I am dead, / My soul's first shape, a soft feathery shape, / And is not that a strange shape for the soul / Of a great fighting-man?' To the Blind Man's 'Your shoulder is there, / This is your neck / Ah! ah! Are you ready, Cuchulain!' he replies, 'I say it is about to sing' (lines 177–83). The Morrigu, Goddess of War, details the 'six mortal wounds' which brought about Cuchulain's death (lines 184–95).

The Statues

First published in the *London Mercury*, March 1939. See *A Vision*: 'Each age unwinds the thread another age had wound, and it amuses one to remember that before Phidias, and his westward-moving art, Persia fell, and that when full moon came round again, amid eastward-moving thought, and brought Byzantine glory, Rome fell; and that at the outset of our westward-moving Renaissance Byzantium fell; all things dying each other's life, living each other's death'.

1–3. *Pythagoras* See note to 'Among School Children', lines 45–7; *planned* Yeats assumes that the mathematical proportions of Greek sculpture can be traced back to the Pythagorean system. 9–16. Asiatic art was succeeded and superseded by Greek; in this artistic development, rather than in the naval victory over the Persians at Salamis in 480 BC, the Greeks defeated their Asian enemies and predecessors. Greek art tended towards the human and the individual, while Asiatic tended towards the inhuman and the plural. The 'many-headed foam' looks towards the imagery of the final stanza and can be linked with a Yeatsian fear and disgust for the crowd and its pull towards incoherence which was particularly acute in his later years, notably in *OTB*. Phidias (*c*. 490–*c*. 432 BC) was responsible for the sculpture of the Parthenon at Athens. In *A Vision* Yeats wrote of him: 'one remembers Titian – and all is transformed by the full moon, and all abounds and flows.' 17–24. After the Eastern conquests of Alexander the Great, Greek influence informed statues of the Buddha, whose postures of well-fleshed meditation contrasted with 'the wavering, lean image of hungry speculation' in the European Hamlet. Eastern religion is evoked by 'gong and conch'. *Grimalkin* Cat, especially an old she-cat. 25ff. For Patrick Pearse, see 'Easter 1916' and notes. The Provisional Government proclaimed Ireland a republic on the steps of the General Post Office, which later became a central focus of conflict between the insurrectionaries and government forces. Pearse had made clear his admiration for the heroes of Irish tradition: 'Fearghus, Conchubar, Cuchulain, Fion, Oisin, Oscar – these were more to the Gael than mere names of great champions and warriors of a former time: they represented to him men who had gone before, who had fought the good fight, . . . who had become gods, but whose spirits, heroic and immortal, still lived after them.' In particular Pearse had a strong personal devotion to the figure of Cuchulain, which was later commemorated by a statue in the Post Office ('A statue's there to mark the place, / By Oliver Sheppard done', *The Death of Cuchulain*, lines 224–5). 'Are those things that men adore and loathe / Their sole reality? / What stood in the Post Office / With Pearse and Connolly? / What comes out of the mountain / Where men first shed their blood? / Who thought Cuchulain till it seemed / He stood where they had stood?' (Singer in *The Death of Cuchulain*, lines 212–19). At the beginning of the play Yeats also offers an exercise in self-mockery. The Old Man who looks 'like something out of mythology' has been selected as producer 'because I am out of fashion and out of date like the antiquated romantic stuff the thing is made of'.

News for the Delphic Oracle

First published in the *London Mercury*, March 1939. The poem should be read in conjunction with 'The Delphic Oracle upon Plotinus' (see notes to this poem); it is a more extensive imagining or re-visioning of the world of eternity to which Plotinus is translated after death, and its emphasis on the physical and the sexual is a corrective to (colloquially 'News for') the eschatological idealism of the oracle. Porphyry begins his *Life of Plotinus* with the statement that 'Plotinus . . . seemed ashamed of being in the body'; Yeats's vision is also a vigorous response to this Neo-Platonic distaste for the physical.

1. *codgers* A familiar or jocosely irreverent term applied to an elderly man, usually with a grotesque or whimsical application (*OED*); a fellow, person, chap; a character (*Dialect Dictionary*). 5–6. For the love of Niamh and Oisin, see note to *The Wanderings of Oisin*. 7–8. For Pythagoras, see note to 'Among School Children', lines 45–7, and 'The Delphic Oracle upon Plotinus', in which the 'stately' Pythagoras is associated with 'the choir of Love'. 9–12. For Plotinus, see 'The Delphic Oracle upon Plotinus' and notes. For the irony of his exhibiting these symptoms of physical desire, see above. See 'that morning when I met / Face to face my rightful man / And did after stretch and yawn' ('Three Things', lines 15–17); compare Ezra Pound's 'yawn and stretch' in *The Spirit of Romance* (1910). 13ff. For dolphins and the afterlife, see 'Byzantium', line 33, and note. 26. *Peleus on Thetis* The marriage of Peleus and Thetis was thought to be the subject of a painting by Nicolas Poussin in the National Gallery of Ireland; it has now been retitled 'Acis and Galatea'. 31. *Pan* In Greek mythology the god Pan was a hybrid of goat and human form and was associated with, among other things, lust.

Long-legged Fly

First published in the *London Mercury*, March 1939.

5. *Caesar* A type of the military leader; 'What had the Caesars but their thrones?' ('Demon and Beast', line 50). 11. *topless towers* The phrase, which is borrowed from Marlowe's *Doctor Faustus*, refers to Troy and invokes, once again, the destructive example of Helen of Troy (see 'When Helen Lived', line 8). 23–5. A reference to Michelangelo's frescoes painted for the Pope on the ceiling and walls of the Sistine Chapel in the Vatican.

A Bronze Head

First published in the *New Republic*, March 1939. The head of Maud Gonne is a plaster cast painted bronze by Lawrence Campbell in the Municipal Gallery of Modern Art in Dublin (see 'The Municipal Gallery Revisited').

7. *Hysterica passio* See note to 'Parnell's Funeral', line 21. 13. *McTaggart* John McTaggart Ellis McTaggart (1866–1925), whose works included *Studies in Hegelian Cosmology* (1907), *The Relation of Time and Eternity* (1908) and *Human Immortality and Pre-existence* (1915), from which Jeffares has cited: 'Units, which were combined in a certain way, are now combined otherwise. The form has changed. But everything which was there before is there now [after something "ceases to exist"].' 18. *Propinquity* Nearness, closeness, proximity. 25. *stocks* Line of descent (or source of a line of descent); race, ethnical kindred; ancestral type from which various races, species, etc., have diverged (*OED*). 'Since about 1900 the better stocks have not been replacing their numbers, while the stupider and less healthy have been more than replacing theirs. Unless there is a change in the public mind every rank above the lowest must degenerate, and, as inferior men push up into its gaps, degenerate more and more quickly' (*OTB*). Also: 'The danger is that there will be no war, that the skilled will attempt nothing, that the European civilisation, like those older civilisations that saw the triumph of their gangrel stocks, will accept decay' (*OTB*; note the close connection of *gangrel* and *gangling*). Lines 24–8 play over in a different key some of the main themes of 'I Ancestral Houses' in 'Meditations in Time of Civil War', of the first section of 'Nineteen Hundred and Nineteen', and of the Coole Park poems; their emphasis on the fall of the aristocratic tradition and on genetic degeneration can be paralleled in many of the *Last Poems*, in *OTB* and in *Purgatory*. For clown and knave, see 'The Fisherman', lines 17–24, and compare the 'knave and fool' of 'Remorse for Intemperate Speech', line 1, and the 'lout' of 'The Fascination of What's Difficult', line 10.

John Kinsella's Lament for Mrs. Mary Moore

First published in the *London Mercury*, December 1938; originally 'A Strong Farmer's Complaint about Death' (Jeffares). John Kinsella and Mary Moore are both Yeatsian inventions.

21. *put a skin on* Give a vivid forcefulness in expression (Irish usage).

NOTES

High Talk

First published in the *London Mercury*, December 1938. 'These new men are goldsmiths working with a glass screwed into one eye, whereas we stride ahead of the crowd, its swordsmen, its jugglers, looking to right & left' (*LDW*, April 1936).

5. A circus procession (see 'The Circus Animals' Desertion'). 9. *Malachi* An Irish name without any further specific significance in this context. *Stilt-Jack* Presumably a conflation of stiltwalker and steeple-jack. 11. *Barnacle goose* See note to *The Wanderings of Oisin*, line 156. See also Cuchulain's words to Emer in the play *The Green Helmet* (1910): 'Would you stay the great barnacle-goose / When its eyes are turned to the sea and its beak to the salt of the air?' (lines 270–71).

The Man and the Echo

First published in the *Atlantic Monthly*, January 1939. Titled 'His Convictions' in draft.

1. *cleft* Probably on Knocknarea. 8. 'Seems to have done but harm until' (draft in *LDW*). 11–12. *that play of mine Cathleen ni Houlihan* was set in the revolutionary context of 1798. Yeats recalled a vision which had inspired his play in which Cathleen was 'Ireland herself, that Cathleen ni Houlihan for whom so many songs have been sung and about whom so many stories have been told and for whose sake so many have gone to their death' (1903). In April 1902 Maud Gonne performed the title role in Dublin with electrical effect. Yeats himself recalled: 'Her great height made Cathleen seem a divine being fallen into our mortal infirmity' (*CW*). Among those who explicitly registered the impact were Arthur Griffith, Stephen Gwynn and Bernard Shaw, who told Lady Gregory, 'When I see that play I feel it might lead a man to do something foolish.' By an appropriate irony, some of the Abbey actors who were to take part in a later production of the play joined the insurrectionary forces on Easter Monday, 1916; the first man to be shot on that day was 'the player Connolly' (not to be confused with James). For Maud Gonne's politics, see especially 'The People' and 'A Prayer for my Daughter', lines 57–64. 13ff. 'Or did my spoken words perplex / That man, that woman now a wreck?' (earlier version in *LDW*). 14. For Margo Collis (Ruddock), see note to 'A Crazed Girl'. 16. Coole Park, which had been sold to the Department of Forestry. 22. *bodkin* Short pointed weapon, dagger; this word alludes to Hamlet's contemplation of the possibility of suicide ('When he himself might his Quietus make / With a bare bodkin', Act III, Scene i, line 76). 46. The poem ends without a final echo.

The Circus Animals' Desertion

First published in the *Atlantic Monthly*, January 1939.

7–8. See 'High Talk'. 10–16. See headnote to *The Wanderings of Oisin*. 17–24. In *The Countess Kathleen* (first performed in Dublin on 8 May 1899) the Countess sells her soul in order to buy bread for the people in a time of famine, although the poet Kevin (later Aleel) attempts to intervene. In Yeats's conception the role was closely identified with the character of Maud Gonne ('my dear') who herself had taken steps to save the people of Donegal from famine, 'at whose suggestion' the play 'was planned out and begun' and to whom it was dedicated. 25–6. At the end of *On Baile's Strand* (first performed in Dublin on 27 December 1904) Cuchulain fights the waves off-stage, while the Fool provides a commentary for the Blind Man and the audience. The play ends with the words of the Blind Man: 'There will be nobody in the houses ... The ovens will be full. We will put our hands into the ovens.' See 'Cuchulain's Fight with the Sea', especially the ending in the 1925 version where he encounters 'the invulnerable tide' (all the draft versions of 'The Circus Animals' Desertion' also have *invulnerable*, not *ungovernable*, reports Bradford). Compare also: 'No body like his body / Has modern woman borne, / But an old man looking on life / Images it in scorn' (*The Death of Cuchulain*, lines 220–23). 33ff. The poem originally ended: 'O hour of triumph come and make me gay. / If burnished chariots are put to flight / Why brood upon old triumph; prepare to die / Even at the approach of un-imagined night / Man has the refuge of his gaiety, / A dab of black enhances every white, / Tension is but the vigour of the mind, / Cannon the god and father of mankind' (draft cited in Bradford). 40. See 'An Acre of Grass', lines 10–11.

Politics

First published in the *Atlantic Monthly*, January 1939. The epigraph from the German novelist Thomas Mann was taken from an article on 'Public Speech and Private Speech in Poetry' by the American poet Archibald Macleish. Macleish celebrated a return to public speech in modern poetry and singled out Yeats for particular praise: his later poetry was 'the first poetry in English in more than a century in which the poem is again an act upon the world'. Yeats was gratified, but 'Politics' suggests that his commitment to public speech was not achieved without conflict.

1–4. Cullingford has commented: 'Berlin was excluded, not solely for reasons of euphony' (but see the draft passage printed in note to 'Under Ben Bulben', line 36). These lines draw upon, if only to repudiate, Yeats's particularly close concern with the activities of Mussolini, his fear of Russian communism and his anxious observation of the Spanish Civil War.

BIBLIOGRAPHY

✦✦✦✦✦

PRIMARY TEXTS AND WORKS OF REFERENCE

Adams, Steve L. and Harper, George Mills (eds.), 'The Manuscript of "Leo Africanus"', *Yeats Annual No. 1* (London and Basingstoke, 1982)

Allt, Peter and Alspach, Russell K. (eds.), *The Variorum Edition of the Poems of W. B. Yeats* (New York, 1957)

Alspach, Russell K. (ed.), *The Variorum Edition of the Plays of W. B. Yeats* (1966; repr. London and Basingstoke, 1979)

Donoghue, Denis (ed.), *W. B. Yeats: Memoirs* (London and Basingstoke, 1972)

Finneran, Richard (ed.), *W. B. Yeats: The Poems – A New Edition* (London and Basingstoke, 1984)

Frayne, John (ed.), *Uncollected Prose by W. B. Yeats*, Vol. I (London, 1970)

Frayne, John and Johnson, Colton (eds.), *Uncollected Prose by W. B. Yeats*, Vol. II (London and Basingstoke, 1975)

Harper, George Mills and Hood, Walter Kelly (eds.), *A Critical Edition of Yeats's* A Vision *(1925)* (London and Basingstoke, 1978)

Hood, Walter Kelly, 'Michael Robartes: Two Occult Manuscripts', *Yeats and the Occult* (ed. George Mills Harper, London and Basingstoke, 1976)

Jeffares, A. Norman, *A New Commentary on the Poems of W. B. Yeats* (London and Basingstoke, 1984)

Jochum, K. P. S., *W. B. Yeats: A Classified Bibliography of Criticism* (Champaign, Ill., 1978)

Kelly, John and Domville, Eric (eds.), *The Collected Letters of W. B. Yeats*, Vol. I 1865–1896 (Oxford, 1985)

Marcus, Philip L., Gould, Warwick and Sidnell, Michael J. (eds.), *The Secret Rose: Stories by W. B. Yeats. A Variorum Edition* (Ithaca, NY, 1981)

O'Donnell, William H. (ed.), *The Speckled Bird* (Toronto, 1976)

Saul, George Brandon, *Prolegomena to the Study of Yeats's Poems* (1957; repr. New York, 1971)

Sidnell, Michael J., Clark, David R. and Mayhew, George P. (eds.), *Druid Craft: The Writing of* The Shadowy Waters (Dublin and London, 1971)

Wade, Allan, *A Bibliography of the Writings of W. B. Yeats* (1951; third ed. revised by Russell K. Alspach, London, 1968)

— (ed.), *The Letters of W. B. Yeats* (London, 1954)

CRITICAL AND CONTEXTUAL STUDIES

Archibald, Douglas, *Yeats* (Syracuse, NY, 1983)

Bloom, Harold, *Yeats* (New York, 1970)

BIBLIOGRAPHY

Bornstein, George, *Yeats and Shelley* (Chicago, Ill. and London, 1970)

Bradford, Curtis, *Yeats at Work* (Carbondale, Ill., 1965)

Bushrui, S. B., *Yeats's Verse-Plays: The Revisions 1900–1910* (Oxford, 1965)

Clark, David R., *Yeats at Songs and Choruses* (Gerrards Cross, 1983)

Cullingford, Elizabeth, *Yeats, Ireland and Fascism* (London and Basingstoke, 1981)

— (ed.), *Yeats: Poems 1919–1935* (London and Basingstoke, 1984)

Deane, Seamus, *Celtic Revivals: Essays in Modern Irish Literature 1880–1980* (London, 1987)

Diggory, Terence, *Yeats and American Poetry: The Tradition of the Self* (Princeton, NJ, 1983)

Donoghue, Denis, *Yeats* (London, 1971)

Ellmann, Richard, *Yeats: The Man and the Masks* (1948; repr. London, 1973)

— *The Identity of Yeats* (1954; repr. London, 1964)

— *Eminent Domain: Yeats among Wilde, Joyce, Pound, Eliot and Auden* (New York, 1967)

— *Four Dubliners: Wilde, Yeats, Joyce and Beckett* (London, 1987)

Engelberg, Edward, *The Vast Design: Patterns in W. B. Yeats's Aesthetic* (Toronto, 1964)

Faulkner, Peter, *Yeats* (Milton Keynes and Philadelphia, 1987)

Finneran, Richard, *Editing Yeats's Poems: A Reconsideration* (London and Basingstoke, 1990)

Flannery, James W., *W. B. Yeats and the Idea of a Theatre: The Early Abbey Theatre in Theory and Practice* (New Haven, Conn. and London, 1976)

Flannery, Mary C., *Yeats and Magic: The Earlier Works* (Gerrards Cross, 1977)

Fletcher, Ian, *W. B. Yeats and His Contemporaries* (Brighton, 1987)

Friedman, Barton R., *Adventures in the Deeps of the Mind: The Cuchulain Cycle of W. B. Yeats* (Princeton, NJ, 1977)

Gordon, D. J. (ed.), *W. B. Yeats: Images of a Poet* (1961; repr. Westport, Conn., 1970)

Gould, Warwick, '"Lionel Johnson comes the first to mind": Sources for Owen Aherne', *Yeats and the Occult*, (ed. George Mills Harper, London and Basingstoke, 1976)

— 'The Definitive Edition', *Yeats's Poems* (ed. A. Norman Jeffares, London and Basingstoke, 1989)

Grossmann, Allan R., *Poetic Knowledge in the Early Yeats: A Study of* The Wind Among the Reeds (Charlottesville, NC, 1969)

Harper, George Mills, *Yeats's Golden Dawn* (London and Basingstoke, 1974)

— (ed.), *Yeats and the Occult* (London and Basingstoke, 1976)

— *W. B. Yeats and W. T. Horton: The Record of an Occult Friendship* (London and Basingstoke, 1980)

— *The Making of Yeats's* A Vision: *A Study of the Automatic Script* (London and Basingstoke, 1987)

Harris, Daniel A., *Yeats, Coole Park and Ballylee* (Baltimore, Md and London, 1974)

BIBLIOGRAPHY

Hassett, J., *Yeats and the Poetics of Hate* (Dublin and New York, 1986)

Heaney, Seamus, 'Yeats as an Example?', *Preoccupations: Selected Prose 1968–1978* (London, 1980)

Henn, T. R., *The Lonely Tower: Studies in the Poetry of W. B. Yeats* (1950; second ed. London, 1965)

Hill, Geoffrey, '"The Conscious Mind's Intelligible Structure": A Debate', *Agenda*, 9–10 (Autumn/Winter 1971/2)

Hough, Graham, *The Mystery Religion of W. B. Yeats* (Brighton and London, 1984)

Jeffares, A. Norman and Cross, K. G. W. (eds.), *In Excited Reverie: A Centenary Tribute to William Butler Yeats 1865–1939* (London and Basingstoke, 1965)

Jeffares, A. Norman (ed.), *W. B. Yeats: The Critical Heritage* (London, 1977)

— *W. B. Yeats: A New Biography* (London, 1988)

Kenner, Hugh, 'The Sacred Book of the Arts', *Yeats: A Collection of Critical Essays* (ed. John Unterecker, Englewood Cliffs, NJ, 1963)

— *A Colder Eye: The Modern Irish Writers* (London, 1983)

Kermode, Frank, *Romantic Image* (London, 1957)

Kinahan, Frank, *Yeats, Folklore and Occultism: Contexts of the Early Work and Thought* (London, 1988)

Kuch, Peter, *Yeats and A E: 'The antagonism that unites dear friends'* (Gerrards Cross and Totowa, NJ, 1986)

Loizeaux, Elizabeth B., *Yeats and the Visual Arts* (New Brunswick, NJ, 1986)

Longenbach, James, *Stone Cottage: Pound, Yeats and Modernism* (New York and Oxford, 1988)

Lyons, F. S. L., *Ireland since the Famine: 1850 to the Present Day* (London, 1971)

McCormack, W. J., *Ascendancy and Tradition in Anglo-Irish Literary History from 1789 to 1939* (Oxford, 1985)

McHugh, Roger (ed.), *Ah, Sweet Dancer. W. B. Yeats Margot Ruddock: A Correspondence* (London and Basingstoke, 1970)

MacNeice, Louis, *The Poetry of W. B. Yeats* (1941; repr. London, 1969)

Malins, Edward, *A Preface to Yeats* (London, 1974)

Meir, Colin, *The Ballads and Songs of W. B. Yeats* (London and Basingstoke, 1974)

Melchiori, Giorgio, *The Whole Mystery of Art: Pattern into Poetry in the Work of W. B. Yeats* (London, 1960)

Miller, Liam, *The Noble Drama of W. B. Yeats* (Dublin and Atlantic Heights, NJ, 1977)

Murphy, William M., *Prodigal Father: The Life of John Butler Yeats (1839–1922)* (Ithaca, NY and London, 1978)

O'Brien, Conor Cruise, 'Passion and Cunning: An Essay on the Politics of W. B. Yeats', *In Excited Reverie: A Centenary Tribute to William Butler Yeats 1865–1939* (eds. A. Norman Jeffares and K. G. W. Cross, London and Basingstoke, 1965)

BIBLIOGRAPHY

O'Donnell, William H., 'Portraits of W. B. Yeats: This Picture in the Mind's Eye', *Yeats Annual No. 3* (1985)

— 'Yeats as Adept and Artist: *The Speckled Bird, The Secret Rose* and *The Wind Among the Reeds*', *Yeats and the Occult* (ed. George Mills Harper, London and Basingstoke, 1976)

O'Driscoll, Robert and Reynolds, Lorna (eds.), *Yeats and the Theatre* (London and Basingstoke, 1975)

Parkinson, Thomas, *W. B. Yeats Self-Critic: A Study of His Early Verse* (Berkeley, Calif. and Los Angeles, Calif. 1951)

— *W. B. Yeats: The Later Poetry* (Berkeley, Calif. and Los Angeles, Calif., 1964)

Pierce, David, *W. B. Yeats: A Guide through the Critical Maze* (Bristol, 1989)

Putzel, Stephen, *Reconstructing Yeats:* The Secret Rose *and* The Wind Among the Reeds (Dublin and Totowa, NJ, 1986)

Raine, Kathleen, *Yeats the Initiate: Essays on Certain Themes in the Work of W. B. Yeats* (Dublin and London, 1986)

Ronsley, Joseph, *Yeats's Autobiography: Life as Symbolic Pattern* (Cambridge, Mass. and London, 1968)

Said, Edward, *Nationalism, Colonialism and Literature: Yeats and Decolonization* (Derry, 1988)

Sidnell, Michael J., 'Mr Yeats, Michael Robartes, and Their Circle', *Yeats and the Occult* (ed. George Mills Harper, London and Basingstoke, 1976)

Skene, Reg, *The Cuchulain Plays of W. B. Yeats* (London and Basingstoke, 1974)

Stallworthy, Jon, *Between the Lines: Yeats's Poetry in the Making* (Oxford, 1963)

— 'The Second Coming', *Agenda*, 9–10 (Autumn/Winter 1971/2)

— *Yeats*: Last Poems. *A Casebook* (London and Basingstoke, 1968)

— *Vision and Revision in Yeats's* Last Poems (Oxford, 1969)

Stead, C. K., *The New Poetic: Yeats to Eliot* (Harmondsworth, 1967)

Thuente, Mary Helen, *W. B. Yeats and Irish Folklore* (Dublin, 1980)

Torchiana, Donald T., *W. B. Yeats and Georgian Ireland* (Evanston, Ill., 1968)

Tuohy, Frank, *Yeats* (London and Basingstoke, 1976)

Unterecker, John, *A Reader's Guide to W. B. Yeats* (1959; repr. London, 1965)

— (ed.), *Yeats: A Collection of Critical Essays* (Englewood Cliffs, NJ, 1963)

Ure, Peter, *Yeats the Playwright: A Commentary on Character and Design in the Major Plays* (London, 1963)

Vendler, Helen Hennessy, *Yeats's 'Vision' and the Later Plays* (Cambridge, Mass. and London, 1963)

Watson, George, *Irish Identity and the Literary Revival: Synge, Yeats, Joyce and O'Casey* (London, 1979)

Welch, Robert, *Irish Poetry from Moore to Yeats* (Gerrards Cross, 1980)

Zwerdling, Alex, *Yeats and the Heroic Ideal* (London, 1966)

INDEX OF FIRST LINES

❖❖❖❖❖❖

The titles of variant first lines appear in italic.

INDEX OF TITLES

The titles of variant poems appear in italic.

READ MORE IN PENGUIN

In every corner of the world, on every subject under the sun, Penguin represents quality and variety – the very best in publishing today.

For complete information about books available from Penguin – including Puffins, Penguin Classics and Arkana – and how to order them, write to us at the appropriate address below. Please note that for copyright reasons the selection of books varies from country to country.

In the United Kingdom: Please write to *Dept. EP, Penguin Books Ltd, Bath Road, Harmondsworth, West Drayton, Middlesex UB7 ODA*

In the United States: Please write to *Consumer Sales, Penguin USA, P.O. Box 999, Dept. 17109, Bergenfield, New Jersey 07621-0120*. VISA and MasterCard holders call 1-800-253-6476 to order Penguin titles

In Canada: Please write to *Penguin Books Canada Ltd, 10 Alcorn Avenue, Suite 300, Toronto, Ontario M4V 3B2*

In Australia: Please write to *Penguin Books Australia Ltd, P.O. Box 257, Ringwood, Victoria 3134*

In New Zealand: Please write to *Penguin Books (NZ) Ltd, Private Bag 102902, North Shore Mail Centre, Auckland 10*

In India: Please write to *Penguin Books India Pvt Ltd, 706 Eros Apartments, 56 Nehru Place, New Delhi 110 019*

In the Netherlands: Please write to *Penguin Books Netherlands bv, Postbus 3507, NL-1001 AH Amsterdam*

In Germany: Please write to *Penguin Books Deutschland GmbH, Metzlerstrasse 26, 60594 Frankfurt am Main*

In Spain: Please write to *Penguin Books S. A., Bravo Murillo 19, 1° B, 28015 Madrid*

In Italy: Please write to *Penguin Italia s.r.l., Via Felice Casati 20, I–20124 Milano*

In France: Please write to *Penguin France S. A., 17 rue Lejeune, F–31000 Toulouse*

In Japan: Please write to *Penguin Books Japan, Ishikiribashi Building, 2–5–4, Suido, Bunkyo-ku, Tokyo 112*

In Greece: Please write to *Penguin Hellas Ltd, Dimocritou 3, GR–106 71 Athens*

In South Africa: Please write to *Longman Penguin Southern Africa (Pty) Ltd, Private Bag X08, Bertsham 2013*

READ MORE IN PENGUIN

A SELECTION OF POETRY

Octavio Paz   Selected Poems
Winner of the 1990 Nobel Prize for Literature

'His poetry allows us to glimpse a different and future place ... liberating and affirming' – *Guardian*

Fernando Pessoa   Selected Poems

'I have sought for his shade in those Edwardian cafés in Lisbon which he haunted, for he was Lisbon's Cavafy or Verlaine' – *Sunday Times*

Roger McGough   Defying Gravity

'The title poem is pure McGough – both ordinary and magical – and is perfect in its way' – *Poetry Review*

Carol Ann Duffy   Selected Poems

'Carol Ann Duffy is one of the freshest and bravest talents to emerge in British poetry – any poetry – for years' – *Independent on Sunday*

John Ashbery   Selected Poems

'America's leading poet ... there is a marvellous free stride in his best work, which extends the territory' – *Irish Times*

Frank O'Hara   Selected Poems

With his unpremeditated, fresh style, O'Hara broke with the academic traditions of the 1950s and became the life and soul of the New York school of poets.

Dannie Abse   Selected Poems

Medicine, music, the myths of Judaism, the cities of London and Cardiff – all recur in poems composed in a spare and witty style that liberates the speaking voice.

READ MORE IN PENGUIN

READ MORE IN PENGUIN

POETRY LIBRARY

Arnold	Selected by Kenneth Allott
Blake	Selected by W. H. Stevenson
Browning	Selected by Daniel Karlin
Burns	Selected by Angus Calder and William Donnelly
Byron	Selected by A. S. B. Glover
Clare	Selected by Geoffrey Summerfield
Coleridge	Selected by Richard Holmes
Donne	Selected by John Hayward
Dryden	Selected by Douglas Grant
Hardy	Selected by David Wright
Herbert	Selected by W. H. Auden
Jonson	Selected by George Parfitt
Keats	Selected by John Barnard
Kipling	Selected by James Cochrane
Lawrence	Selected by Keith Sagar
Milton	Selected by Laurence D. Lerner
Pope	Selected by Douglas Grant
Rubáiyát of Omar Khayyám	Translated by Edward FitzGerald
Shelley	Selected by Isabel Quigley
Tennyson	Selected by W. E. Williams
Wordsworth	Selected by Nicholas Roe
Yeats	Selected by Timothy Webb